21世纪内容语言融合（CLI）系列英语教材

"十二五"普通高等教育本科国家级规划教材

国家社会科学基金项目成果
高等教育国家级教学成果奖获奖项目成果
辽宁省普通高等教育本科教学成果奖获奖项目成果

美 国 国 情
美国历史文化

（第3版）

UNDERSTANDING THE U.S.A.
AMERICAN HISTORY
(THIRD EDITION)

常俊跃 夏 洋 赵永青 主编

北京大学出版社
PEKING UNIVERSITY PRESS

图书在版编目(CIP)数据

美国国情.美国历史文化 / 常俊跃,夏洋,赵永青主编.—3版.—北京：北京大学出版社，2023.10
21世纪内容语言融合（CLI）系列英语教材
ISBN 978-7-301-32726-5

Ⅰ.①美… Ⅱ.①常…②夏…③赵… Ⅲ.①英语—阅读教学—高等学校—教材②文化史—美国 Ⅳ.①H319.4

中国国家版本馆CIP数据核字(2023)第192584号

书　　　名	美国国情：美国历史文化（第3版） MEIGUO GUOQING: MEIGUO LISHI WENHUA（DI-SAN BAN）
著作责任者	常俊跃　夏洋　赵永青　主编
责 任 编 辑	李　颖
标 准 书 号	ISBN 978-7-301-32726-5
出 版 发 行	北京大学出版社
地　　　址	北京市海淀区成府路205号　100871
网　　　址	http://www.pup.cn　　新浪微博：@北京大学出版社
电 子 邮 箱	编辑部 pupwaiwen@pup.cn　总编室 zpup@pup.cn
电　　　话	邮购部 010-62752015　发行部 010-62750672　编辑部 010-62754382
印 刷 者	三河市博文印刷有限公司
经 销 者	新华书店
	787毫米×1098毫米　16开本　14印张　454千字 2009年9月第1版　2016年6月第2版 2023年10月第3版　2023年10月第1次印刷
定　　　价	69.00元

未经许可，不得以任何方式复制或抄袭本书之部分或全部内容。
版权所有，侵权必究
举报电话：010-62752024　电子邮箱：fd@pup.cn
图书如有印装质量问题，请与出版部联系，电话：010-62756370

第三版前言

长期以来,"以语言技能训练为导向"(SOI)的教学理念主导了我国高校外语专业教育,即通过开设语音、语法、基础英语、高级英语、听力、口语、阅读、写作、翻译等课程进行语言教学,帮助学生提高语言技能。该理念对强化学生的语言技能具有一定的积极作用,但也导致了学生知识面偏窄、思辨能力偏弱、综合素质偏低等问题。

为了探寻我国外语专业教育的新路,大连外国语大学英语专业教研团队在总结西南联大等高校外语教育经验的基础上,在北美内容依托教学(CBI)的启发下,于2006年开展了校级和省级英语专业课程改革改革项目,还于2007—2022年连续开展了三个国家哲学社科项目,系统推进英语专业课程体系改革探索,推出中国特色鲜明的内容语言融合教育理念(CLI)(Content and Language Integration),即"将目标语用于教授、学习内容和语言这两个重点,达到多种教育目的的教育理念"。CLI不仅具有自己独特的育人观、课程观、教材观、教学观、测评观、教师发展观,而且展示了如下特点:

(1)教育目标 有别于诸多外语教学理念,CLI不局限于语言教学,而是服务知识、能力和素质培养三大目标,将价值塑造、知识传授和能力培养三者融为一体,寓价值观引导于知识传授和能力培养之中,帮助学生塑造正确的世界观、人生观、价值观,着力落实立德树人根本任务。知识目标包含专业知识、相关专业知识、跨学科知识;能力目标包含语言能力、认知能力、交际能力、思辨能力等;素质目标包含人生观、价值观、世界观、人文修养、国际视野、中国情怀、责任感、团队意识等。

(2)教学特点 有别于单纯训练语言的教学,CLI指导下的语言训练依托内容,内容教学依靠语言;语言、内容融合教学,二者不再人为割裂。

(3)师生角色 有别于传统教学和学生中心理念对师生角色的期待,CLI倡导在充分发挥教师主导作用的同时发挥学生的主体作用。教师可以扮演讲授者、评估者、建议者、资源提供者、组织者、帮助者、咨询者,同时也不排斥教师的权威角色等角色。学生角色也更加多元,包括学习者、参与者、发起者、创新者、研究者、问题解决者。

(4)教学材料 有别于我国传统的外语教科书,在CLI指导下开发的教材具有多样化的特点,包括课本、音频资料、视频资料、网站资料、教学课件、学生作品等。教材的每个单元都围绕内容主题设计,内容具有连续性和系统性。

(5)教学侧重 CLI倡导教师要根据教学阶段或教学内容的特点确定教学重点,或侧重语言知识教学,或侧重语言技能教学,或侧重专业知识教学,或在语言教学和内容教学中达成某种平衡。

(6)教学活动 CLI主张教学活动不局限于某一种教学方法所规定的某几种技巧,倡导充分吸收各种教学方法促进语言学习、内容学习、素质培养的技巧,运用多种教学手段,通过问题驱动、输出驱动等方法调动学生主动学习;运用启发式、任务式、讨论式、结对子、小组活动、课堂展示、项目依托教学等行之有效的方法,活动与学科内容教学有机结合,提高学生的语言技能,激发学生的学习兴趣,培养学生的自主性和创造性,提升学生的思辨能力和综合素质。

(7)教学测评　　CLI 主张测评要吸收测试研究和评价研究的成果,开展形成性评价和终结性评价。形成性评价可以有小测验、课堂发表、角色扮演、小组活动、双人活动、项目、撰写论文、撰写研究报告、创意写作、创意改写、反馈性写作、制作张贴作品等;终结性评价可以包括传统的选择题等各种测评方法。

(8)互动性质　　CLI 有别于传统教学从教师向学生的单向信息传送,课堂互动包括师生互动基础上的生生互动、生师互动乃至师生与其他人员的互动。

(9)情感处理　　CLI 重视对学生的人文关怀,主张教师关注学生的情感反应,教学中有必要有效处理影响学生学习的各种情感因素。

(10)母语作用　　CLI 尊重外语环境下师生的母语优势并加以利用。不绝对禁止母语的使用,母语的使用取决于教学的需要,母语用于有效支持教育目标的达成。

(11)应对失误　　CLI 认可失误是学生获得语言或知识内容不可避免的现象,对学生的失误采取包容的态度。针对具体情况应对学生的失误,或不去干预,允许学生自我纠正,或有针对性地适时给予纠正。

(12)理论支撑　　CLI 得到语言、认知、社会互动、学习等多种理论的支撑。包括:语言是以文本或话语为基础的;语言的运用借助各种技能的融合;语言具有目的性;当人们把语言当成获取信息的工具而不是目的时学习语言更成功,作为语言学习的基础使得一些内容比另外一些内容更有用;当教学关注学生的需求时学生的学习效果会更好;教学应该以学生以前的学习经历为基础。

在 CLI 指导下,依托 3 个国家哲学社科项目,我们将教育部《高等学校英语专业英语教学大纲》规定的语言技能课程(包括英语语音、英语语法、英语听力、英语口语、英语阅读、英语写作、英语语音、英语语法、基础英语、高级英语、英语视听说、英汉笔译、英汉口译等)和专业知识课程(包括英语国家概况、英国文学、美国文学、语言学概论、学术论文写作)进行系统改革,构建了全新的英语专业课程体系,包括九个系列的核心课程:

1. 提高综合英语能力的课程包括:美国文学经典作品、英国文学经典作品、世界文学经典作品、西方思想经典。依托美国、英国、世界的英语文学作品经典和西方思想经典的内容,提高学生综合运用英语的能力,丰富对文学及西方思想的认知,提高综合能力和综合素养。

2. 提高英语视听说能力的课程包括:美国社会文化经典电影、英国社会文化经典电影、环球资讯、专题资讯。依托美英社会文化经典电影、环球资讯、专题资讯内容,提高学生的英语听说能力,同时增加学生对相关国家社会文化的了解。

3. 提高英语口语表达的课程包括:功能英语交际、情景英语交际、英语演讲、英语辩论。依托人际交往的知识内容,提高学生的英语口语交际能力,增进对人际沟通的了解。

4. 提高英语写作能力的课程包括:段落写作、篇章写作、创意写作、学术英语写作。依托笔头交际的知识内容,提高学生的英语笔头表达能力。

5. 提高英汉互译能力的课程包括：英汉笔译、汉英笔译、交替传译、同声传译、专题口译。依托相关学科领域的知识内容，提高学生的英汉笔译、交译、同传、专题口译技能，增加学生对相关领域的了解。

6. 拓展社会文化知识的课程：美国社会与文化、美国自然人文地理、美国历史文化、英国社会与文化、英国自然人文地理、英国历史文化、澳新加社会与文化、欧洲文化、中国文化、古希腊罗马神话、《圣经》与文化、跨文化交际。依托相关国家区域的社会、文化、史地等知识，扩展学生的社会文化知识，增加学生专业知识的系统性，拓宽学生的国际视野，同时提高学生的英语能力。

7. 提升英语文学修养的课程包括：英语短篇小说、英语长篇小说、英语散文、英语戏剧、英语诗歌。依托各种体裁的优秀文学作品内容，强化学生对英语文学文本的阅读，提高学生的文学欣赏能力及语言表达能力，提升学生的文学素养。

8. 提升语言理论修养的课程包括：英语语言学、英语词汇学、语言与社会、语言与文化、语言与语用。依托英语语言学知识内容，帮助学生深入了解英语语言，增加对语言与社会、文化、语用关系的认识，同时提升学生的专业表达能力。

9. 提升区域国别问题探究能力的课程包括：欧洲英语国家研究、北美英语国家研究、大洋洲英语国家研究、拉美英语国家研究、亚洲英语国家研究、非洲英语国家研究。通过指导学生获取区域国别学知识、开展区域国别问题研究项目，提高学生获取国情区情知识、拓宽国际视野、探究国别问题、进行语言沟通等综合能力和综合素养。

研究表明，CLI指导下的课程改革对学生的语音、词汇、语法、听力、口语、写作、交际、思辨、情感、知识等诸多方面产生了显著的积极影响。此外，对学生的研究、创新等能力也产生了积极影响。

CLI教育理念及其指导下的实践探索成果在国内外研讨会进行交流，产生了广泛的积极影响。CLI教育理念指导下开发的系列课程和教材在北京大学出版社、上海外语教育出版社等出版社出版并被广泛使用。培育的校级、省级和国家级教学研究成果在我国高校广泛借鉴，出版的教学研究著作及在国内外学术期刊发表的研究论文对推进外语专业教育理念变革、改善教学实践发挥了积极的作用。高校教师积极参与CLI教育教学研讨与交流，200多所高校引进了理念、课程、教材并结合本校实际开展了课程改革，取得了积极成果。

该理念不仅得到一线教师的广泛支持，也得到了戴炜栋、王守仁、文秋芳等知名专家的高度肯定。蔡基刚教授认为其具有"导向性"作用。孙有中教授认为，该理念指导的教学改革"走在了全国的前列"。教育部前外语教学指导委员会主任委员戴炜栋建议推广探索的课程。内容语言融合教育理念被作为教学要求写入《外国语言文学类教学质量国家标准》及《普通高等学校英语类专业教学指南》，用于指导全国的外语专业教育，必将对我国的外语教育产生更大的影响。

《美国国情：美国历史文化》是CLI教育理念指导下英语专业知识课程体系中美国历史文化课程所使用的教材。教材针对的学生群体是具有中学英语基础的大学生，适用于英语专业一、二年级学生，也适用于具有中学英语基础的非专业学生和英语爱好者。总体看来，本教材具有以下主要特色：

美国国情 美国历史文化(第3版)

1. 打破了传统的教学理念。本教材改变了"为学语言而学语言"的传统教材建设理念，在具有时代特色且被证明行之有效的内容依托教学理论指导下，改变了片面关注语言知识和语言技能忽视内容学习的做法。它依托学生密切关注的西方文明和文化内容，结合社会文化内容组织学生进行语言交际活动，在语言交流中学习有意义的知识内容，既训练语言技能，也丰富相关知识，起到的是一箭双雕的作用。

2. 涉及了丰富的教学内容。《美国国情：美国历史文化》共分为十五个单元。教材主要呈现了美国从英属十三个殖民地到第二次世界大战后美国的主要历史发展脉络，涵盖了较为系统的美国历史基础知识。美国历史的一般性主题和话题将贯穿教材始终，并对其中重要历史事件和历史人物有所侧重，其中包括北美十三个殖民地、独立战争、联邦政府的发展与成长、美国的领土扩张、西进运动、镀金时代、世界大战中的美国、多种文化融合的演进以及不断发展的美国经济与社会等诸多方面。

3. 引进了真实的教学材料。英语教材是英语学习者英语语言输入和相关知识输入的重要渠道。本教材使用大量真实、地道的语言材料，为学生提供了高质量的语言输入。此外，为了使课文内容更加充实生动，易于学生理解接受，编者在课文中穿插了大量的插图、表格、照片等真实的视觉材料，表现手段活泼，形式多种多样，效果生动直观。

4. 设计了新颖的教材板块。本教材每一单元的主体内容均包括 Before You Read，Start to Read，After You Read 和 Read More 四大板块，不仅在结构上确立了学生的主体地位，而且系统的安排也方便教师借助教材有条不紊地开展教学活动。它改变了教师单纯灌输、学生被动接受的教学方式，促使学生积极思考、提问、探索、发现、批判，培养自主获得知识、发现问题和解决问题的能力。

5. 提供了有趣的训练活动。为了培养学生的语言技能和综合素质，本教材在关注英语语言知识训练和相关知识内容传授的基础上精心设计了生动多样的综合训练活动，例如头脑风暴、话题辩论、角色表演、主题陈述、故事编述等等。多样化的活动打破了传统教材单调的训练程式，帮助教师设置真实的语言运用情境，组织富于挑战性的、具有意义的语言实践活动，培养学生语言综合运用能力。

6. 推荐了经典的学习材料。教材的另一特色在于它对教学内容的延伸和拓展。在每个章节的最后部分，编者向学生推荐经典的书目、影视作品、名诗欣赏以及英文歌曲等学习资料，这不仅有益于学生开阔视野，也使教材具有了弹性和开放性，方便不同院校不同水平学生的使用。

本教材是我国英语专业综合课程改革的一项探索，凝聚了全体编写人员的艰苦努力。然而由于水平有限，还存在疏漏和补足，希望使用本教材的老师和同学们能为我们提出宝贵意见和建议。您的指导和建议将是我们提高的动力。

编者
2023 年 2 月 20 日
于大连外国语大学

目录

Unit 1 The Age of Exploration / 1
- Text A Early Exploration and Settlements / 2
- Text B Columbus's Discovery of America / 4
- Text C The Legacy of the Puritans / 7
- Text D The Thanksgiving Story / 8

Unit 2 The Colonial America / 13
- Text A The Original 13 Colonies / 14
- Text B Colonial Life of the Early Settlers / 20
- Text C Slavery in Colonial America / 22

Unit 3 The Road to Independence / 26
- Text A The War of Independence / 27
- Text B The American Revolution / 33
- Text C Causes of the American Revolution / 34

Unit 4 The Young Republic / 39
- Text A The Creation of a National Government / 40
- Text B Benjamin Franklin / 48
- Text C The Essence of the Constitution / 49

Unit 5 The Westward Movement / 54
- Text A The Frontier of the American West / 55
- Text B The Donner Party / 61
- Text C Louisiana Purchase / 62

Unit 6 The Civil War / 66
- Text A Causes of the Civil War / 67
- Text B The Gettysburg Address / 72
- Text C Eye Witness Accounts of the Assassination / 74

Unit 7 Reconstruction / 79
  Text A Reconstruction after the Civil War / 80
  Text B Education after the Civil War / 85
  Text C A Shattered Fairy Tale / 86

Unit 8 The Gilded Age / 90
  Text A The Gilded Age / 91
  Text B Industrialization / 98
  Text C The Gilded Age Society / 99

Unit 9 America in World War I / 104
  Text A The U.S.A. and World War I / 105
  Text B Wilson's Declaration of Neutrality / 113
  Text C U.S. Entry into World War I / 114

Unit 10 The Roaring Twenties / 118
  Text A The Roaring Twenties / 119
  Text B Mass Entertainment in the 1920s / 123
  Text C The Lost Generation / 125

Unit 11 The Great Depression / 130
  Text A The Great Depression in America / 131
  Text B Iowa in the 1920s and the 1930s / 137
  Text C Franklin D. Roosevelt / 138

Unit 12 America in World War II / 141
  Text A World War II / 142
  Text B The Origins of World War II / 148
  Text C American Domestic Situation During World War II / 150

Unit 13 Postwar American Society / 155
  Text A American Society in the 1950s / 156
  Text B The Postwar Economy: 1945—1960 / 161
  Text C Desegregation / 163

Unit 14 America in Transition / 168
  Text A America in the 1960s / 170
  Text B America in the 1970s / 171
  Text C The Cuban Missile Crisis / 175

Unit 15   Toward a New Century / 181
    Text A   America Entering a New Century / 182
    Text B   The Gulf War / 187
    Text C   No Ordinary Day / 188

Appendixes
    Appendix 1   States, Their Entry into Union & Their Settlement / 193
    Appendix 2   Presidents & Vice Presidents of the U.S. / 195
    Appendix 3   U.S. History Timeline / 198

重点参考书目和网站/ 213

Unit 1
The Age of Exploration

> Those who cannot learn from history are doomed to repeat it.
> —George Santayana
>
> I have but one lamp by which my feet are guided, and that is the lamp of experience. I know no way of judging of the future but by the past.
> —Edward Gibbon

Unit Goals

- To understand the motivations of the exploration of the New World.
- To know the Puritan beliefs and the origin of Thanksgiving.
- To learn the historical terms that describe the age of exploration of America.
- To learn the important words and expressions that describe the age of exploration.
- To improve English language skills.
- To develop critical thinking and intercultural communication skills.

Before You Read

1. Read the quotes at the beginning of the unit. Consider whether the quotes make sense in your study of the American history.
2. Suppose there is a piece of land little known to us on this globe. If you, captain of a ship made in the 15th century, were on a voyage crossing the Pacific or the Atlantic for the land, what problems were you likely to encounter?

Possible Problems
_____
_____
_____
_____
_____

3. Do you know why many Europeans left their homelands for the New World?

Possible Reasons
- _____
- _____
- _____
- _____

4. Form groups of three or four students. Try to find, on the Internet or in the library, more information about the age of exploration which interests you. Prepare a 5-minute classroom presentation.

Start to Read

Text A　　Early Exploration and Settlements

1. The age of exploration beginning in the late 1400s was an important era in the discovery and development of land yet unknown to Europeans. During this period, Europeans sought new sea routes to Asia in pursuit of economic gain, glory, and opportunities to spread Christianity. Although these were motivations for explorers, the impact of the discoveries resulted in significant changes and achievements that created possibilities, and opened a new world for all of Europe.

2. The desire to explore the unknown has been a driving force in human history since the dawn of time. From the earliest documented accounts, ancient civilizations have explored the earth by sea. Early adventurers were motivated by religious beliefs, the desire for conquest, the need to establish trade routes, and hunger for gold. Modern history books begin the age of exploration with the fourteenth century, but there is evidence that exploration between Europe and Asia began much earlier. The Han Dynasty of China and the Roman Empire, likewise, had regular trade relations and even exchanged a few diplomats.

3. Early explorers did not sail into the unknown without some idea of their final destination. Although they were searching for a specific land or route, they oftentimes were surprised at what they discovered. Sometimes the country they were seeking was only known in legend or rumor.

4. The captain of the ship needed funding and manpower and could not get

underway without support from a rich benefactor. Most voyages during the fourteenth century were made in the name of the royal ruler of a particular government. The crewmen who signed on to these long and dangerous voyages were not the most experienced seamen, but large numbers of them were needed to help man the sails and to allow for attrition due to illness and death. The ships that the royal leaders provided were not always new, but the captain took what he was given.

5. The captain himself was not always an experienced seaman. Desires for wealth or political favor were often his only motivations for undertaking dangerous voyages. He could be a merchant, adventurer, soldier, or gentleman of the court. Under his command were the pilot or first mate (who was in charge of navigation), and the crew (who worked the sails and rigging and made repairs to the ship while in uncharted waters).

6. Little cooking was done at sea. Food stores often consisted of pickled or dried meat and ship's biscuits (made from flour with a little water to make them hard). By the end of the voyage, these biscuits would be full of black insects called weevils. Other foods included cheese, onions, dried beans, and salted fish or recently caught fresh fish. Without fresh fruit and vegetables which contain vitamin C, sailors suffered from a fatal condition called scurvy. Water supply was another serious problem. Fresh water did not always keep in barrels and wine turned sour. Fresh water was the first thing the crew looked for whenever the ship reached land.

7. The first English immigrants to what is now the United States crossed the Atlantic long after thriving Spanish colonies had been established in Mexico, the West Indies and South America. Like all early travelers to the New World, they came in small, overcrowded ships. During their 6 to 12 week voyages, they lived on meager rations. Many died of disease; ships were often battered by storms and some were lost at sea.

8. Most European emigrants left their homelands to escape political oppression, to seek the freedom to practice their religion or for adventure and opportunities denied to them at home. Between 1620 and 1635, economic difficulties swept England. Many people were jobless and could not survive. Even skilled artisans could earn little more than a bare living. Poor crop yields added to the distress. In addition, the Industrial Revolution had created a burgeoning textile industry, which demanded an ever-increasing supply of wool to keep the looms running. Landlords enclosed farmlands and evicted the peasants in favor of sheep cultivation. Colonial expansion became an outlet for this displaced peasant population.

Text B Columbus's Discovery of America

1. Five hundred years ago, Europeans did not have accurate maps. Many people thought they knew what the earth looked like, but they could only guess. Many ancient maps do not look anything like the true surface of the earth because they were based on incorrect information.

2. One man who thought he knew what the earth's surface looked like was Christopher Columbus. Columbus was an Italian from Genoa, Italy, who had spent much of his life as a sailor.

3. Marco Polo was a merchant who had traveled east to China. After seeing the great wealth of China, Marco Polo returned to Europe and wrote about the wonders he had seen. Some Europeans did not believe Polo's amazing stories. Others, however, were eager to visit Asia and get some wealth for themselves.

4. Christopher Columbus read and believed Marco Polo's story and devised a plan to sail to Asia. He wanted to visit the lands of China. Columbus thought that if he sailed west from Europe he would eventually come to Asia. Columbus landed on the island of San Salvador on October 12, 1492. Because Columbus thought he had reached India, a part of Asia, he referred to the people on the island as Indians. Even though Columbus was thousands of miles away from India, the name he gave to the Native Americans remains to this day, and the islands he reached are now called the West Indies.

5. Columbus visited several islands in the West Indies as he continued his search for gold. On this first journey, Columbus never actually landed on the coast of North or South America. Columbus made three more journeys to America. On each one he showed his superior talents as a navigator.

6. Columbus was a great man because he showed others the way to do something that was supposedly impossible—sail across the unknown ocean. Soon after Columbus's early voyages, other men sailed west. Columbus led the way for the settlement of the New World, part of which was to become the United States of America.

7. After news of Columbus's discovery spread, other sea captains lost their fear of sailing across the Atlantic Ocean. They were eager to make their own discoveries. One such explorer, an Italian named Amerigo Vespucci, claimed that he had crossed the Atlantic Ocean four times between 1497 and 1500. He wrote a letter saying, "I have found a new world."

8. Although Columbus really found the New World before Vespucci, Vespucci was the first person to call it the "New World." In 1507, a German mapmaker did not know what name to give the New World. After reading Vespucci's letters, the mapmaker decided to name the New World "America" in honor of the man he thought had discovered it—Amerigo Vespucci.

Unit 1 The Age of Exploration

After You Read

Knowledge Focus

1. **Pair Work: Discuss the following questions with your partner.**
   (1) What were the motivations of the early explorers? Why did an explorer want to go on a long and dangerous voyage to an unknown place?
   (2) What is the significance of the early exploration?
   (3) What kind of relationship did the early explorers and the indigenous Indians maintain?
   (4) How do you account for the emigration of Europeans to the New World?

2. **Solo Work: Tell whether the following are true or false according to the knowledge you have learned. Consider why.**
   (1) In the late 1400s, Europeans sought new land routes to Asia in pursuit of economic gain, glory, and opportunities to spread Christianity. (　)
   (2) The discovery of the New World resulted in significant changes and achievements that created possibilities. (　)
   (3) The first English immigrants to what is now the United States crossed the Atlantic long after thriving Spanish colonies had been established in Mexico, the West Indies and North America. (　)
   (4) Most European emigrants left their homelands to escape political oppression, to seek the freedom to practice their religion or for adventure and opportunities denied to them at home. (　)
   (5) The Industrial Revolution had created a burgeoning textile industry, which demanded an ever-increasing supply of wool to keep the looms running. Colonial expansion became an outlet for the displaced peasant population. (　)
   (6) Christopher Columbus was an Spanish sailor, who had spent much of his life as a sailor. (　)
   (7) Marco Polo was a merchant who had traveled east to China. (　)
   (8) Columbus landed on the island of San Salvador on October 12, 1495. (　)
   (9) Columbus was a great man because he showed others the way to do something that was supposedly impossible—sail across the unknown ocean. Soon after Columbus's early voyages, other men sailed west. Columbus led the way for the settlement of the New World, part of which was to become the United States of America. (　)
   (10) Although Columbus really found the New World before Vespucci, Vespucci was the first person to call it the "New World." In 1507, a German mapmaker named the New World "America" in honor of the man he thought had discovered it—Amerigo Vespucci. (　)

Language Focus

1. Fill in the blanks with the following words from the texts.

> motivation benefactor undertake fatal thrive
> yield burgeoning abundant batter considerable

(1) The experiments we conducted with the aid of our teaching assistant _____ new insights.

(2) The huge wave _____ the wrecked ship to pieces.

(3) This crash course serves to prevent stumbling blocks in learning and boost the study _____ of the students.

(4) A business cannot _____ without investment.

(5) They did _____ work to acquaint the masses of the United States with the problems of Latin America.

(6) The mainstream journalists and Hollywood can no longer afford to ignore the _____ video game industry.

(7) A _____ is someone who gives help, usually through financial means, to another; the person who receives the benefits or help is called a beneficiary.

(8) Father who lost three children in a(n) _____ accident calls for tough penalty against drunk drivers.

(9) Hydrogen is the most _____ element in the known Universe.

(10) She _____ the organization of the whole scheme.

2. Find the appropriate prepositions or adverbs that collocate with the neighboring words.

(1) Europeans sought new sea routes _____ Asia in pursuit of economic gain, glory, and opportunities to spread Christianity.

(2) Early adventurers were motivated by religious beliefs, the desire _____ conquest, the need to establish trade routes, and hunger _____ gold.

(3) Although they were searching _____ a specific land or route, they oftentimes were surprised _____ what they discovered.

(4) _____ his command were the pilot or first mate, and the crew.

(5) New York City consists _____ five boroughs.

(6) During their 6 to 12 week voyages, the voyagers lived _____ meager rations.

(7) _____ addition, the Industrial Revolution had created a burgeoning textile industry. Landlords enclosed farmlands and evicted the peasants _____ favor _____ sheep cultivation.

(8) Colonial expansion became an outlet _____ this displaced peasant population.

(9) Many ancient maps do not look anything like the true surface of the earth because they were based _____ incorrect information.

(10) Columbus thought he had reached India, so he referred _____ the people on the island as Indians.

(11) Columbus continued his search _____ gold. _____ this first journey, he never actually landed _____ the coast of North or South America.

(12) Columbus made three more journeys _____ America, but a mapmaker named

the New World "America" _____ honor _____ the man he thought had discovered it instead of Columbus.

Comprehensive Work

Pair Work

Read the following quotes and discuss with your partner why we learn about American history.

"History is a guide to navigation in perilous times. History is who we are and why we are the way we are."

—David C. McCullough

"Our ignorance of history causes us to slander our own times."

——Gustave Flaubert

"History is Philosophy teaching by examples."

—Thucydides

"I worshipped dead men for their strength, forgetting I was strong."

—Vita Sackville-West

"We are made wise not by the recollection of our past, but by the responsibility for our future."

—George Bernard Shaw

"American history is longer, larger, more various, more beautiful, and more terrible than anything anyone has ever said about it."

—James Arthur Baldwin

Essay Writing

Here are several controversial questions about Columbus's discovery of the New World. Read the excerpt first and then write an essay around 300 words to air your views.

Should Columbus be remembered as a great discoverer who brought European culture to a previously unknown world? Or should he be condemned as a man responsible for an "American Holocaust," a man who brought devastating European and Asian diseases to unprotected native peoples, who disrupted the American ecosystem, and who initiated the Atlantic slave trade? What is Columbus's legacy—discovery and progress, or slavery, disease, and racial antagonism?

Read More

Text C　The Legacy of the Puritans

During the early 1600's, a period called the Reformation saw changes in the way Europeans looked at religion. The Catholic Church split apart and many new Christian organizations called Protestants were formed. In England, a protestant religion called the Anglicans became the dominant force in

social and political life. Some people in England, however, viewed religion differently. As a result, a new protestant religion called Puritans evolved. The ruling Anglican church disapproved of Puritan beliefs and persecuted the Puritans. Though Puritans did gain control of England for a short time (Oliver Cromwell), many fled England and came to the New World (America) to escape religious persecution. So the early settlers in New England were Puritans.

Puritans believed that all men were born sinners, this was known as the idea of "original sin." For the Puritans, the only way to be saved was by the grace of God. Puritans also believed in "predestination." The Bible, according to the Puritans, was the direct word of God. Because of this, the Bible was seen as an infallible guide to all aspects of life including political, social and economic matters.

The Puritans believed that man must follow the Bible exactly and live a holy life. Since everything is treated to glorify God, Puritans immersed themselves in their work and made great contribution to art, sculpture, poetry, drama, economy, science, technology, etc. But their life style was so simple that it was austere in the eyes of people today. Even home furnishings were simply made of wood. The result of this lifestyle of hard work was a community that was wealthy and industrious. Since God was an all knowing and powerful force, the Puritans saw their wealth as a gift from God. The Puritans sought to stamp out anything that might interfere in the word of God. Puritans made their ideals realized in this new world.

The long term impact of Puritanism are felt throughout America because they were amongst the first settlers and spread their ideas and values throughout the land. The Puritan work ethic became a staple of American idealism. Likewise this nation remains a Protestant country with a legacy of conservatism. The Puritans lasted only a century or a little longer, but their ideals remain.

Questions for Discussion or Reflection

1. Can you briefly summarize the fundamental beliefs of the Puritans?
2. Why did many Puritans sail to this New World?
3. What is your understanding of "Puritanism"? Do you see any value of "Puritanism" in this money-oriented world?

Text D The Thanksgiving Story

Multiple-Choice Questions

Directions: *In this part, you will discover some unusual things about the history of Thanksgiving. Take the quiz first and then read about the history of Thanksgiving to find out the answers you missed.*

1. When did the Pilgrims have their first Thanksgiving Feast?
    A. In 1619.   B. In 1620.
    C. In 1621.   D. In 1935.
2. What food was probably NOT on the Pilgrims' Thanksgiving menu?
    A. Potatoes.   B. Corn.
    C. Fish.   D. Dried Fruit.
3. The Horn of Plenty or Cornucopia symbolizes abundance. In what country did it originate?
    A. Holland.   B. Greece.
    C. America.   D. Turkey.
4. During which month was a day of Thanksgiving proclaimed in 1676?
    A. May.   B. June.
    C. October.   D. November.
5. Which president did not like the idea of having a national Thanksgiving Day?
    A. Washington.   B. Nixon.
    C. Truman.   D. Jefferson.
6. Who is credited with leading the crusade in establishing Thanksgiving Day?
    A. Sarah Jessica Parker. B. Sarah Lee.
    C. Sarah Josepha Hale.   D. Sarah Ferguson.
7. Which president first established the date of Thanksgiving as a national celebration?
    A. Jefferson.   B. Adams.
    C. Lincoln.   D. Wilson.
8. Which president moved the date of Thanksgiving twice?
    A. Lincoln.   B. T. Roosevelt.
    C. F.D. Roosevelt.   D. Eisenhower.

The Pilgrims who sailed to this country aboard the *Mayflower* were originally members of the English Separatist (a Puritan sect). They had earlier fled their home in England and sailed to Holland (The Netherlands) to escape religious persecution. There, they enjoyed more religious tolerance, but they eventually became disenchanted with the Dutch way of life, thinking it ungodly. Seeking a better life, the Separatists negotiated with a London stock company to finance a pilgrimage to America.

The Pilgrims set ground at Plymouth Rock on December 11, 1620. Their first winter was devastating. At the beginning of the following fall, they had lost 46 of the original 102 who sailed on the *Mayflower*. But the harvest of 1621 was a bountiful one. And the remaining colonists decided to celebrate with a feast—including 91 Indians who had helped the Pilgrims survive their first year. It is believed that the Pilgrims would not have made it through the year without the help of the natives. The feast was more of a

traditional English harvest festival than a true "thanksgiving" observance. It lasted three days.

It is not certain that wild turkey was part of their feast. However, it is certain that they had venison. The term "turkey" was used by the Pilgrims to mean any sort of wild fowl.

Another modern staple at almost every Thanksgiving table is pumpkin pie. But it is unlikely that the first feast included that treat. The supply of flour had been long diminished, so there was no bread or pastries of any kind. However, they did eat boiled pumpkin, and they produced a type of fried bread from their corn crop. There was also no milk, cider, potatoes, or butter. There was no domestic cattle for dairy products, and the newly-discovered potato was still considered by many Europeans to be poisonous. But the feast did include fish, berries, lobster, dried fruit, clams, venison, and plums.

This "thanksgiving" feast was not repeated the following year. But in 1623, during a severe drought, the pilgrims gathered in a prayer service, praying for rain. When a long, steady rain followed the very next day, Governor Bradford proclaimed another day of Thanksgiving, again inviting their Indian friends. It wasn't until June of 1676 that another Day of Thanksgiving was proclaimed.

On June 20, 1676, the governing council of Charlestown, Massachusetts, held a meeting to determine how best to express thanks for the good fortune that had seen their community securely established. By unanimous vote they instructed Edward Rawson, the clerk, to proclaim June 29 as a day of thanksgiving. It is notable that this thanksgiving celebration probably did not include the Indians. October of 1777 marked the first time that all 13 colonies joined in a thanksgiving celebration. It also commemorated the patriotic victory over the British at Saratoga. But it was a one-time affair.

George Washington proclaimed a National Day of Thanksgiving in 1789, although some were opposed to it. There was discord among the colonies, many feeling the hardships of a few Pilgrims did not warrant a national holiday. And later, President Thomas Jefferson scoffed at the idea of having a day of thanksgiving.

It was Sarah Josepha Hale, a magazine editor, whose efforts eventually led to what we recognize as Thanksgiving. Hale wrote many editorials championing her cause in her Boston *Ladies' Magazine*, and later, in *Godey's Lady's Book*. Finally, after a 40-year campaign of writing editorials and letters to governors and presidents, Hale's obsession became a reality when, in 1863, President Lincoln proclaimed the last Thursday in November as a national day of Thanksgiving.

Thanksgiving was proclaimed by every president after Lincoln. The date was changed a couple of times, most recently by Franklin Roosevelt, who set it up one week to the next-to-last Thursday in order to create a longer Christmas shopping season. Public uproar against this decision caused the president to move Thanksgiving back to its original date two years later. And in 1941, Thanksgiving was finally sanctioned by Congress as a legal holiday, as the *fourth* Thursday in November.

Proper Names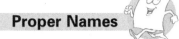

Amerigo Vespucci 阿美利哥·韦斯浦奇(1454—1512)
Christopher Columbus 克里斯托夫·哥伦布(1451—1506)
The Mayflower Compact 《五月花号公约》
the Protestants 新教徒
the Puritans 清教徒
the Reformation 宗教改革

Notes

1. **Amerigo Vespucci**: He was an Italian explorer who claimed to have explored what is now the American mainland in 1497 and believed that he had reached a "New World." Since he was the first person to refer to the lands he had visited as a "New World," a German geographer suggested in 1507 that the land should be named "America."
2. **Christopher Columbus**: He was an Italian explorer in the service of Spain. Columbus was determined that the earth was round and attempted to reach Asia by sailing west from Europe, thereby discovering America. When he finally arrived at the land in October, 1492, he believed that he arrived in the Far East, a part of Asia known as "Indies." So he gave the natives a name "Indians." He made three subsequent voyages to the Caribbean in his quest for a sea route to China.
3. **The Puritans**: A group of English Protestants who advocated strict religious discipline along with simplification of the ceremonies and creeds of the Church of England in the 16th and 17th centuries.

For Fun

Works to Read
(1) John Bakeless, *America as Seen by Its First Explorers: The Eyes of Discovery*
  This is an excellent reference. Bakeless uses journals, diaries, and letters to reconstruct the experiences of these explorers as they encountered a seemingly untouched New World.
(2) Grosseck Joyce and Elizabeth Attwood, *Great Explorers*
  It is about the daring people bold enough to venture into the unfamiliar New World from the Vikings to Neil Armstrong. Chapters on John Cabot, Vasco da Gama, Ferdinand Magellan, Jacques Cartier, Hernando de Soto, and Henry Hudson are helpful in the study of this unit.

Song to Enjoy

The *Mayflower*

By Jon & Vangelis

The sea like the sea
The wind like the wind
The stars in the sky

The sea like the sea
The moon like the moon
The stars in the sky

In the wind, on the ship, a lullaby
We sailing pass the moment of time
We sailing' round the point
The kindly light, the kindly light

We go sailing through the waters
Of the summers end
Long ago, search for land
Looking to and fro

We searching in the day
We searching in the night
We looking everywhere
For land a helping hand

For there is hope if truth be there
How much more will we share
We pilgrims of the sea
Looking for a home

Stars in the sky
Shining so bright
Looking for light
On this earth
On this earth

Unit 2
The Colonial America

> Heaven and earth never agreed better to frame a place for man's habitation.
> —John Smith

Unit Goals

- To get familiar with the natural surroundings of the colonies.
- To know the history and geographical locations of the colonies.
- To acquire information about the daily life in the colonies in general.
- To learn the useful words and expressions that can describe the colonial America.
- To improve English language skills.
- To develop critical thinking and intercultural communication skills.

Before You Read

1. Do you still remember the story about the Puritans and the *Mayflower*? Can you retell the story?
2. Decide whether each of the following is a Puritan belief according to what you learned in Unit 1.

Statements	YES/NO
Puritans believed in predestination.	
All men were born sinners.	
They led pleasure-seeking lives.	
They valued austere and simple life.	
Puritans saw *Bible* as the infallible guide to everything.	

3. What would have happened on the new land if the Westerners had never moved to the

New World? Use your imagination!
Answer 1: _____
Answer 2: _____
Answer 3: _____

4. Form groups of three or four students. Try to find, on the Internet or in the library, more information about the colonial period of America which interests you. Prepare a 5-minute classroom presentation.

Start to Read

Text A The Original 13 Colonies

1. Within the span of a hundred years, in the 17th and early 18th centuries, a tide of emigration—one of the great folk wanderings of history—swept from Europe to America. This movement, impelled by powerful and diverse motivations, built a nation out of a wilderness and, by its nature, shaped the character and destiny of an uncharted continent.

2. Today, the United States is the product of two principal forces—the immigration of European peoples with their varied ideas, customs, and national characteristics and the impact of a new country which modified these distinctly European cultural traits. But, inevitably, the force of geographic conditions peculiar to America, the interplay of the varied national groups upon one another, and the sheer difficulty of maintaining old-world ways in a raw, new continent caused significant changes. These changes were gradual and at first scarcely visible. But the result was a new social pattern which, although it resembled European society in many ways, had a character that was distinctly American.

In New York's fertile Hudson River Valley, soil and climate favored diversified agriculture. On farms such as this one, grain crops, especially wheat, were abundant, and flour was one of the colony's important exports.

3. To the anxious travelers, the sight of the American shore brought almost inexpressible relief. Said one chronicler, "The air at twelve leagues' distance smelt as sweet as a new-blown garden." The colonists' first glimpse of the new land was a vista of dense woods. The virgin forest with its profusion and variety of trees was a real treasure-house which extended over 1,300 miles from Maine in the north to Georgia in the south. Here was abundant fuel and lumber. Here was the raw material of houses and furniture, ships and naval stores.

4. "Heaven and earth never agreed better to frame a place for man's habitation." wrote John Smith (founder of the colony of Virginia) in praise of Virginia, the colony he helped found. As inviting as the climate were the native foods. The sea abounded in oysters and crabs, cod and lobster.

5. In 1620, a group of Pilgrims sailed to the New World on the ship *Mayflower*. These Pilgrims came to be known as Separatists. They had separated from the Church of England and came to America for religious freedom. Before landing, their leaders signed *the Mayflower Compact*. In this document, they agreed to make and obey just and equal laws for the common good. They landed at Plymouth in what is now Massachusetts and founded a colony there.

6. The Pilgrims suffered greatly during the first winter. Shelters were poor, disease widespread, and food scarce. About half the members died. Fortunately, the Indians proved friendly. In the following year, the colonists worked hard in the fields and had a good harvest. So in early autumn of 1621, they set aside a day for celebrating peace and plenty, and invited the Indians to join them. That was the first Thanksgiving ever celebrated.

7. In 1629, Puritans founded the Massachusetts Bay Colony. Plymouth became part of Massachusetts Colony in 1691. Between 1629 and 1640, about 20000 more English colonists crossed the Atlantic Ocean to settle in New England. These Puritan settlers valued hard work and commercial success, and they also believed in the importance of education. These Puritanical values strongly influenced the culture of the American colonies and later of the United States. The Puritans also contributed to democracy in America. They held town meetings, where the adult males worked together to make laws.

8. From the foundation of the colonies beginning with the founding of Jamestown until the beginning of the Revolutionary War, different regions of the eastern coast had different characteristics. Once established, the thirteen British colonies could be divided into three geographic areas: New England,

Middle, and Southern. Each of these had specific economic, social, and political developments that were unique to the regions.

The New England Colonies: New Hampshire, Massachusetts, Rhode Island, and Connecticut.

9. The New England was basically founded by Puritans who had suffered a lot of religious persecution in England. They came to the New World for the sake of free worship. Harbors were located throughout the region. The area was not known for good farmland. Therefore, the farms were small, mainly to provide food for individual families. New England flourished instead with fishing, shipbuilding, manufacturing, and fur trading along with trading goods with Europe. People were considered relatively equal, at least in the eyes of God.

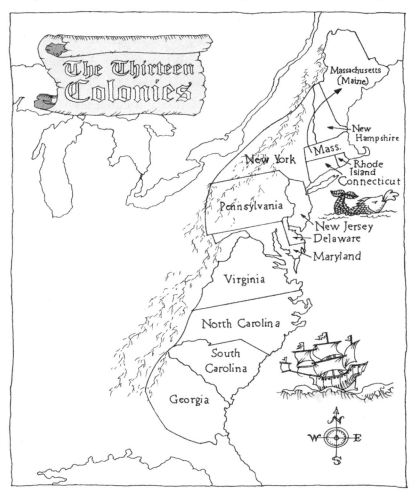

The Middle Colonies: New York, New Jersey, Pennsylvania, and Delaware.
10. Due to their geographical locations, these colonies had some of the characteristics of the South and some of the North. This area was excellent for farming and

included natural harbors. Farmers grew grain and raised livestock. The Middle Colonies also practiced trade like New England, but typically they were trading raw materials for manufactured items.

The Southern Colonies: Maryland, Virginia, North Carolina, South Carolina, and Georgia.

11. Southern colonies grew their own food along with growing three major cash crops: tobacco, rice, and indigo. These were grown on plantations typically worked by slaves and indentured servants. The reason for establishing the colonies in the south was to provide Britain with a new trade market. Plantations kept people widely separate which prevented the growth of many towns. People in this area fell into several categories as for the hierarchical order, namely the aristocracy (wealthy but very few), the middle class farmers and the slaves.

Colony Name	Year Founded	Founded By	Became Royal Colony
Virginia	1607	London Company	1624
Massachusetts	1620	Puritans	1691
New Hampshire	1623	John Wheelwright	1679
Maryland	1634	Lord Baltimore	N/A
Connecticut	c. 1635	Thomas Hooker	N/A
Rhode Island	1636	Roger Williams	N/A
Delaware	1638	Peter Minuit and New Sweden Company	N/A
North Carolina	1653	Virginians	1729
South Carolina	1663	Eight Nobles with a Royal Charter from Charles II	1729
New Jersey	1664	Lord Berkeley and Sir George Carteret	1702
New York	1664	Duke of York	1685
Pennsylvania	1682	William Penn	N/A
Georgia	1732	James Edward Oglethorpe	1752

After You Read

Knowledge Focus

1. Answer the following questions:
   (1) Which country does the thirteen colonies belong to?

(2) Which colony was farthest north?

(3) Which colony was farthest south?

(4) The colonies were bounded by the Appalachian Mountains on the west. What ocean bordered the colonies on the east?

(5) The oldest colony was Virginia founded in 1607. Which colony was just south of Virginia?

(6) The colony of Virginia contained what are now the states of Virginia and West Virginia. What colony bordered Virginia on the northeast?

(7) The colony of Massachusetts was composed of what are now the states of Massachusetts and Maine. What colony was between the two parts?

(8) What colony was located east of Connecticut?

(9) The colony of New York contained what are now the states of Vermont and New York. What two colonies bordered the colony of New York on the south?

(10) In what year did the 13 colonies declare their independence from Britain?

2. Make a comparison between the Southern colonies and New England.

	Southern colonies	New England
Economy		
Reasons for establishing a colony		
People		
Social structure		

Language Focus
1. **Fill in the blanks with the following words or expressions from the text.**

impel	diverse	resemble	just (*adj.*)
abound in	substantial	flourish	permanent
persecution	for the sake of		

(1) The Mediterranean countries _____ in historic remains.

(2) _____ convenience, many students prefer to use small pocket dictionaries or palmtop electronic dictionaries.

(3) He is writing a history of the _____ endured by his race.
(4) No new business can _____ in the depressing economic climate.
(5) Henry sincerely believed that he was fighting a _____ war.
(6) After the earthquake, the booming metropolis _____ a battlefield.
(7) Over the past year, industry leaders have made _____ efforts to build self-regulatory programs.
(8) He entered the United States in 1988 as a _____ resident because of his marriage to a U.S. citizen.
(9) Most historians claim that New York is a very culturally _____ city.
(10) She was in such a mess I felt _____ to offer you services.

2. **Complete the following sentences with the proper forms of the words in the brackets.**
   (1) All the _____ (emigration) were arrested for the illegal activity.
   (2) The chef spared no effort to _____ (diversity) the menu.
   (3) The construction was designed by a master with great _____ (peculiar).
   (4) All possible measures have been taken to _____ (relief) the symptoms of the patient.
   (5) This summer resort is not only a place of interest for visitors, but also a natural _____ (habitation) for birds.
   (6) A group of _____ (influence) media exchanged their views on media censorship.
   (7) The _____ (uniqueness) existing example of Donn's handwriting fascinated many scholars.
   (8) Christians are those who follow the _____ (religion) belief based on the life and teachings of Jesus.
   (9) The implementation of this measure greatly enhanced the economy and _____ (commercial) of the nation.
   (10) We intend to form a _____ (democracy) government with the help of these party members.

Comprehensive Work
Team Work

The Colonial Era in America provided a new beginning for many, and an unfortunate end for others. The new colonies offered prosperity, wealth, adventure, and hardship. Each of the original 13 colonies played a vital role in the development of America, and it is your responsibility to research and report your discovery of these colonies.

The Original Thirteen Colonies	
1. New Hampshire	7. Pennsylvania
2. Massachusetts	8. Delaware
3. New York	9. Maryland
4. Rhode Island	10. Virginia
5. Connecticut	11. North Carolina
6. New Jersey	12. South Carolina
	13. Georgia

Your task is to uncover this information through research and make a class presentation. Your final presentation will include:

◇ Identify the original colony;
◇ Identify the founders of the colony and the year it was founded;
◇ Explain why the colony was founded and where the settlers came from;
◇ Explain the origin of the name and why the name was given to the colony;
◇ Describe the geography of the colony;
◇ Describe the economic characteristics of the colony (What products were produced in your colony and what were the major industries? How did people earn their living?);
◇ Explore three unique qualities about this colony that would draw families from Europe to live here;
◇ Explore the predominant religion;
◇ Explain other important facts about the colony.

Essay Writing

Please read Text B and get a bird's-eye view about the colonial life of early settlers. Suppose you were living in one of the original 13 colonies, what was your life like? Write a short essay with 300 words to describe your life in colonial America and express your feelings about living in Colonial days.

Read More

Text B Colonial Life of the Early Settlers

The earliest settlers lived in the roughest sort of shelter. Some lived in the caves they had dug in the side of steep banks, and some built houses with bark peeled from trees. A common American home during colonial times was the "log cabin." Some houses were built of bricks, but wood was still the common building material.

The American colonists got their food from several places. The modern supermarket that we know today, where you can get all kinds of food, was not an option back then. People who lived on the Atlantic coast often caught fish and whales. They sold fish and whale blubber at fish markets, which were usually down by the docks. Farmers who grew wheat, barley, corn, tobacco, or rice hauled their crops to a town market, where the crops were sold to people in that town or to traders who would ship the goods to other colonies. (These traders would send the goods by boat, on rivers or along the ocean coast, or on wagons.) A great many American colonists also took care of their own food needs. It was not uncommon for a farm family to have crops growing near the ocean while chickens, pigs, and cows were grazing nearby and for that same family to fish for clams and other fish down at the ocean-side. In this way, the family would not have to buy food from anyone else. They might have apple trees and rows of corn and wheat. They might turn that corn into cornbread or cornmeal mush. They might turn that wheat into flour themselves and use it to bake bread. They might also hunt wild animals, like deer, rabbits, and turkeys. The farms of the 13 colonies took up a much larger amount of the total land available than do farms today. Still, farming is very much a way of life for many people today, just as it was for the American colonists.

If you were a school-age person in colonial America, you might have gone to a public or private school, just like you would today. But what you learned and how you learned it have changed throughout the years.

In the New England colonies, parents believed that their children should learn about Christianity. To that end, parents taught their children to read so they could read the Bible. And once those kids knew how to read, they could read school books as well. New England villages having more than 100 families set up grammar schools, which taught boys Latin and math and other subjects needed to get into college. And although girls could read, they were not allowed to go to grammar school or to college.

Middle Colonies schools were also largely religious but taught the teachings of one religion. If you were a Catholic, you learned about the Catholic religion. Most schools were private. Students also learned other subjects so they could get into college. Again, girls were not allowed to attend, unless they were Quakers.

School-age kids in the Southern Colonies were taught at home, for the most part, by their parents or by private tutors. When these kids became teenagers, they would then go off to college or to Europe. As in the other colonies, Southern girls did not go to school. Schools were generally small, not like the large ones many kids go to today. Kids learned to read from special books called hornbooks. Kids in colonial America were taught a trade, usually the one their fathers did, so they could continue the family business when their fathers retired. Often, kids would go to school and learn a trade.

Farming in colonial differed in many ways from farming today. The most significant difference was in what crops were grown and where. Farmers in the New England Colonies had a rough time of it. Much of the soil was not good for growing crops, especially near the ocean. Also, the early and long-lasting winters killed many crops quickly. Still, New England farmers often grew enough food to feed their families and maybe even help feed other families. The main kind of food New Englanders contributed to the economy was fish. Farmers in the Middle Colonies were the most prosperous of all.

They grew wheat, barley, oats, rye, and corn. The Middle Colonies were often called the "breadbasket" because they grew so much food. Wheat could be ground to make flour, and both wheat and flour could be sold in other colonies or in Europe. Farmers in the Southern Colonies grew several things. The most popular crop was tobacco. The Jamestown colonists had grown tobacco originally, and tobacco farms sprung up all over Virginia and North Carolina. The two southernmost states (South Carolina and Georgia) also grew indigo and rice. Farm equipment was also different. Colonial farmers did not have the large machines that today's farmers have and so had to rely on manpower and animal power.

Clothing was simple and rough. The most common clothes were "homespun," with materials of wool or flax. Many people expected to wear the same clothes year after year until they were completely worn out.

1. Questions for Discussion or Reflection
   (1) What was the common building material? What sort of house did early settlers live in?
   (2) What do you know about the farm produce and sea foods available to the early settlers?
   (3) What did people learn in the New England colonies?
   (4) What does it mean by "grammar school"?
   (5) Can you briefly state the differences in the educational systems of the three regions of colonial America?
   (6) Summarize the differences of farming in the three regions of colonial America.

2. Complete the following chart, and compare the life of the Pilgrims in the 1600's with your life today.

	Pilgrims' Life	Your Life Today
Housing		
Food		
Education		
Farming		
Clothing		

Text C Slavery in Colonial America

In colonial America, there was no sharp division between a slave South and a free-labor North. New England was involved in the Atlantic slave trade from the mid-1600s to the 1780s. In the years preceding the American Revolution, slavery could be found in all the American colonies. By the mid 18th century, slaves made up almost 8 percent of the population in Pennsylvania, 40 percent in Virginia, and 70 percent in South Carolina. During the second quarter of the 18th century, a fifth of Boston's families owned slaves; and in New York City in 1746, slaves performed about a third of the city's manual labor.

In the North, slaves were used in both agricultural and non-agricultural employment, especially in highly productive farming and stock-raising for the West Indian market in southern Rhode Island, Long Island, and New Jersey. Slaves not only served as household servants for an urban elite—cooking, doing laundry, and cleaning stables—they also worked in rural industry, in salt works, iron works, and tanneries. In general, slaves were not segregated into distinct racial ghettoes; instead, they lived in back rooms, lofts, attics, and alley shacks. Many slaves fraternized with lower-class whites. But in the mid-18th century, racial separation increased, as a growing proportion of the white working-class began to express bitter resentment over competition from slave labor. The African American response in the North to increased racial antagonism and discrimination was apparent in a growing consciousness and awareness of Africa and the establishment of separate African churches and benevolent societies.

Questions for Discussion or Reflection
(1) What would have happened if there were no indentured servants or slaves in colonial America? How would America be different?
(2) Can you tell the reasons why the black people were exploited as slaves of the white after the latter settled down in colonial America?

Proper Names

Connecticut 康涅狄格
Delaware 德拉华
Georgia 佐治亚
Jamestown 詹姆斯敦
Maryland 马里兰
Massachusetts Bay Colony 马萨诸塞湾殖民地
Massachusetts 马萨诸塞
New Hampshire 新罕布什尔
New Jersey 新泽西

New York 纽约
North Carolina 北卡罗来纳
Pennsylvania 宾夕法尼亚
Pilgrims 朝圣者
Plymouth 普利茅斯
Rhode Island 罗德岛
South Carolina 南卡罗来纳
Virginia 弗吉尼亚

Notes

1. **The indentured servant**: An indentured servant was one who agreed to work for his master for a couple of years without pay. In return, the master provided the servant with food, clothing and shelter. When the years was served, the master gave him a piece of land and he became a free man.

2. *The Mayflower Compact*: It is a written agreement composed by the new Settlers arriving at New Plymouth in November of 1620. *The Mayflower Compact* was drawn up with fair and equal laws, for the general good of the settlement and with the will of the majority. All 41 of the adult male members on the *Mayflower* signed the Compact. Being the first written laws for the new land, the Compact determined authority within the settlement and was the observed as such until 1691. This established that the colony (mostly persecuted Separatists), was to be free of English law. It was devised to set up a government from within themselves and was written by those to be governed.

3. **Pilgrims (Pilgrim Fathers)**: The term "Pilgrims" is commonly applied to the early settlers of the Plymouth Colony in present-day Plymouth, Massachusetts. In 1620 one hundred Puritans boarded the *Mayflower* bound for the New World. The colony, established in 1620, became the second successful English settlement (after the founding of Jamestown, Virginia in 1607) in what was to become the United States of America.

Websites to Visit(本书出现的网站访问日期为 2023 年 4 月 6 日)

1. http://www.congressforkids.net/games/thirteencolonies/2_thirteencolonies.htm
   This website presents various classroom activities about the original thirteen colonies.
2. http://mrkash.com/activities/colonies.html
   The website provides information about the original thirteen colonies.
3. http://www.timepage.org/spl/13colony.html
   The website offers information on the original thirteen colonies and their origins.

Movie to See
The Crucible (1996)
   The Crucible is a 1996 film, written by Arthur Miller and based on his play of the same name. It was directed by Nicholas Hytner. The story was set in 1692 Salem, Massachusetts Bay Colony.

Song to Enjoy

"**America**" by Samuel F. Smith

"**My Country, 'Tis of Thee,**" also known as "America," is an American patriotic song. Its lyrics were written by Samuel Francis Smith. The melody is that of the British national anthem "God Save the King or Queen" with adaptation. The song served as a de facto national anthem of the United States before the adoption of "The Star-Spangled Banner" as the official anthem.

America

Lyrics by Samuel Francis Smith

My country, 'tis of thee,
Sweet land of liberty,
Of thee I sing:
Land where my fathers died!
Land of the Pilgrims' pride!
From every mountainside
Let Freedom Ring!
My native country, thee,
Land of the noble free,
They name I love:
I love thy rocks and rills,
Thy woods and templed hills;
My heart with rapture thrills
Like that above.
Let music swell the breeze,
And ring from all the trees
Sweet Freedom's song:
Let mortal tongues awake;
Let all that breathe partake;
Let rocks their silence break,
The song prolong.
Our father's God, to Thee,
Author of liberty,
To Thee we sing:
Long may our land be bright
With freedom's holy light;
Protect us by Thy might,
Great God, our King!

Unit 3
The Road to Independence

> We hold these truths to be self-evident, that all men are created equal, that they are endowed by their Creator with certain unalienable Rights, that among these are Life, Liberty, and the pursuit of Happiness.
> —*The Declaration of Independence*

Unit Goals

- To know the situation before the War of Independence.
- To learn the significant events of American revolutionary period.
- To understand the significance of *The Declaration of Independence*.
- To learn the useful words and expressions about the War of Independence.
- To improve English language skills.
- To develop critical thinking and intercultural communication skills.

 Before You Read

1. What is your interpretation of "independence"? Are you independent now in any sense? Are you independent financially or spiritually? Do you agree with the following statements about "independence"? Share your views with your classmates.

Statement	Pros	Cons
The financial independence is the basis of all other rights.		
One can be spiritually independent, though not financially independent.		
Nobody can be completely independent in that everyone has to be dependent on others one way or another.		

2. What do you know about the causes of the War of Independence?
3. Find some information about the author of *The Declaration of Independence*. And share the information with your classmates.
4. Form groups of three or four students. Try to find, on the Internet or in the library, more information about the War of Independence which interests you most. Prepare a 5-minute classroom presentation.

Start to Read

Text A　　The War of Independence

1. Although some believe that the history of the American Revolution began long before the first shots were fired in 1775, England and America did not begin an overt parting of the ways until 1763. In that year the Seven Years' War (1756—1763) ended, during which Britain and France fought over the control of North American colonies. In the end, Great Britain defeated France and removed the long-standing threat to the colonies. However, Britain also accumulated a large debt over the course of war. To help pay off the debt, Britain turned to the colonies to generate revenue and in so doing they came into conflict with the interest of the colonies.

2. The colonies had grown vastly in economic strength and cultural attainment, and actually all had long years of self-government behind them. Long accustomed to a large measure of independence, the colonies were demanding more freedom. Fast increasing in population and needing more land for settlement, various colonies claimed the right to extend their boundaries as far west as the Mississippi River.

3. The British government, which needed more money to support its growing empire, took measures. The first step was the enforcement of the "Sugar Act" of 1764. This act outlawed the importation of foreign liquor; it also put a modest duty on molasses from all sources and levied taxes on wines, silks, coffee, and a number of other luxury items. Another measure, known as the "Stamp Act," sparked the greatest resistance. It provided that revenue stamps be attached to all newspapers, pamphlets, licenses or other legal documents, the revenue to be used for "defending, protecting and securing" the colonies. Trade with the mother country fell off sharply in the summer of 1765, as prominent men organized themselves into the "Sons of Liberty"—secret organizations formed to protest the Stamp Act, often through violent means.

4. The powerful East India Company, finding itself in critical financial situation, appealed to the British government, which granted it the sole right on all tea exported to the colonies. Aroused by the loss of the tea trade, the colonial traders agitated for independence. On the night of December 16, 1773, Sons of Liberty disguised as Indians and led by Samuel Adams boarded three British ships and dumped their tea cargo into Boston harbor. This action was called the Boston Tea Party.

5. The Boston Tea Party made the British government irritated. It passed a series of acts generally called "the Intolerable Acts" in America early in 1774 to punish the Bostonians. The British government had intended to punish one colony, but the Acts alarmed all other colonies. Contrary to Britain's expectation, the Intolerable Acts became a driving force in uniting the 13 colonies.

6. On September 5, 1774, in response to the British "the Intolerable Acts", the colonies held the First Continental Congress. Representatives from each colony, except Georgia, met in Philadelphia. The purpose of the First Continental Congress was not to seek independence from Britain. The Congress had three objectives: to compose a statement of colonial rights, to identify British parliament's violation of those rights, and to provide a plan that would convince Britain to restore those rights. They agreed to meet again in May 1775, if the British did not change their policies.

7. Before Congress met again, the situation had changed. Moving against the possibility of armed violence by the colonists, Britain sent around 2000 soldiers from Boston on the night of April 18, 1775, to confiscate munitions that the colonists were storing at Concord—twenty-six miles northeast of Boston. During the night, the fellow riders went from house to house, quietly giving warning to people who belonged to a group called Minutemen—so named because they were said to be ready to fight in a minute. On the morning of

April 19, 1775, the first shots of the Revolutionary War were fired at Lexington, Massachusetts. It was, in the often quoted phrase of Ralph Waldo Emerson, "the shot heard round the world."

8. While the alarms of Lexington and Concord were still resounding, the Second Continental Congress met in Philadelphia, Pennsylvania, on May 10, 1775. By May 15, the Congress voted to go to war, establishing the militia as the Continental Army to represent the thirteen states and appointing Colonel George Washington of Virginia as commander-in-chief of the American forces.

9. In January 1776, Thomas Paine, a political theorist and writer who had come to America from England in 1774, published a 50-page pamphlet, *Common Sense*. Within three months, 100,000 copies of the pamphlet were sold. Paine attacked the idea of hereditary monarchy. Circulated throughout the colonies, *Common Sense* helped to crystallize the desire for separation.

10. However, there still remained the task, of gaining each colony's approval of a formal declaration. Immediately, a committee of five, headed by Thomas Jefferson of Virginia, was appointed to prepare a formal declaration. Largely Jefferson's work, *The Declaration of Independence*, adopted July 4, 1776, not only announced the birth of a new nation, but also set forth a philosophy of human freedom.

11. To further the American cause, Benjamin Franklin was sent to Paris in 1776. His wit and intellect soon made their presence felt in the French capital, and played a major role in winning French assistance. France began providing aid to the colonies in May 1776, and the Franco-American alliance soon broadened the conflict. In June 1778, British ships fired on French vessels, and the two countries went to war.

12. After several years of being at war, British government decided to pursue peace negotiations in Paris in early 1782. Signed on September 3, 1783, the *Treaty of Paris* acknowledged the independence, freedom, and sovereignty of the 13 former colonies, now states. The new United States stretched west to the Mississippi River, north to Canada, and south to Florida, which was returned to Spain. The task of knitting together a nation remained.

After You Read

Knowledge Focus

1. **Pair Work: Discuss the following questions with your partner.**
   (1) What is the major cause of the Seven Years' War?

(2) When and where were the first independent shots fired?

(3) What do you know about the "Sugar Act"?

(4) Who wrote the famous pamphlet *Common Sense*?

(5) What did Jefferson mean by "all men are created equal, that they are endowed by their Creator with certain unalienable Rights"?

2. Solo Work: Tell whether the following are true or false according to the knowledge you have learned. Consider why.

(1) The seven Years' war was concluded in 1763, and the Great Britain was finally defeated. ( )

(2) In order to support its growing empire, the British government enforced the "Stamp Act" in 1764. ( )

(3) The East India Company long held a privileged position in relation to the English, and later the British government. As a result, it was frequently granted special rights and privileges, including trade monopolies and exemptions. ( )

(4) "The Intolerable Acts" came into effect after the Boston Tea Party, which was used to punish the Bostonians. ( )

(5) The purpose of the First Continental Congress was to seek independence from Britain. ( )

(6) The objectives of the First Continental Congress were to identify British parliament's violation of those rights, and to provide a plan that would convince Britain to restore those rights. ( )

(7) "The shot heard round the world" refers to the shot fired at Lexington. ( )

(8) Thomas Jefferson was the third President of the United States, the principal author of *The Declaration of Independence*, and one of the most influential Founding Fathers for his promotion of the ideals of republicanism in the United States. ( )

3. Pair Work: Fill in the blanks with words in the box and check the answers with your partner.

| assert | outbreak | announce |
| approve | vote | adopt |

The United States Declaration of Independence is a statement _____ by the Second Continental Congress on July 4, 1776, which _____ that the thirteen American colonies then at war with Great Britain were now independent states, and thus no longer a part of the British Empire. Written primarily by Thomas Jefferson, the Declaration is a formal explanation of why Congress had _____ on July 2 to declare independence from Great Britain, more than a year after the _____ of the American Revolutionary War. In addition, the *Declaration* _____ certain natural rights, including a right of revolution. The birthday of the United States of America—Independence Day—is celebrated on July 4, the day the wording of the *Declaration* was _____ by Congress.

Language Focus

1. **Fill in the blanks with the following words or expressions from the text.**

overt	attainment	provoke	ensure
accustomed	levy	hostility	outlaw
prominence	appeal to		

   (1) Church leaders have _____ the government to halt the war.
   (2) The unfriendly newcomers showed obvious _____ towards their neighbors.
   (3) Bands of _____ lived in the forest and never came back home to avoid being caught.
   (4) It is the first time that a lawyer of such _____ has been given the freedom to air his views on TV.
   (5) A(n) _____ attitude is shown in an open and obvious way. Although there is no overt hostility, black and white students do not mix much.
   (6) The criminal who slit his wife's throat made the excuse that he was _____ into the attack by her infidelity.
   (7) Airport tax is _____ on all passengers upon embarkation of international flights at the airport.
   (8) Their 2-0 victory today has _____ a place in the Cup Final for the Italian team.
   (9) I had hoped to send him a telegram to congratulate him on his _____ of Nobel Prize.
   (10) Have we become so _____ to being passive in class that we've forgotten how to be active?

2. **Complete the following sentences with the proper forms of the words in the brackets.**

   (1) The _____ (accumulate) effect is crucial to learning a foreign language.
   (2) This particular charity is responsible for organizing the _____ (remove) of supplies to famine-stricken areas.
   (3) The people of Africa have successfully fought against _____ (colony) rule.
   (4) The results of the experiment shook the basic _____ (assume) of his theory.
   (5) Her husband took a long _____ (luxury) hot bath.
   (6) The prime minister was greeted by a rather _____ (hostility) crowd.
   (7) The young fashion designer is rising to _____ (prominent).
   (8) The idea of a free holiday is _____ (appeal) to those white collars.
   (9) She were confronted with a(n) _____ (tolerate) situation the other day.
   (10) This _____ (restore) of a prehistoric village shows what it must have looked like.

Comprehensive Work
Pair Work

The historical document *The Declaration of Independence* listed the rights of man, described the abuses of George III and declared independence. Its significance is deeply rooted in the belief in people's unalienable rights. You must be familiar with the

following quotes:

"*We hold these truths to be self-evident, that all men are created equal, that they are endowed by their Creator with certain unalienable Rights, that among these are Life, Liberty, and the pursuit of Happiness.*"

The belief bounded the thirteen colonies together and planted firm resolution to fight for independence. You are highly suggested to read the Declaration text on the website "http://www.ushistory.org/declaration/document/", and then work with your partner to accomplish the following tasks:

(1) If you were a colonist, would you struggle for your independence from Britain? Why?

(2) Do you think American people from all walks of life today have really achieved full equality?

(3) Among the unalienable rights are "life, liberty and the pursuit of happiness." Which one do you give priority to? Write your responses in the blanks that follow, and discuss them with your partner.

◇ **Life is the most important, because...**
  Reason 1: without life, nothing is possible.

  Reason 2: _____

  Reason 3: _____

◇ **The pursuit of happiness is more important, because ...**
  Reason 1: the pursuit of happiness is the ultimate goal of life and liberty.

  Reason 2: _____

  Reason 3: _____

◇ **Liberty should be of No. 1 importance, because ...**
  Reason 1: without liberty, life is meaningless.

  Reason 2: _____

  Reason 3: _____

Essay Writing

Sort out some persuasive points in the discussion above and organize those points into an essay within 300 words.

Read More

Text B The American Revolution

The American Revolution was much more than a war for national independence. It was also much more than a revolt against taxes and trade regulations.

The American Revolution was truly the first modern revolution. It enjoyed widespread popular support and marked the first time in history that a people fought for their independence in the name of certain universal principles of human rights and civil liberties.

The American Revolution touched off an "age of revolution." Its example helped inspire revolutions across the entire western world. During the late 1700s and early 1800s, revolutions and popular uprisings erupted from the Ural Mountains in Russia to the Andes Mountains in South America: in Greece, Ireland, Italy, Mexico, Poland, Switzerland, and in many other countries. In Haiti, for the first time in history, slaves succeeded in winning their independence by force of arms. These revolutions were justified in terms of such ideas as "the rights of man" and "national independence," principles popularized by the American Revolution.

What were the principles that the American revolutionaries fought for? One was popular sovereignty. The American patriots believed that all governments exist for the benefit of the governed. Whenever a government violated the peoples' fundamental rights, they had the right to change or overthrow it.

Another basic principle was equality before the law. At a time when most people in the western world were ruled by kings, the American patriots rejected the idea that the people should be royal subjects. Instead, they insisted that the people should be regarded as citizens with equal rights, including the right to participate in governmental affairs.

A third fundamental principle was constitutional rights and rule of law. The American revolutionaries believed in natural rights—the idea that the people have certain fundamental rights that must be protected against tyrannical oppression, including the right to trial by jury, freedom of speech and conscience, and freedom from arbitrary arrest and punishment. They also believed in constitutionalism—the idea that the peoples' rights and government's functions and powers needed to be spelled out in a written document.

1. Questions for Discussion or Reflection
   (1) What were the principles that the American revolutionaries fought for?
   (2) Do you think the principle "equality before the law" can ensure 100% equality of the citizens in a nation? Why?

2. **Fill in the blanks with words you learned in the passage above.**
    The American Revolution was not only a war for national _____ or a revolt

against taxes and trade _____ but also truly the _____ modern revolution. It _____ off an "age of revolution" and helped _____ revolutions across the entire western world. The American patriots believed that all governments exist for the benefit of the _____. They insisted that the people should be regarded as citizens with equal rights, including the right to participate in _____ affairs. The American revolutionaries believed in natural rights and also in _____.

Text C Causes of the American Revolution

In explaining why the Revolution took place, it is necessary to look both at underlying causes and at the precipitating events. The Revolution was, in part, the consequence of long-term social, political, and cultural transformations. Between 1680 and 1776, a distinctly American society emerged, a society that differed significantly from Britain. In the course of a century, the colonies had diverged markedly from Britain. A variety of long-run trends gave the 13 American colonies certain common characteristics which made them very different from England.

1) **The absence of a titled aristocracy**

The colonies had no legally privileged social classes, and they did not have many of the other characteristics of a monarchical society. They had no standing army and had a government bureaucracy that was smaller and far less powerful than that found in Britain. While there were wealthy merchants and planters in the colonies, economic stratification was less pronounced than in Britain and membership in this affluent segment of the population was volatile and changing. To be sure, colonial society in the 18th century was, in certain respects, becoming more aristocratic. Colonial elites increasingly emulated the values and lifestyle of the English aristocracy. They aped the English elites' dress and manners, and copied their furniture and architecture. Nevertheless, compared with Britain, few Americans had fortunes large enough to lead lives of leisure.

2) **The widespread ownership of property**

Except for slaves, most physical labor was performed by people who owned their own farms or shops or could expect eventually to be economically independent. Relatively few of the colonists were tenant farmers, and most yeomen maintained a remarkable degree of independence. Even in the Chesapeake region or the Hudson River Valley, where much of the land was leased, farmers still could acquire long-term leases on relatively easy terms.

3) _____

The colonies not only displayed a religious diversity unmatched in the western world, they were also more willing to tolerate religious difference. Four colonies—Delaware, New Jersey, Pennsylvania, and Rhode Island—had no established church. Five other states disestablished the Church of England even before the Revolution broke out.

4) **The relative absence of poverty**

In the 18th century England, half the population was at least occasionally dependent on charity for subsistence. Apart from slaves, the American population was far better off. Nothing better illustrates the relative affluence of the white population than the fact that the colonists were on average three inches taller than their English counterparts.

5) A lack of urban development

In 1760, the largest city in the colonies, Philadelphia, had just 20,000 inhabitants. In that year, the total number of Americans living in cities or towns with more than 3,000 residents was no greater than 70,000. The colonies had few of the attributes of an urban society: there was no large-scale manufacturing, no stock markets, few large cities, and virtually no banks in British North America.

6) A relative lack of deference to authority

The American colonists were far less deferential and less willing to accept subordination than their British or European counterparts. The colonists enjoyed the broadest suffrage of any people in the western world. Although the right to vote in colonial America was restricted to property owners, property owning was so widespread that roughly 80 percent of white adult males could vote. Although relatively few men actually voted in elections, the principle of self-government was well-developed. To gain political office, social leaders felt increasingly forced to make direct appeals to the people. Compared with Britain, popular participation in decision making was much more pronounced. Militia officers were often selected by their companies, and ministers were often hired by their congregations.

7) _____

In 1776, one-fifth of the inhabitants of the American colonies lived in bondage. Most of the growth of slavery had taken place since 1680. In 1680, Africans accounted for just five percent of the population in Maryland and Virginia. But in 1760, enslaved Africans comprised nearly 40 percent of Virginia's population. By 1776, the number of slaves in the colonies had reached 500,000. Slavery in 18th century America was not confined to the South. Slaves could be found in each of the 13 colonies, and were especially numerous in New Jersey and in New York's Hudson River Valley.

The widespread presence of slavery made adult white males acutely aware of the difference between independence and dependence. Colonial Americans knew what it was like to be subjected to the will, authority, and domination of another person. By the 1770s, a growing number of Americans had begun to see their society as fundamentally different from European society. Their society was a "republican" society, a society free of many of the trappings of aristocracy and of the corruptions associated with cities and large-scale manufacturing and financial institutions. From this perspective, Americans were simpler, more independent, and more virtuous than Europeans.

Question for Discussion or Reflection

1. **The passage elaborates on the common characteristics of the thirteen colonies. However, some sub-titles remain vacant. Please read the two paragraphs first and then supply the missing sub-title for each.**

2. Finish the following multiple-choice questions according to what you learned in the passage above.

(1) Between _____, a distinctly American society emerged. It was a society that differed significantly from Britain.
   A. 1680 and 1776   B. 1682 and 1772
   C. 1680 and 1767   D. 1676 and 1776

(2) Which of the following is NOT the common characteristic of the 13 American colonies?
   A. A lack of urban development.
   B. The relative absence of poverty.
   C. The widespread ownership of property.
   D. A relative lack of deference to democracy.

(3) Most physical labor, except for _____, was performed by people who owned their own farms or shops or could expect eventually to be economically independent.
   A. tenant farmers   B. slaves
   C. yeomen   D. aristocracy

(4) Which of the following was done by the American colonists to make people defer to authority?
   A. Making direct appeals to the people.
   B. Participation in decision making.
   C. Militia officers were selected and ministers were hired.
   D. All of the above.

(5) Slaves could be found in all of the 13 colonies, and they were especially numerous in _____.
   A. Maryland and Virginia
   B. New York's Hudson River Valley
   C. New Jersey and in New York's Hudson River Valley
   D. Philadelphia and in New York's Hudson River Valley

Proper Names

Boston Tea Party 波士顿倾茶事件
Common Sense《常识》
The Declaration of Independence《独立宣言》
the East India Company 东印度公司
the First Continental Congress 第一次大陆会议
the Intolerable Acts 不可容忍法令

the Second Continental Congress 第二次大陆会议
the Seven Years' War 七年战争
the "Sons of Liberty" 自由之子
the "Stamp Act" 印花税法
the "Sugar Act" 糖税法
the *Treaty of Paris*《巴黎协定》

Notes

1. **Thomas Jefferson**: He was the author of *The Declaration of Independence* and the third president of the United States. Jefferson also founded the University of Virginia and built one of America's most celebrated houses, Monticello, in Charlottesville, Virginia.

2. **The Liberty Bell**: It refers to the bell in Philadelphia, Pennsylvania, an enduring symbol of American freedom. First rung on July 8, 1776 to celebrate the adoption of the Declaration of Independence, it cracked in 1836 during the funeral of John Marshall, Chief Justice of the U.S. Supreme Court.

3. **The Seven Years' War (1756—1763)**: The Seven Years' War, a global conflict known in America as the French and Indian War, officially began when England declared war on France. However, fighting and skirmishes between England and France had been going on in North America for years. The Seven Years' War ended with the signing of the treaties of Hubertusburg and Paris in February 1763. In the *Treaty of Paris*, France lost all claims to Canada and gave Louisiana to Spain, while Britain received Spanish Florida, Upper Canada, and various French holdings overseas. The treaty ensured the colonial and maritime supremacy of Britain and strengthened the 13 American colonies by removing their European rivals to the north and the south.

For Fun

Websites to Visit

1. http://www.historyofwar.org/articles/wars_american_independence.html
   It is a comprehensive website about the War of Independence, offering information about battles, timeline and weapons, etc.
2. http://en.wikipedia.org/wiki/Declaration_of_independence
   It is a website where you can find declarations of independence in other countries.

Movies to See

1. *The Crossing* (2000)

   This is a historical non-fiction movie. The main character is George Washington played by Jeff Daniels. This movie is about how the colonists crossed the Delaware River. At the time George Washington was not the president, but a general. The colonists were losing the revolution badly to the British. The Delaware River was about to freeze. General Washington decides that they need to cross the river to get away from the British. If you would like to learn about when

Washington crossed the Delaware or if you love to study history, this movie would definitely be the best recommendation.

2. *Rebels and Redcoats*(2003)

We've been told that the War of Independence was the American people's struggle for liberty against an oppressive colonial power. However, many Americans were loyal to the British Crown throughout the war; men and women often chose sides not because they wanted freedom, but because they wanted their neighbor's land. Using vivid reconstruction, eye-witness accounts, original documents and paintings, and Richard's proven story-telling skills, this film overthrows traditional perceptions about these compelling years. As the story unfolds, the truth emerges—a truth far more fascinating than we were ever led to believe.

Song to Enjoy
"Yankee Doodle"

Singing a song in Revolutionary America was not necessarily an innocent act. At the time, almost everyone sang in public on occasions either for entertainment, for worship, or as part of their work. However, songs were also important instruments of satire and mockery. People used them to make fun of public figures, to pass ugly rumors, or to playfully insult their enemies—and sometimes their friends.

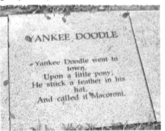

As opposition to the British rule in the American colonies heated up, satirical songs took on a new edge. Rebellious colonists sang songs insulting Britain's king, George III, as a drunken tyrant, and British soldiers answered with songs ridiculing the Americans as backwoods yokels.

One of these songs, which told the story of a poorly dressed Yankee simpleton, or "doodle," was so popular with British troops that they played it as they marched to battle on the first day of the Revolutionary War. The rebels quickly claimed the song as their own, though, and created dozens of new verses that mocked the British, praised the new Continental Army, and hailed its commander, George Washington.

By 1781, when the British surrendered at Yorktown, being called a "Yankee Doodle" had gone from being an insult to a point of pride, and the song had become the new republic's unofficial national anthem.

Unit 4
The Young Republic

> Any society that would give up a little liberty to gain a little security will deserve neither and lose both.
> —Benjamin Franklin

Unit Goals

- To learn about the process of establishing centralized government.
- To know the essence of American Constitution.
- To understand the reason of Louisiana Purchase.
- To learn the useful words and expressions about the American Constitution and the Young Republic.
- To improve English language skills.
- To develop critical thinking and intercultural communication skills.

Before You Read

1. If you were forming a new organization, how would you run it? Would there be one leader or representatives from each section? Would larger ones have more representatives and more votes than smaller ones?
2. What do you know about the Constitution of the United States? Have you ever heard of "check and balance" of a government? Comment on it.
3. Do you know that United States purchased Louisiana with only $15 million, which is an average of 4 cents an acre? Why did people argue for or against it at that time?

Pros	Cons

4. Form groups of three or four students. Try to find, on the Internet or in the library, more information about the U.S. Constitution. Prepare a 5-minute classroom presentation.

Start to Read

Text A   **The Creation of a National Government**

1. The revolutionary generation of Americans bequeathed to posterity a workable system of national government. No national political institutions existed in America before the war. To fight the war against Britain, the states in 1781 agreed to *Articles of Confederation*, which created a weak but workable national government. Then

in 1787, nationalist-minded Patriots devised a constitution, creating a "national republic" whose powers were drawn from the people at large and which established a much stronger central government.

2. The movement toward centralized government began slowly and sporadically. The First and Second Continental Congresses, held at Philadelphia in 1774 and 1775, were attended by delegates from most colonies and claimed to speak for the entire American population.

3. Following the *Declaration of Independence* in 1776, the states voluntarily joined together in the Continental Congress, in which each state had one vote. The Congress mediated disputes among the states, raised and maintained the Continental Army, secured loans from European bankers, and made military and commercial alliances with France. Its success laid the basis for more permanent national political institutions.

4. The Continental Congress was a temporary government without clearly defined powers. To establish its authority, the Congress in November 1777 enacted the *Articles of Confederation*, drafted by John Dickinson of Pennsylvania, and declared they would go into effect when ratified by all of the states. The Articles proposed a loose confederation in which each state kept its sovereign independence and control over all of its internal affairs. However, certain powers, primarily relating to diplomacy and defense, were entrusted to the Confederation Congress. It was given the power to declare war, make treaties, borrow and print money, and requisition funds from the states.

5. At first, a number of states refused to ratify the Articles. Some state governments hesitated to create a central political authority that might restrict their autonomy like the British Parliament had done. Gradually, the pressures of war overcame this reluctance. And the Congress did its part, persuading the states to give up their western land claims and to allow creation of a national domain. Finally, in 1781, under the threat of British invasion, Maryland became the final state to ratify the Articles.

6. The central government created by the Articles was simple in structure and limited in authority. There was no governor or chief executive and no system of courts. In the Congress, each state had one vote, regardless of  population or wealth. Furthermore, the powers of the Confederation could be changed only by the unanimous consent of the states.

7. Even as the *Articles of Confederation* were ratified, some Patriots were campaigning for a stronger central government. One group that wanted a more powerful Confederation was composed of nationalists. These men—military officers, diplomats, delegates to Congress, and bureaucrats—had served the Confederation during the war and had acquired a national perspective and outlook. In their thinking, there was a self-evident need for central control over the western lands, commercial policies and dealings with foreign states.

8. The 55 delegates gathered in Philadelphia's Independence Hall in May 1787 to revise the *Articles of Confederation*, including some of the most prestigious men in the United States—among them were George Washington, Benjamin Franklin, and Alexander Hamilton. Most of the delegates were mostly merchants, slave-owning planters, and landlords.

9. Some members objected that it discriminated against states with large populations by leaving all states with a single vote in the one-house Confederation legislature. Many other delegates were convinced that it left too many powers to the states.

10. The convention turned its attention to the plan for a national republic presented by James Madison of Virginia, known as the "Father of the Constitution." Madison was determined to create a powerful central government. His Virginia Plan would limit the sovereignty of the individual states and ensure "the supremacy of national authority." The Virginia Plan proposed a three-part national government, with a lower house—the House of Representatives, elected by the voters, an upper house—the Senate, selected by the lower body, and an executive and judiciary chosen by the entire legislature.

11. The delegates endorsed the basic principles of Madison's plan in June. During the following month, they fashioned two compromises. The first compromise sought to balance the political power of states with large and small populations. Under the terms of the compromise, the states would be represented in the lower house on the basis of population. In the upper house, each state would have an equal number of votes.

12. Although the main conflict over representation was between the large and the small states, a second compromise was necessary to solve an important regional issue. The Southern states contained a large number of black slaves. Since these slaves were not allowed to vote, Northern delegates argued that they should not be counted for purposes of representation. They maintained that the number of seats held by Southern states in the lower house should be based on their white population. Southerners wanted slaves to be counted equally with free people. The delegates compromised. Three-fifths of a state's enslaved population would be counted for purposes of representation and taxation.

13. After reaching these compromises over representation and slavery, the delegates spent two months working out the details of the new plan of government.

14. In the middle of September, 38 of the delegates still in Philadelphia signed the *Constitution of the United States* (3 refused to sign). The document stipulated that it would go into effect upon ratification by special conventions

in 9 of the 13 states.

15. The new constitution produced exciting debates and bitter political battles both in the state conventions and among the public at large. Supporters of the new document called themselves Federalists. Merchants as well as the commercial-minded farmers were the advocates of the Constitution, hoping it would spur business activity.

16. The Anti-federalists, who opposed ratification of the Constitution, were drawn from all sections and classes and included political leaders in many states. However, their arguments appealed primarily to small-scale farmers, who would have little voice in the new government and feared its power. Anti-federalist leaders argued that republican institutions were possible only in cities or small states. They contended that the new central government would be far removed from the people; and that the lack of a bill of rights would expose citizens to arbitrary national power.

17. Some Federalists saw merit in this last criticism and, in order to win ratification in the crucial states of Virginia, Massachusetts, and New York, promised that a bill of rights would be added. The other Anti-federalist arguments were answered by Madison, Hamilton, and John Jay in a series of newspaper articles known as *The Federalist Papers* (1788). They stressed that the state governments, which were closer to the people, would retain substantial powers. The authors also asserted that the three branches of the new government would "check and balance" one another, thus preventing an arbitrary exercise of power.

18. These arguments of *The Federalist Papers* and the promise of a bill of rights secured the ratification of the Constitution. By 1789 the Constitution had been ratified in 11 states and was put into effect with the election of the first Congress of the United States and a first president, George Washington.

After You Read

Knowledge Focus

1. **Pair Work: Discuss the following questions with your partner.**
   (1) What was the Continental Congress largely responsible for?
   (2) What do you know about the *Articles of Confederation*?
   (3) What are the three parts of a national government according to the Virginia Plan?
   (4) What are the viewpoints of federalists and anti-federalists?
   (5) How do you understand the "check and balance" of the U.S. government?

2. **Sole Work**: Tell whether the following are true or false according to the knowledge you have learned. Consider why.

   (1) Some national political institutions existed in America before the War of Independence. (　)

   (2) The Continental Congress was a temporary government without clearly defined powers. (　)

   (3) In the *Articles of Confederation*, each state kept its sovereign dependence and control over all of its internal affairs. (　)

   (4) The powers of the Confederation could be changed only by the unanimous consent of the states. (　)

   (5) Although the *Articles of Confederation* was a hard move, all the states ratified the Articles without hesitation. (　)

   (6) In the Congress, each state had one vote, regardless of population or wealth. (　)

   (7) Most of the 55 delegates who gathered in May 1787 to revise the *Articles of Confederation* were mostly soldiers, slave-owning planters, and aristocracy. (　)

   (8) Merchants as well as the commercial-minded farmers were the advocates of the Constitution because they wished to benefit from the *Constitution of the United States*. (　)

   (9) The Anti-federalists, who opposed ratification of the Constitution, were widely supported. (　)

   (10) Because of the effort of George Washington, by 1789 the Constitution had been ratified. (　)

3. **Fill in the blanks according to the historical knowledge you have learned in the text above.**

   (1) To fight the war against Britain, the states in _____ agreed to _____, which created a weak but workable national government.

   (2) To establish its authority, the Congress in _____ enacted the *Articles of Confederation*, _____ by John Dickinson of Pennsylvania, and declared they would go into effect when ratified by all of the states.

   (3) The 55 delegates gathered in Philadelphia's Independence Hall in May 1787 to revise the *Articles of Confederation*, including some of the most prestigious men in the United States—among them, _____, _____ and Alexander Hamilton.

   (4) In the middle of September, 38 of the delegates still in Philadelphia signed the _____ although 3 refused to sign.

   (5) Anti-federalist leaders argued that _____ were possible only in cities or small states.

   (6) _____ stressed that the state governments, which were closer to the people, would retain substantial powers.

   (7) By _____, the Constitution had been ratified in _____ states and was put into effect with the election of the first Congress of the United States and the first president _____.

Language Focus

1. Fill in the blanks with the following words or expressions from the text.

sporadically	mediate	ratify	entrust
reluctance	unanimous	stipulate	ensure
prestigious	discriminate		

(1) I am afraid he is going to stay in his protective shell forever. I could understand his _____ to involve in any relationships.

(2) World Health Organization stresses the need to _____ the safety of children's medicines.

(3) All the representatives of local union _____ voted to endorse the tentative national agreement.

(4) The law in effect does not _____ clearly any penalty of those criminals of this kind.

(5) The committee members overwhelmingly voted to _____ a new four-year agreement with the U.S. Postal Service, since this agreement was in the interest of all.

(6) It is illegal to _____ against an individual because of birthplace, ancestry, culture, or language common to a specific ethnic group.

(7) In the first two month I did not experience any errors, but now I find them _____ happen on different machines of mine.

(8) The challenges have not lessened the reputation of the Pulitzer Prizes as the country's most _____ awards.

(9) Whenever I succeed in resolving a conflict, I recall my mother's wise words, "It is not a trivial matter to _____ and resolve disputes."

(10) The construction of the new metro line will be probably _____ to the private corporation as the municipal government does not have enough money to build two new metro lines at the same time.

2. Complete the following sentences with the proper forms of the words in the brackets.

(1) Several local _____ (establish) have had to shut down.

(2) Students usually find _____ (temporarily) jobs during their summer holidays.

(3) Last few decades witnessed great increase in _____ (internalize) trade.

(4) His _____ (hesitate) attempts to speak English bothered himself for a long time.

(5) The old universities of Oxford and Cambridge have a lot of _____ (prestigious) in the academic circle.

(6) Johnson is largely regarded as a man of _____ (consider) by his colleagues.

(7) The _____ (autonomy) region has been established since the 1950s.

(8) Most scientists in the lab risk _____ (expose) to harmful radiation.

(9) The _____ (promise) singer made his debut at national theater.

(10) Once the jewels were safely locked up in the bank, he had no more anxiety about their _____ (secure).

Comprehensive Work

Essay Writing

Amendment II of Constitution says: "A well regulated Militia being necessary to the security of a free State, the Right of the People to keep and bear Arms shall not be infringed."

The right to bear arms is one of the controversies of American policies. On the one hand, people increasingly worry about the increased violence; on the other hand, they are not willing to give up the legacy of history, i.e. the right to bear arms. As they claimed, it is one of the basic rights they are entitled to as an American, and it is guaranteed by the Second Amendment of American Constitution. Examine the issue critically and make comments on it.

Learning to Write an Outline

Directions: An outline is a document that briefly summarizes the information that will be included in a paper, book, speech, or similar document. It shows the order in which the information will be presented and indicates the relationship of the pieces of information to each other. Please try to complete the following outline of Text A in this unit.

Text A   The Creation of a National Government

(1) Introduction: The road to a national government
   Before the war _____
   In 1781 _____
   In 1787 _____

(2—3) The two Continental Congresses, 1774—1775
   What was the Continental Congress responsible for?
      [1] To mediate _____
      [2] To raise and maintain _____
      [3] To secure _____
      [4] To make _____

(4—7) The Articles of Confederation, 1781
   (Para 4)
      1. What were the powers of each state?
         [1] To keep _____
         [2] To control over _____
      2. What were the powers entrusted to the Congress?
         [1] To declare _____

[2] To make _____
[3] To borrow and print _____
[4] To requisition _____

(Para 5)
Why were the *Articles of Confederation* enacted in 1777, but ratified in 1781?
[1] at first _____
[2] gradually _____
[3] finally _____

(Para 6)
The dissatisfaction with _____

(Para 7)
The need for _____

(8—10) The Constitutional Convention, 1787

James Madison and the three-part national government
[1] The legislature (the Senate & the House of Representatives)
[2] The executive
[3] The judiciary

(11—13) The compromises over representation and slavery

(Para 11) the first compromise: to balance _____
[1] In the lower house, _____
[2] In the upper house, _____

(Para 12) the second compromise: an important regional issue is _____
[1] Northern delegates argued that _____
[2] Southerners replied that _____

(Para 13) Summary:
Compromises over _____ and _____

(14—18) The Constitution and struggle over ratification

(Para 14) The delegates signed the _____ of the United States
(Para 15) the Federalists
The advocates of _____
(Para 16) the anti-federalists
[1] Republican institutions were _____
[2] The new central government would _____
[3] The lack of a bill of rights would _____
(Para 17) "Check and balance"
(Para 18) The first Congress and the first president

Text B   Benjamin Franklin

Directions: Go through the following passage quickly and finish the multiple-choice questions.

1. Benjamin Franklin did not invent _____.
   A. Franklin's stove   B. bifocals
   C. lightning rod   D. electricity
2. Franklin lived in the _____ century.
   A. nineteenth   B. seventeenth
   C. twenty-first   D. eighteenth
3. Franklin did not use _____ to test for electricity in a thunderstorm.
   A. lightning rod   B. lightning bells
   C. bifocals   D. kite
4. David Rittenhouse was _____.
   A. a scientist who studied electricity
   B. an inventor who improved on Franklin's stove
   C. a famous athlete
   D. a customer who bought Franklin stoves
5. Rittenhouse made his improvements on Franklin's stove in the _____.
   A. 1790s   B. 1750s
   C. 1600s   D. 1760s

What makes a person famous—great looks, athletic ability, musical talent, or star quality?

Benjamin Franklin has been famous for a long time. Maybe he had all of those qualities, or maybe he did not. Either way, that is not what he is remembered for. Ben Franklin is remembered for his many great achievements, including some great inventions. None of those "star qualities" would have helped him invent the Franklin stove, but another great quality did, curiosity. Franklin was curious about how things worked. When something did not work very well, he liked to go to his workshop and see what he could come up with. He liked to experiment to see if his ideas were right. His curiosity led to some more inventions too, including bifocal glasses and the lightning rod.

Benjamin Franklin invented the lightning rod in 1752, during the time that he was experimenting with electricity. Everyone has heard the tale about how he flew a kite in a thunderstorm to see if lightning was really electricity. He also used other creations to test out his ideas about electricity. One of them was called lightning bells, which were bells that would jingle when there was electricity in the air. He first set up a lightning rod to test for electricity too. Later when he observed a house that had been struck by lightning he noticed that the entire house had burned down except for the parts that had metal in them. This gave him the idea to use his lightning rod to protect a house in a storm.

In 1760, Franklin invented bifocal glasses. He had reached the age where he needed glasses both to read and to see things far away. Of course this meant two pairs of glasses: one that focused near, for reading and looking at things up close, and one that focused far away, for the rest of the time. Ben always had to change from one pair of glasses to the other, and that probably became a nuisance. He thought that there must be a better way, and so he cut the lenses from two pair of glasses in half, fastened half of each together, and created the first pair of bifocals. This was an invention that Ben could use everyday.

In 1790, he invented the Franklin stove. This time, the problem that he had been thinking about was fireplaces. Fireplaces used lots of wood, wasted lots of heat, made lots of smoke, and could be dangerous. Franklin's idea for an improvement was an iron stove that would take in cool air through the bottom, and radiate heat from all sides. There was one problem with Franklin's design, and that had to do with the chimney. Another inventor, David Rittenhouse, improved Franklin's stove with a better chimney. Franklin stoves have been around ever since.

How did Benjamin Franklin learn all that he needed to know to create these great inventions? He did not spend a lot of years in school, like most people do today, but he did spend many years on his education. How was that possible? Franklin was mainly self-taught. His own curiosity led him to search for information. Franklin educated himself in the fields of math, science, and English, as well as several foreign languages. By experimenting and trying our new inventions, he continued his education throughout his whole life.

Benjamin Franklin accomplished many things during his lifetime. If you follow Ben's simple advice, maybe you will too. He said, "Employ thy time well."

Text C The Essence of the Constitution

The government is to be run for the people and by the people. The purposes of the new government are "to form a perfect union, establish justice, insure domestic tranquility, provide for the common defense, promote the general welfare, and secure the blessings of liberty."

Separation of Powers

It is the doctrine and practice of dividing the powers of a government among different branches to guard against abuse of authority. A government of separated powers assigns different political and legal powers to the legislative, executive, and judicial branches. The legislative branch has the power to make laws—for example, the declaration of what acts are to be regarded as criminal. The executive branch has the authority to administer the law—primarily by bringing lawbreakers to trial—and to appoint officials and oversee the administration of government responsibilities. The judicial branch has the power to try cases brought to court and to interpret the meaning of laws under which the trials are conducted. Most democratic systems have some degree of separation of powers, but the United States stands as the preeminent example of the practice.

In the United States, the separation of powers is a fundamental constitutional principle. The legislative power is vested in Congress, the executive power in the president, and the judicial power in the Supreme Court and other federal courts.

An important aspect of the separation of powers is that the power of one branch should not be exercised by anyone who also holds a position in another branch. In other words, a lawmaker may not also administer the laws. Another important feature of the separation of powers in the United States is judicial review. The courts, not Congress or the president, say what the law means when a case is before them. In appropriate cases, the courts may even strike down a law enacted by Congress, or order the executive branch to halt enforcement of a law or government policy, if they determine that the law or policy conflicts with the Constitution.

Checks and Balances

It is the doctrine and practice of dispersing political power and creating mutual accountability among political entities such as the courts, the president or prime minister, the legislature, and the citizens. The diffusion of power and the mutual accountability are designed to prevent any single group or individual from dominating the political system. Political systems with checks and balances sometimes have a separation of powers—that is, an allocation of different political and legal functions to separate and independent branches of the government.

Federalism

It also referred to as federal government, a national or international political system in which two levels of government control the same territory and citizens. The word federal comes from the Latin term *fidere*, meaning "to trust." Countries with federal political systems have both a central government and governments based in smaller political units, usually called states, provinces, or territories. These smaller political units surrender some of their political power to the central government, relying on it to act for the common good.

In a federal system, laws are made both by state, provincial, or territorial governments and by a central government. In the United States, for example, people who live in the state of Ohio must obey the laws made by the Ohio legislature and the Congress of the United States.

The Bill of Rights

It refers to the 10 amendments to restrict the central government and assure individual rights. During the debates on the adoption of the Constitution, its opponents repeatedly demanded a "bill of rights" that would spell out the immunities of individual citizens. Several state conventions in their formal ratification of the Constitution asked for such amendments.

Questions for Discussion or Reflection
1. What are the branches in the American government with separated powers? And what is the responsibility of each branch?
2. What do you know about the "Bill of Rights"? Why is it fit for America?
3. What does "Separation of Powers" refer to?

Proper Names

Alexander Hamilton 亚历山大·汉密尔顿
Benjamin Franklin 本杰明·富兰克林
Bill of Rights 《权利法案》
Checks and Balances 政府机关彼此之间的相互制衡
Federalism 联邦政治,联邦制度
George Washington 乔治·华盛顿

James Madison 詹姆斯·麦迪逊
Separation of Powers 三权分立
Articles of Confederation 《邦联条例》
the House of Representatives 众议院
the Senate 参议院

Notes

1. **Alexander Hamilton** (1755 or 1757—1804): He was the first U.S. Secretary of the Treasury, a founding Father, an economist, and a political philosopher. He was one of America's first Constitutional lawyers, and co-writer of the *Federalist Papers*, a primary source for Constitutional interpretation.
2. **James Madison** (1751—1836): He was the fourth U.S. president. Because of his central role in the Constitutional Convention, he became known as the "Father of the Constitution."
3. **"In God We Trust"**: The national motto of the United States. The phrase is derived from the line "And this be our motto, 'In God is our trust,'" in the battle song that later became the U.S. national anthem, "*The Star-Spangled Banner.*" The phrase first appeared on U.S. coins in 1864 and became obligatory on all U.S. currency in 1955. In 1956, it was made the national motto by an act of Congress.
4. **The Bill of Rights**: Because the Constitution of the United States granted the federal government so much power, several states demanded several amendments to guarantee individual rights against the power of the federal government. The first ten amendments are known as the "Bill of Rights," which includes items like the freedom of speech and the right to bear arms, etc.

For Fun

Websites to Visit

http://en.wikipedia.org/wiki/Articles_of_Confederation

This is a website that provides information on *Articles of Confederation* including its background, article summaries and its functions, etc.

http://www.usconstitution.net/const.html

This page presents all the articles of the American Constitution.

http://www.usconstitution.net/consttop_sepp.html

This topic page concerns the separation of powers.

Song to Enjoy

"Hunters of Kentucky"

The War of 1812 was a major turning point for the United States, and a severe test of the young republic's resolve. During the three years of war, the country endured many hardships. However, it also achieved a number of decisive battlefield victories—triumphs that demonstrated the American people's ability to overcome great odds, and that helped forge a new sense of national identity.

The last battle of the war, the Battle of New Orleans, was such a dramatic and unexpected victory that it immediately took a prominent place in American popular culture. Under the leadership of General Andrew Jackson, a few thousand U.S. troops, including militiamen from Kentucky, Mississippi, Tennessee, and Louisiana, successfully held off a much larger force of British troops and kept New Orleans from falling into enemy hands. This triumph made Jackson a legend and set him on the road to the White House. The battle itself, meanwhile, was celebrated in poems, paintings, dances, and songs.

A favorite theme of many songs was the key role rural militiamen and backwoods hunters played in the victory. The War of 1812 was the first conflict to bring men from many Southern states and territories together to fight for the U.S. Soldiers from each region sang songs praising their own superhuman abilities and exaggerating their accomplishments, in a sort of humorous boasting competition with the men from other parts of the country. As you read this song about Kentucky militiamen in the Battle of New Orleans, you might ask yourself how stories and songs about the battle might have shaped the way people at the time thought about themselves—both as Kentuckians and Americans.

Hunters of Kentucky

YE gentlemen and ladies fair
Who grace this famous city,
Just listen, if you've time to spare,
While I rehearse a ditty;
And for the opportunity
Conceive yourselves quite lucky,
For 'tis not often that you see
A hunter from Kentucky.
Oh Kentucky, the hunters of Kentucky!
Oh Kentucky, the hunters of Kentucky!

We are a hardy, free-born race,
Each man to fear a stranger;
Whate'er the game, we join in chase,
Despising toil and danger.
And if a daring foe annoys,
Whate'er his strength and forces,
We'll show him that Kentucky boys
Are alligator horses.
Oh Kentucky, & c.
I s'pose you've read it in the prints,
How Packenham attempted
To make old Hickory Jackson wince,
But soon his scheme repented;
For we, with rifles ready cock'd,
Thought such occasion lucky,
And soon around the gen'ral flock'd,
The hunters of Kentucky.
Oh Kentucky, & c.

You've heard, I s'pose, how New-Orleans
Is fam'd for wealth and beauty—
There's girls of ev'ry hue, it seems,
From snowy white to sooty.
So Packenham he made his brags,
If he in fight was lucky,
He'd have their girls and cotton bags,
In spite of old Kentucky.
Oh Kentucky, & c.
But Jackson he was wide awake,
And was not scar'd at trifles,
For well he knew what aim we take,
With our Kentucky rifles:
So he led us down by cypress swamp,
The ground was low and mucky;
There stood John Bull in martial pomp,
And here was old Kentucky.
Oh Kentucky, & c.

Unit 5

The Westward Movement

> The whole country, from San Francisco to Los Angeles... resounds with the cry of Gold! Gold! Gold! While the field is left half-planted, the house half-built, and everything neglected but the manufacture of picks and shovels.
>
> —From *The Californian*

Unit Goals

- To understand the motivations of people's moving westward.
- To learn about the territory expansion of the U.S.
- To be acquainted with the Gold Rush.
- To learn the useful words and expressions concerning the history of Westward Movement of America.
- To improve English language skills.
- To develop critical thinking and intercultural communication skills.

Before You Read

1. What impact did the migration have on Native Americans and the environment?

   Impacts {
   _____
   _____
   _____
   _____
   }

2. Do you think the westward expansion could repeat itself in another part of the world?
3. What could be the possible motivations of the westward expansion?

4. Form groups of three or four students. Try to find, on the Internet or in the library, more information about the Westward Movement which interests you most. Prepare a 5-minute classroom presentation.

Start to Read

Text A The Frontier of the American West

1. American Westward Movement, movement of people from the settled regions of the United States to lands farther west. Between the early 17th and late 19th centuries, Anglo-American peoples and their societies expanded from the Atlantic Coast to the Pacific Coast. This westward movement, across what was often called the American frontier, was of enormous significance. By expanding the nation's borders to include more than three million square miles, the United States became one of the most powerful nations of the 20th century. However, this expansion also resulted in great suffering, destruction, and cultural loss for the Native Americans of North America.

"At the proper seasons, one sees in the long main street of the town, lines of emigrant wagons."

2. Before Anglo-American westward expansion, North America had been shaped by many other forces and cultures. There were hundreds of Native American tribes who had been living on the continent for thousands of years before any Europeans arrived. Many of these tribes disappeared because of the assault of European exploration and settlement.

3. England established its first Atlantic colonies in Virginia at Jamestown in 1607 and in Massachusetts. These first English frontiers illustrated two of the most common motivations for people moving westward. The first motivation

was the hope of finding great wealth quickly through developing and trading the colonies' resources. Jamestown was settled for this reason. The earliest dreams of mining for gold and producing wine and silk came to nothing, but in time Virginians found prosperity in the rich soil, especially by raising and exporting tobacco. Over the next 400 years, the economic motive, in particular the desire for good and cheap farmland would be the most powerful attractions for people moving west.

4. The second common motivation was the hope of practicing their religion without government intervention. The Puritan settlers of Massachusetts wanted to build a community based on religious ideas that were opposed by the British government. The frontier was home to dozens of colonies looking for freedom, religious and otherwise.

5. Those first Atlantic colonies also illustrated the contradictory roles that government played in westward expansion. The Puritans settled in Massachusetts with the permission, and sometimes the protection, of the same government whose policies they were trying to escape. Governments, first England and then the United States, always encouraged movement westward in a variety of ways. These governments bought or seized land from others and gave it away or sold it cheaply to emigrants. The governments used their military to protect settlers and financed developments, such as transportation, that made settlement easier.

6. People heading west came to expect the government's aid and support. At the same time, settlers often resisted efforts by distant authorities to regulate how they used and lived on their new lands. From the first colonies to the final farming frontiers of the 20th century, this conflicting relationship between pioneers and government was a large part of the frontier story.

7. It took Americans a century and a half to expand as far west as the Appalachian Mountains, a few hundred miles from the Atlantic coast. It took another 50 years to push the frontier to the Mississippi River. By 1830, fewer than 100,000 pioneers had crossed the Mississippi.

8. Only a small number of explorers and traders had ventured far beyond the

Mississippi River. These trailblazers drew a picture of the American West as a land of promise, a paradise of plenty, filled with fertile valleys and rich land. During the 1840s, tens of thousands of Americans began the process of settling the West beyond the Mississippi River. Thousands of families chalked GTT ("Gone to Texas") on their gates or on their wagons, and joined the trek westward. By 1850, pioneers had pushed the edge of settlement all the way to Texas, the Rocky Mountains, and the Pacific Ocean.

9. On January 24, 1848, less than 10 days before the signing of the peace treaty ending the Mexican War, James W. Marshall, a 36-year old carpenter and handyman, noticed several bright bits of yellow mineral near a sawmill that he was building. To test if the bits were "fool's gold," which shatters when struck by a hammer, Marshall "tried it between two rocks, and found that it could be beaten into a different shape but not broken." He told the men working with him: "Boys, by God, I believe I have found a gold mine."

10. On March 15, a San Francisco newspaper, *The Californian*, printed the first account of Marshall's discovery. Within two weeks, the paper had lost its staff and was forced to shut down its printing press. In its last edition it told its readers:

11. "The whole country, from San Francisco to Los Angeles... resounds with the cry of Gold! Gold! Gold! While the field is left half-planted, the house half-built, and everything neglected but the manufacture of picks and shovels."

12. In 1849, 80,000 men arrived in California. Only half were Americans; the rest came from Britain, Australia, Germany, France, Latin America, and China. Sailors jumped ship; husbands left wives; apprentices ran away from their masters; farmers and business people deserted their livelihoods. By July, 1850, sailors had abandoned 500 ships in San Francisco Bay. Within a year, California's population had swollen from 14,000 to 100,000. The population of San Francisco, which stood at 459 in the summer of 1847, reached 20,000 within a few months.

13. The Gold Rush transformed California from a sleepy society into one that was wild, unruly, ethnically-diverse, and violent. Philosopher Josiah Royce, whose family arrived in the midst of the gold rush, declared that the Californian was "morally and socially tried as no other American ever has been tried." In San Francisco alone there were more than 500 bars and 1,000 gambling dens. In the span of 18 months, the city burned to the ground six times.

14. The Gold Rush era in California lasted less than a decade. By 1860, the

romantic era of California gold mining was over. Prospectors had found more than $350 million worth of gold.

15. The exploration and settlement of the Far West is one of the great epics of the 19th century history. But America's dramatic territorial expansion also created severe problems. In addition to providing the United States with its richest mines, greatest forests, and most fertile farm land, the Far West intensified the sectional conflict between the North and South and raised the ultimately divisive question of whether slavery would be permitted in the western territories.

After You Read

Knowledge Focus

1. Pair Work: Discuss the following questions with your partner.
   (1) What was the significance of American Westward Movement?
   (2) What motivated people to expand the nation's borders westward?
   (3) What were the conflicting roles of the government in the westward expansion?
   (4) How did those explorers and traders view the American West?
   (5) Why was the Californian "morally and socially tried as no other American ever has been tried"?

2. Sole Work: Tell whether the following are true or false according to the knowledge you have learned. Consider why.
   (1) Between the early 17th and late 19th centuries, Anglo-American peoples and their societies expanded from the Atlantic Coast to the Pacific Coast. (　)
   (2) England established its first Atlantic colonies in Virginia at Jamestown in 1607 and in California. (　)
   (3) One of the motivations to move westward was to find great wealth quickly through developing and trading the colonies' resources. (　)
   (4) It took Americans a century and a half to expand as far west as the Appalachian Mountains. (　)
   (5) Among the common motivations of moving westward are finding great wealth and practicing religion without government intervention. (　)
   (6) James W. Marshall was the first person to discover a gold mine in California. (　)
   (7) The vast majority of those who arrived in California were Americans. (　)
   (8) The Gold Rush transformed California from a sleepy society into one that was wild, unruly, ethnically-diverse, and violent. (　)
   (9) The Gold Rush provided the United States with its richest mines, greatest forests, and most fertile farm land and made America one of the richest

countries. (　)

(10) The Gold Rush was a period of feverish migration of workers into the area which witnessed a dramatic discovery of commercial quantities of gold. (　)

Language Focus

1. **Fill in the blanks with the following words or expressions from the text.**

expand	assault	exploration	motivation
resound with	contradictory	transform	restrict
attempt	come to nothing		

(1) The school's activities have been _____ to include climbing and mountaineering.

(2) A woman and a man have been convicted of _____ a police officer in last month's demonstration.

(3) They are making _____ into the cultural problems of South Africa.

(4) There seems to be a lack of _____ among the staff.

(5) I keep getting _____ advice—some people tell me to keep it warm while some tell me to put ice on it.

(6) The concert hall _____ cheers and applause.

(7) Whenever a camera was pointed at her, Marilyn would instantly _____ herself into a radiant star.

(8) The government has _____ freedom of movement into and out of the country.

(9) There's no point in even _____ to explain—he'll never listen.

(10) Much effort and planning _____.

2. **Complete the following sentences with the proper forms of the words in the brackets.**

(1) Foreigners are, more often than not, amazed at the vast _____ (expand) of the Chinese territory.

(2) A large number of weapons for mass _____ (destructive) were put into use in the Second World War.

(3) The _____ (explore) of space has long been a topic that fascinates the scholars in the Academy.

(4) The internal affairs cannot be _____ (intervention) by external forces.

(5) His theory on cultural shock was _____ (contradict) to what he mentioned in his speech delivered in the conference.

(6) Any visitor is not allowed to take photo without _____ (permit).

(7) This is a place where _____ (conflict) ideas clash.

(8) He was informed of the specific time and place about the _____ (arrive) of the Indian delegation.

(9) All his colleagues were stunned by the _____ (drama) change in his appearance and manner.

(10) We did not notice the _____ (severe) of the earthquake until the inside story

was publicized.

Comprehensive Work

Time Magazine is creating a special issue to highlight the periods of American history. Your historical news team has been assigned to create a four-page magazine spread for the westward expansion period.

Each person in your group will assume one of the following roles to make up your news team:

Reporter
Scientist
Correspondent
Historian

A. Each member of your group must decide on a role to create for the news team. And the duties for each role are as follows.

Reporter will be responsible for writing a news story that explains the westward migration movement. He/she should cover the following questions.

1. Who were the people traveling west? Where did they come from? What were they like?
2. What items would the pioneers need to take on their journey west?
3. Where were the pioneers going? What did they expect to find at their destination?
4. When did this migration west take place? How many people made this journey?
5. Why did the pioneers migrate west?
6. How did they travel? Was wagon train the only option?

Scientist will report on the wildlife, natural hazards and physical hazards that the wagon train may encounter along the journey. They are based on the questions below.

1. What wildlife would pioneers expect to see as they travel west?
2. How was wildlife helpful to the pioneers on their journey?
3. Why could wildlife be dangerous to the travelers?
4. Pioneers could expect to face many natural hazards along the trail. Research and explain several natural hazards the pioneers may encounter, such as too much water, too little water, deserts, mountains.
5. Pioneers also expected to face many physical hazards. Research and explain several of the many physical hazards encountered, such as disease, accidents, and Native Americans.

Correspondent will be responsible for keeping a diary or journal for a typical wagon train. The journal must have a minimum of 4 entries like the beginning of trip, 1-2 months into the trip, 3—4 months into the trip, and reaching destination. It should be based on the following questions.

1. What emotions did pioneers experience as they prepared to make the long, hard journey west?
2. Research some common experiences and emotions as people adjusted to life on the trail. Give specific details of their day to day lives.

3. What responsibilities did the women have on the wagon train? How about the children?
4. What effect did several months of harsh, trail life have on the members of the wagon trains? Explore several actual diaries and journals from true pioneers to better understand the effect the long, hard journey had on the pioneers.
5. Reaching their destination was often bittersweet. Explain how this could be possible. Describe their destination and the feelings on reaching their new home.

Historian will be responsible for capturing some of the unusual stories, dispelling common myths of wagon trains, and researching two of the Native American tribes the pioneers may encounter.

There are questions to refer to:
1. People often get an inaccurate picture of history in traditional books and movies. Research what wagon trains were really like. Try to dispel a few common myths.
2. History is also full of funny and unusual occurrences. Find some examples of unusual or different events from real wagon trains.
3. At this period in history, Native American tribes inhabited most of the western lands. Research at least two tribes whose land was crossed by the wagon trains heading west. Be sure to include accurate information about the relationship between these tribes and the pioneers.

B. Once you have decided on your roles, research the Internet and other resources for information that will help you to write your article.
C. Write and edit your articles. Allow teammates to read the articles and offer advice for improvement.
D. Layout and publish your magazine.

Read More

Text B The Donner Party

 Early in April, 1846, 87 pioneers led by George Donner, a well-to-do 62-year-old farmer, set out from Springfield, Illinois, for California. Like many emigrants, they were ill-prepared for the dangerous trek. The pioneers' 27 wagons were loaded with foods, liquor, and built-in beds and stoves.

On July 20, at Fort Bridger, Wyoming, the party decided to take a shortcut. Lansford Hastings, had suggested in a guidebook that pioneers could save 400 miles by cutting south of the Great Salt Lake. Hastings himself had never taken his own shortcut. He was trying to overthrow California's weak Mexican government and hoped to bring in enough emigrants to start a revolution.

Soon huge boulders, arid desert, and dangerous mountain passes slowed the expedition to a crawl. During one stretch, the party traveled only 36 miles in 21 days. A desert crossing that Hastings said would take two days actually took six days and nights.

Twelve weeks after leaving Fort Bridger, the Donner Party reached the eastern Sierra Nevada Mountains and prepared to cross Truckee Pass, the last remaining barrier before they arrived in California's Sacramento Valley. On October 31, they climbed the high Sierra ridges in an attempt to cross the pass, but five-foot high snow drifts blocked their path.

Trapped, the party built crude tents and tepees, covered with clothing, blankets, and animal hides. To survive, the Donner party was forced to eat mice, their rugs, and even their shoes. In the end, surviving members of the party escaped starvation only by eating the flesh of those who died.

In mid-December, a group of 12 men and 5 women made a last-ditch effort to cross the pass to find help. They took only a 6-day supply of rations, consisting of finger-sized pieces of dried beef—two pieces a person per day. During a severe storm, two of the group died. The surviving members of the party "stripped the flesh from their bones, roasted and ate it, averting their eyes from each other, and weeping." More than a month passed before seven frost-bitten survivors reached an American settlement. By then, the rest had died and two Indian guides had been shot and eaten.

Relief teams immediately sought to rescue the pioneers still trapped near Truckee Pass. During the winter, four successive rescue parties broke through and brought out the survivors. The situation that the rescuers found was unspeakably gruesome. Thirteen were dead. Surviving members of the Donner party were delirious from hunger and overexposure. One survivor was found in a small cabin next to a cannibalized body of a young boy. Of the original 87 members of the party, only 47 survived.

Questions for Discussion or Reflection
(1) Were George Donner and his party well-prepared when they started their trip?
(2) Why did the party decide on a shortcut?
(3) How did those trapped members of the party survive at last?
(4) What happened to the Donner Party finally?

Text C Louisiana Purchase

One of the most significant acquisitions of land came during James Madison's tenure as Secretary of State. The Louisiana Purchase nearly doubled the size of the young nation, changing its borders from Canada to the Gulf of Mexico and from the Mississippi River to the Rocky Mountains. Today, there are thirteen states that were part of the lands added from the Louisiana Purchase. These states are: Louisiana, Arkansas, Missouri, Iowa, North Dakota, South Dakota, Nebraska, Kansas, Wyoming, Minnesota, Oklahoma, Colorado and Montana.

In 1803, France sold over 900,000 square miles west of the Mississippi River to the United States for $15 million, which is an average of 4 cents an acre. This new addition made the U.S. one of the largest geographic nations in the world and showed the growing power of the nation.

The Louisiana Territory had been given to Spain by France in 1762 after forty years of Spanish rule; the Spanish were willing to give the territory back to pay off some of its debts. Thomas Jefferson and James Madison soon heard of the pending deal and sent Robert Livingston to negotiate for a small piece of land along the Mississippi so America could build its own seaport. Becoming impatient with the lack of news, Jefferson and Madison sent James Monroe to attempt to acquire New Orleans and West Florida. France realized that war with Great Britain was coming and knew that it could not defend Louisiana against the naval might of Great Britain. It offered to sell the entire territory to the U.S.

The deal was completed through a series of three documents between the United States and France. A treaty of cession had to be agreed upon first, then two agreements on the exchange of monies were made. Both parties gained what they had sought from the deal. The United States acquired the land they desired, while France needed the money from the deal to help pay the cost of the Napoleonic Wars and pay off the debt it already owed to the U.S. This was a remarkable feat for the time, most large empires had been obtained with the use of force, but the transfer of land from France to the United States occurred without any bloodshed.

By purchasing the Louisiana Territory, President Jefferson and Secretary of State Madison insured that the French could no longer dominate trade and restrict American ships from using the Mississippi River. This had a major impact on American trade, as now the Mississippi was open from New Orleans and St. Louis. Traders from around the world now dealt directly with the United States for goods that could easily be shipped down the river. Along with protecting American trade interests, the purchase provided a sense of protection from French aggression and territorial disputes. The threat of Napoleon's new world empire was real to the United States and Jefferson knew it was important to defend the nation's boarders. The deal also helped the transformation of the United States from a country that was centered around the Eastern Seacoast to a nation that would stretch from Atlantic to Pacific.

To commemorate the historic purchase, the Louisiana Purchase State Park has been created by the state of Louisiana. The park is an area that has been kept like the wilderness found by Lewis and Clark during their exploration. In 1904, the World's Fair was held in St. Louis. An exposition at the fair celebrated the Louisiana Purchase and President Teddy Roosevelt expressed his feelings about the triumphs of the Jefferson and his decision to make the deal with France. In conjunction with the World's Fair, the U.S. Postal Service released a stamp to mark the anniversary of the purchase.

Questions for Discussion or Reflection
(1) What impacts did the purchase of Louisiana exert on the United States and on American trade in particular?
(2) If you are a leading figure at the time, do you think you have that kind of vision to buy a land?

Proper Names

George Donner 乔治·当纳
James W. Marshall 詹姆斯·W. 马歇尔
the Appalachian Mountains 阿巴拉契亚山脉
the Donner Party 当纳聚会——美国史上人吃人传说
the Gold Rush 淘金热
the Mississippi River 密西西比河
the Westward Movement 西进运动

Notes

1. **James Wilson Marshall**（1810—1885）: He was an American carpenter and sawmill operator, whose discovery of gold in the American River in California on January 24, 1848 set the stage for the California Gold Rush. Marshall was forced from his own land by the resulting wave of gold seekers, and never profited from his discovery.
2. **The Donner Party**: It was a group of California-bound American emigrants who were caught up in the "western fever" of the 1840s. After becoming snowbound in the Sierra Nevada in the winter of 1846—1847, some of the emigrants resorted to cannibalism.

For Fun

Movies to See

1. *The Gold Rush*（1925）

   A lone prospector ventures into Alaska looking for gold. He gets mixed up with some burly characters and falls in love with the beautiful Georgia. He tries to win her heart with his singular charm. Finally he finds more than gold; he finds love and an uproarious adventure that forever change the lives of the people he meets.

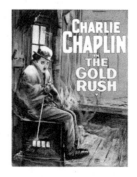

2. *The Donner Party*（1992）

   It is a cautionary tale of human endeavor and failure, hope and despair, greed and ambition. The Donner Party chronicles the tale of the ill-fated emigrant group who set out for the promised land of California in the spring of 1846, only to meet with disaster in the snows of the Sierra Nevada the following winter.

Websites to Visit

1. http://www.newton.k12.ks.us/tech/wm.htm

   On this website, you can find westward movement timeline, events, trails, maps, etc.

2. http://www.isu.edu/~trinmich/home.html

   This page is a comprehensive guide to the epic quest for gold.

3. http://www.pbs.org/wgbh/amex/donner/index.html

   This website features the Donner Party, including film, maps and teacher's guide.

Song to Enjoy

"Oh! Susanna" was first published on February 25, 1848. Popularly associated with the California Gold Rush, the song is occasionally but incorrectly called "Banjo on My Knee."

Oh! Susanna

lyrics by Stephen Foster

I come from Alabama with my banjo on my knee;
I'm goin' to Lousiana my true love for to see.
It rained all night the day I left,
the weather it was dry;
The sun so hot I froze to death,
Susanna don't you cry.
Oh! Susanna, don't you cry for me;
I come from Alabama,
with my banjo on my knee.
I had a dream the other night,
When everything was still;
I thought I saw Susanna dear,
A-coming down the hill.
The buckwheat cake was in her mouth,
The tear was in her eye,
Said I, I'm coming from the south,

Susanna don't you cry.
Oh! Susanna, don't you cry for me;
I come from Alabama,
with my banjo on my knee.
I soon will be in New Orleans,
And then I'll look all round,
And when I find Susanna,
I'll fall upon the ground.
But if I do not find her,
This darkey'll surely die,
And when I'm dead and buried,
Susanna don't you cry.
Oh! Susanna, don't you cry for me;
I come from Alabama,
with my banjo on my knee.

Unit 6
The Civil War

> ... that this nation, under God, shall have a new birth of freedom; and that government of the people, by the people, for the people, shall not perish from the earth.
> —*The Gettysburg Address*

Unit Goals

- To understand the causes of the Civil War.
- To know the significance of the Civil War.
- To be familiar with Lincoln and his key role in the Civil War.
- To learn the useful words and expressions that describe the Civil War.
- To improve English language skills.
- To develop critical thinking and intercultural communication skills.

Before You Read

1. Do you know the 16th president of the U.S.A.? Share what you know about Abraham Lincoln with your classmates.
2. Compare the South and the North of the United States before the Civil War.

the South	the North

3. What do "freedom" and "equality" mean? Do they have one unchanging meaning over time, or do they change over time?

4. Form groups of three or four students. Try to find, on the Internet or in the library, more information about the causes and the significance of the Civil War which interests you most. Prepare a 5-minute classroom presentation.

Start to Read

Text A Causes of the Civil War

1. The American Civil War is sometimes called the War Between the States, the War of Rebellion, or the War for Southern Independence. It began on April 12, 1861, when Confederate General opened fire on Fort Sumter, South Carolina, and lasted until May 26, 1865, when the last Confederate army surrendered. The war took more than 600,000 lives, destroyed property valued at $5 billion, brought freedom to 4 million black slaves, and opened wounds that have not yet completely healed many years later.

2. The chief and immediate cause of the war was slavery. Southern states, including the 11 states that formed the Confederacy, depended on slavery to support their economy. Southerners used slave labor to produce crops, especially cotton. Although slavery was illegal in the Northern states, only a small proportion of Northerners actively opposed it. The main debate between the North and the South on the eve of the war was whether slavery should be permitted in the Western territories recently acquired during the Mexican War (1846—1848), including New Mexico, part of California, and Utah. Opponents of slavery were concerned about its expansion, in part because they did not want to compete against slave labor.

Economic and Social Factors

3. By 1860, the North and the South had developed into two very different regions. Divergent social, economic, and political points of view, dating from colonial times, gradually drove the two sections farther and farther apart. Each tried to impose its point of view on the country as a whole. Although compromises had kept the Union together for many years, the situation was explosive in 1860. The election of Abraham Lincoln as president was viewed by the South as a threat to slavery and ignited the war.

4. During the first half of the 19th century, economic differences between the regions also increased. By 1860, cotton was the chief crop of the South, and it represented 57 percent of all U.S. exports. The profitability of cotton, known as King Cotton, completed the South's dependence on the plantation system and its essential component, slavery.

5. The North was by then firmly established as an industrial society. Labor was needed, but not slave labor. Immigration was encouraged. Immigrants from Europe worked in factories, built the railroads of the North, and settled the West. Very few settled in the South.

6. The South, resisting industrialization, manufactured little. Almost all manufactured goods had to be imported. Southerners, therefore, opposed high tariffs, or taxes that were placed on imported goods and increased the price of manufactured articles. The manufacturing economy of the North, on the other hand, demanded high tariffs to protect its own products from cheap foreign competition.

7. The expanding Northwest Territory, which was made up of the present-day states of Ohio, Indiana, Illinois, Michigan, Wisconsin, and part of Minnesota, was far from the markets for its grain and cattle. It needed such internal improvements for survival, and so supported the Northeast's demands for high tariffs. In return, the Northeast supported most federally financed improvements in the Northwest Territory.

8. As a result, the West allied itself with the Northern, rather than the Southern, point of view although both the South and the West were

agricultural, Economic needs sharpened sectional differences, adding to the interregional hostility.

Political Factors

9. In the early days of the United States, loyalty to one's state often took precedence over loyalty to one's country. A New Yorker or a Virginian would refer to his state as "my country." The Union was considered a "voluntary compact" entered into by independent, sovereign states for as long as it served their purpose to be so joined. In the nation's early years, neither North nor South had any strong sense of the permanence of the Union.

10. As Northern and Southern patterns of living diverged, their political ideas also developed marked differences. The North needed a central government to build an infrastructure of roads and railways, protect its complex trading and financial interests, and control the national currency. The South depended much less on the federal government than did other regions, and Southerners, therefore, felt no need to strengthen it. In addition, Southern patriots feared that a strong central government might interfere with slavery.

After You Read

Knowledge Focus
1. **Pair Work: Discuss the following questions with your partner.**
    (1) When did the American Civil War break out?
    (2) What was the immediate cause of the war?
    (3) What was Confederacy?
    (4) Why did the Southern and Northern states hold opposite attitudes towards slavery?
    (5) How did the Southerners feel about the election of Abraham Lincoln? Why?
    (6) Why did the Southerners want to keep slavery?
    (7) What was the situation like in the North after Lincoln's election?
    (8) Why did the South take a different attitude towards tariffs from the North?
    (9) What did the South prefer to do in order to keep the tariffs low?
    (10) In what way did the political ideas of the South differ from those of the North?

2. **Tell whether the following statements are true or false according to the knowledge you have learned.**
    (1) The American Civil War is sometimes called the War Between the States, the War of Rebellion, or the War for Southern Independence. ( )
    (2) Southern states, including the 12 states that formed the Confederacy, depended on slavery to support their economy. ( )

(3) The election of Abraham Lincoln as president was viewed by the South as a threat to slavery and ignited the war. ( )

(4) By 1860, sugar was the chief crop of the South, and it accounted for 57% of all U.S. exports. ( )

(5) The North was established as an industrial society where slave labor was needed. ( )

(6) The south was in favor of industrialization. However almost all manufactured goods had to be imported into the south. ( )

(7) Interregional hostility sharpened by the economic needs was the most important cause of the war. ( )

(8) In the early days of the United States, loyalty to one's state often took precedence over loyalty to one's country. ( )

(9) Throughout the history of the U.S.A., neither the North nor the South had any strong sense of the permanence of the Union. ( )

(10) The southerners felt an urgent need to establish a strong central government. ( )

Language focus

1. Fill in the blanks with the following words or expressions from the text.

surrender	heal	oppose	compromise
essential	manufacture	tariffs	precedence
loyalty	infrastructures		

(1) The lowering of trans-ocean communications _____ may make global data pipelines nearly as cheap to operate as national networks.

(2) The needs of the community must take _____ over individual requirements.

(3) As one of the best friends of human beings, the dog shows great _____ to its owner.

(4) I am surprised that the Labor Party has decided to _____ it.

(5) The car was _____ in Germany until 1961.

(6) Madame Bernice claimed to be able to _____ people simply by laying her hands on their bodies.

(7) The _____ point is that you both need to treat each other with much more respect.

(8) Officials hope to find a _____ between Britain and other EU members.

(9) All three gunmen had _____ by the end of the day.

(10) Some aspects of the technical _____ for electronic commerce are already in place.

2. Complete the following sentences with proper forms of the words in the brackets.

(1) _____ (slave) was the immediate cause of the war.

(2) Bootlegging was an act to make, sell or transport alcoholic liquor _____ (legal) for sale.

(3) Virginia Woolf once said: "the history of men's _____ (oppose) to women's emancipation is perhaps more interesting than the story of that emancipation itself."

(4) In the House of Representatives, _____ (diverge) ideas on the education of disabled teenagers were presented.

(5) The _____ (explode) of illegal drug use in the coastal cities gave rise to social unrest.

(6) A nationwide campaign was launched for the _____ (survive) of the endangered dolphin.

(7) The _____ (finance) support was immediately provided by the municipal government.

(8) The president made a _____ (hostility) remark on the opening ceremony of the conference.

(9) Those compatriots once solemnly declared that their _____ (loyal) would always lie with their motherland.

(10) The universal human yearn for the _____ (permanence) and enduring peace without shadow of change.

3. **Find the appropriate prepositions or adverbs that collocate with the neighboring words.**

(1) The war took more than 600,000 lives, destroyed property valued _____ $5 billion, brought freedom _____ 4 million black slaves, and opened wounds that have not yet completely healed more than 100 years later.

(2) Southern states, including the 11 states that formed the Confederacy, depended _____ slavery to support their economy.

(3) Divergent social, economic, and political points of view, dating _____ colonial times, gradually drove the two sections farther and farther _____.

(4) The election of Abraham Lincoln as president was viewed by the South as a threat _____ slavery and ignited the war.

(5) _____ the first half of the 19th century, economic differences between the regions increased.

(6) Southerners opposed high tariffs, or taxes that were placed _____ imported goods and increased the price of manufactured articles.

(7) Although both the South and the West were agricultural, the West allied itself _____ the Northern, rather than the Southern, point of view.

(8) In the early days of the United States, loyalty _____ one's state often took precedence _____ loyalty to one's country.

(9) A New Yorker or a Virginian would refer _____ his state as "my country."

(10) Southern patriots feared that a strong central government might interfere _____ slavery.

Comprehensive Work
Essay Writing

Have you ever read the famous speech "The Gettysburg Address" by President

Abraham Lincoln?

On June 1, 1865, Senator Charles Sumner commented on it by calling it a "monumental act" in his eulogy on the slain president. And he said Lincoln was mistaken that "the world will little note, nor long remember what we say here." Rather, the Bostonian remarked, "The world noted at once what he said, and will never cease to remember it. The battle itself was less important than the speech."

"That government of the people, by the people, for the people" is the best American Government anticipated by Abraham Lincoln. How do you understand the government of this kind? Comment on it.

Team Work

"The Homestead Act" of 1862 allowed anyone who was over 21 and the head of a household to own land. "The Homestead Act" became a symbol of new found freedom for many African Americans. The day that "The Homestead Act" went into effect—January 1, 1863—was the same day that President Abraham Lincoln issued "The Emancipation Proclamation." Many Black Americans began looking to the west as a place where they would have the freedom to own their own land.

Do you know that the following four numerals are important in "The Homestead Act" of 1862? Figure out the specific meanings of the numerals, and restate what you know about "The Homestead Act" to your team members, taking these four numerals as clues.

21	
10	
160	
5	

Read More

Text B　　The Gettysburg Address

Four score and seven years ago our fathers brought forth on this continent, a new nation, conceived in liberty, and dedicated to the proposition that all men are created equal.

Now we are engaged in a great civil war, testing whether that nation or any nation so conceived and so dedicated, can long endure. We are met on a great battlefield of that war. We have come to dedicate a portion of that field, as a final resting place for those who here gave their lives that that nation might live. It is altogether fitting and proper that we should do this.

But in a larger sense, we cannot dedicate, we cannot consecrate, we cannot hallow this ground. The brave men, living and dead, who struggled here, have consecrated it, far above our poor power to add or detract.

The world will little note, nor long remember, what we say here, but it can never forget what they did here. It is for us the living, rather, to be dedicated here to the unfinished work which they who fought here have thus far so nobly advanced.

It is rather for us to be here dedicated to the great task remaining before us: that from these honored dead we take increased devotion to that cause for which they gave the last full measure of devotion; that we here highly resolve that these dead shall not have died in vain; that this nation, under God, shall have a new birth of freedom; and that government of the people, by the people, for the people, shall not perish from the earth.

Questions for Discussion or Reflection

1. **Answer the following questions**
   (1) Who did Lincoln refer to by "our fathers"?
   (2) From which document did the idea come that the United States was a "nation dedicated to the proposition that all men are created equal?"
   (3) What is the purpose of the Civil War in Lincoln's opinion?
   (4) Why did Lincoln give this speech?
   (5) How did Lincoln comment on the men who died in the battle here?
   (6) What did Lincoln say about the responsibility of those who are still living?
   (7) What do you think Lincoln meant by the phrase "government of the people, by the people, for the people"?

2. **Match the key words to their corresponding definitions.**

   (1) score   A. to take away
   (2) conceived   B. to die; disappear
   (3) liberty   C. to make sacred
   (4) proposition   D. idea
   (5) dedicate   E. to set apart; make special
   (6) consecrate   F. 20 years
   (7) hallow   G. created
   (8) detract   H. freedom
   (9) devotion   I. to make holy
   (10) perish   J. feeling of love

Text C Eye Witness Accounts of the Assassination

On the evening of the 14th of April, at about twenty minutes past 8 o'clock, I, in the company with Miss Harris, left my residence at the corner of Fifteenth and H streets, and joined the President and Mrs. Lincoln, and went with them, in their carriage, to Ford's Theater, on Tenth Street. On reaching the theater when the presence of the President became known, the actors stopped playing, the band struck up "Hail to the Chief," and the audience rose and received him with loud cheering. The party proceeded along in the rear of the dress-circle and entered the box that had been set apart for their reception.

On entering the box, there was a large arm chair that was placed nearest the audience, farthest from the stage, which the President took and occupied during the whole of the evening, with one exception, when he sat down again. When the second scene of the third act was being performed, and while I was intently observing the proceedings upon the stage, with my back towards the door and the president. The distance from the door and where the president sat was about four feet. At the same time, I heard the man shout some word, which I thought was "Freedom!" I instantly sprang toward him and seized him. He wrested himself from my grasp, and made a violent thrust at my breast with a large knife. I blocked the blow by striking it up, and received a wound several inches deep in my left arm. The opening of my wound was about an inch and a half in length, and extended upward toward the shoulder several inches. The man rushed to the front of the box and I tried to seize him again, but only caught his clothes as he was leaping over the railing of the box. The clothes, as I believe, were torn in the attempt to hold him. As he went over upon stage, I cried out, "Stop that man!" I then turned to the President, his position was not changed; his head was slightly bent forward, and his eyes were closed. I saw that he was unconscious, and, supposing him mortally wounded (a wound which he would die from), rushed to the door for the purpose of calling medical aid.

On reaching the door of the passageway, I found it barred by a heavy piece of plank, on one end of which was secured in the wall, and the other resting against the door. It had been so securely fastened that it required considerable force to remove it. This wedge or bar was about four feet from the floor. Persons upon the outside were beating against the door for the purpose of entering. I removed the bar, and the door was opened. Several persons, who represented themselves as surgeons, were allowed to enter. I saw there Colonel Crawford, and requested him to prevent other persons from entering the box.

I then returned to the box, and found the surgeons examining the President's body. They had not yet discovered the wound. As soon as it was discovered, they were determined to remove him from the theater. He was carried out, and I then proceeded to assist Mrs. Lincoln, who was intensely excited, to the stairs, I requested Major Potter to aid me in assisting Mrs. Lincoln across street to the house where the president was being conveyed. The wound which I had received had been bleeding a lot, and on reaching the house, feeling very faint from the loss of blood, I seated myself in the hall and soon after fainted away, and was laid upon the floor. Upon the return of consciousness, I was taken to my residence ... In my opinion the first shot and the assassin leaving the box did not exceed thirty seconds.

Questions for Discussion or Reflection
1. How was the president greeted when he entered the theater?
2. Who was with him when he was assassinated?
3. What was the writer doing when the man attacked the president?
4. Did the eye-witness succeed in stopping the man?

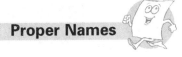

Proper Names

Fort Sumter 萨姆特堡   the American Civil War 美国内战
the Mexican War 墨西哥战役   The Confederacy 南部邦联

Notes

1. **The Mexican War**: The War between the United States and Mexico began with a Mexican attack on American troops along the southern border of Texas on Apr. 25, 1846. Fighting ended when the U.S. general Winfield Scott occupied Mexico City on Sept. 14, 1847. A few months later, a peace treaty was signed at Guadalupe Hidalgo on Feb. 2, 1848.

2. **King Cotton**: It is a phrase frequently used by Southern politicians and authors prior to the American Civil War, indicating the economic and political importance of cotton production. After the invention of the cotton gin in 1793, cotton surpassed tobacco as the dominant cash crop in the agricultural economy of the South, soon comprising more than half the total U.S. exports.

3. **War of 1812**: The conflict between the United States and Britain began in 1812 and lasted until early 1815. President James Madison requested a declaration of war to protect American ships on the high seas and to stop the British from impressing or seizing U.S. sailors. U.S. ships were being stopped and searched by both Great Britain and France who were fighting each other in Europe. President Madison also wanted to prevent Britain from forming alliances with Native Americans on the American frontier. His decision was influenced by Americans in the West and South who hoped to expand the United States by seizing control of both Canada and Florida. Critics called the War of 1812 "Mr. Madison's War," but others saw it as a "second war of independence," an opportunity for Americans to defend their freedom and their honor

in the face of European disrespect. Neither Britain nor the United States was particularly well prepared to fight this war, and the conflict eventually ended in a stalemate.

Books to Read

1. David Herbert Donald, *Lincoln*

   The book draws extensively on Lincoln's personal papers and legal writings to present a biography of the president.

2. Donald Herbert, *Why the North Won the Civil War*

   Six essays explore the political, military, economic, social, and diplomatic reasons for the Union victory over the Confederacy.

3. James M. McPherson, *The American Civil War*

   The United States saw long-simmering sectional tensions erupt into fighting at Fort Sumter, South Carolina, in April 1861, beginning what would become the most cataclysmic military struggle in the western world between Waterloo and the First World War. This book traces the course of the war in both Eastern and Western theatres, looking at strategic, geographical and logistic factors as well as the soldiers, officers, and civilians who were caught up in the conflict.

4. Stephen B. Oates, *With Malice toward None: The Life of Abraham Lincoln*

   This book is a complete account of Abraham Lincoln's life. This is the book for those who think of reading just one book about Lincoln.

Websites to Visit

(1) **Library of Congress — The Gettysburg Address**

http://www.loc.gov/exhibits/gadd/

The website includes numerous rare documents and photographs relating to "The Gettysburg Address."

(2) **AmericanCivilWar.com**

http://americancivilwar.com/

The website includes timelines, battle maps, pictures, and materials on American Civil war.

(3) **CivilWar.com**

http://www.civilwar.com/

The website includes a timeline, the introduction to battles in the Civil War and lesson plan for teachers, etc.

(4) Home of the American Civil War
http://www.civilwarhome.com/
It is a comprehensive site that features the battles, the armies, and the strategies used during the war.

(5) The Civil War Home Page
http://www.civil-war.net/
The website is a great resource featuring battle maps, photographs and Civil War documents.

Movies to See

1. *Gettysburg* (1993)

The movie features the Battle of Gettysburg, turning point of the Civil War. It is based on the novel *The Killer Angels* by Pulitzer Prize winner Michael Shaara.

2. *Gods and Generals* (2003)

Based on the best-selling historical novel by Jeff Shaara, *Gods and Generals* covers the events of the American Civil War before the climactic battle of Gettysburg. Seen from the points of view of leaders such as Thomas Jackson, Joshua Lawrence Chamberlain, Winfield Scott Hancock and Robert E. Lee, the film begins just after the attack on Fort Sumter in April 1861, and culminates with the battle of Chancellorsville in May 1863. Directed by Ronald F. Maxwell, the film is an epic, dramatic prequel to *Gettysburg*, the classic 1993 film also directed by Maxwell.

3. *The Red Badge of Courage* (1951)

This movie tells story about middle years of the Civil War, a soldier's story of bravery overcoming fear. It is based on the novel with the same title by steven Crane.

Song to Enjoy
"Dixie" by Daniel Decatur Emmett

The song "Dixie" originated in the blackface minstrel shows of the 1850s and quickly became popular across the United States. Its lyrics, written in a comic, exaggerated version of African American Vernacular English, tell the story of a homesick southerner. During the American Civil War, "Dixie" was adopted as a de facto anthem of the Confederacy. New versions appeared at this time that more explicitly tied the song to the events of the Civil War. Since the advent of the North American Civil Rights Movement, many have identified the lyrics of the song with the iconography and ideology of the Old South. Today, "Dixie" is sometimes considered offensive, and its critics link the act of singing it to sympathy for slavery or racial separation in the American South. Its supporters, on the other hand, view it as a legitimate aspect of Southern culture and heritage and the campaigns against it as political correctness. The song was a favorite of President Abraham Lincoln; he had it played at some of his political rallies and at the announcement of General Robert E. Lee's surrender.

Dixie

Oh, I wish I was in the land of cotton,
Old times there are not forgotten.
Look away, look away, look away Dixie Land!
In Dixie's Land, where I was born in,
early on one frosty mornin'.
Look away, look away, look away Dixie Land!
I wish I was in Dixie, Hooray! Hooray!
In Dixie's Land I'll take my stand,
to live and die in Dixie.
Away, away, away down south in Dixie!
Away, away, away down south in Dixie!
There's buckwheat cakes and Injun batter,
Makes you fat or a little fatter.
Look away! Look away! Look away! Dixie Land
Then hoe it down and scratch your gravel,
To Dixie's Land I'm bound to travel.
Look away! Look away! Look away! Dixie Land
I wish I was in Dixie, Hooray! Hooray!
In Dixie's Land I'll take my stand,
to live and die in Dixie.
Away, away, away down south in Dixie!
Away, away, away down south in Dixie!

Unit 7

Reconstruction

> The people were generally impoverished. The farms had gone to waste; the fields were covered with weeds and bushes. ... Business was at a standstill; banks and commercial places had either been suspended or closed. And the disbanded soldiers returned to their homes to find desolation and starvation staring them in face.
>
> —Garner, *Reconstruction in Mississippi*

Unit Goals

- To understand the situation in the U.S. after the Civil War.
- To learn about the major aspects of Reconstruction and its impacts.
- To learn the useful words and expressions that describe the Reconstruction era of America.
- To improve English language skills.
- To develop critical thinking and intercultural communication skills.

Before You Read

1. What were the problems left unsolved after the Civil War?

   Problems {
   _____
   _____
   _____
   _____
   _____
   }

2. What was the status of Southerners at the end of the Civil War?
3. What roles did the President and the Congress play in Reconstruction?
4. Put yourself in the shoes of the President confronted with the post-civil war situation.

Discuss with your partner how to solve the following problems:

Problems
(1) What was the relationship between the former Confederate states and the Union?
(2) How should the 11 seceded states be readmitted?
(3) Who should be punished for the Confederate rebellions, if anyone?
(4) What should be the position of the newly-freed slaves?
(5) How do you reintegrate the Southern States into the Union?
(6) How should the war-torn South be rebuilt?

5. Form groups of three or four students. Try to find, on the Internet or in the library, more information about the Reconstruction which interests you most. Prepare a 5-minute classroom presentation.

Start to Read

Text A — Reconstruction after the Civil War

1. Reconstruction was the attempt from 1865 to 1877 in U.S. history to resolve the issues of the American Civil War, especially known as the process of rebuilding the seceded States.

2. By the end of the Civil War, the South was in a state of political upheaval, social disorder and economic decay. The war destroyed southern crops, plantations, and entire cities. Inflation became so severe that by the end of the war a loaf of bread cost several hundred Confederate dollars. Thousands of southerners starved to death, and many who did not starve lost everything they owned: clothing, homes, land, and slaves. As a result, by 1865, policy makers in Washington had the nearly impossible task of southern Reconstruction.

3. Reconstruction encompassed three major aspects: restoration of the Union, transformation of southern society, and enactment of progressive laws favoring the rights of emancipated slaves.

4. President Abraham Lincoln mapped out his Ten-Percent Plan in hope of restoring the Union. Under the plan, each southern state would be readmitted to the Union after 10 percent of its voting population had

pledged future loyalty to the United States, and all Confederates except high-ranking government and military officials would be pardoned. After Lincoln was assassinated in 1865, President Andrew Johnson adopted the Ten-Percent Plan and pardoned thousands of Confederate officials. Radical Republicans in Congress, however, denounced the plan for being too lenient on the South and for not securing any rights for the freed slaves. The Republicans called for harsher measures, demanding a loyalty pledge from 50 percent of each state's voting population rather than just 10 percent. Although such points of disagreement existed, both presidents and Congress agreed on one major point—that the southern states needed to abolish slavery in their new state constitutions before being readmitted to the Union.

5. The Radical Republicans also believed that southern society would have to be completely transformed to ensure that the South would not try to secede again. The Radicals, therefore, attempted to reshape the South by emancipating blacks. As some northerners streamed into the South, southerners denounced them as traitors and falsely accused many of corruption. However, the U.S. government did manage to distribute confiscated lands to former slaves and poor whites and help improve education and sanitation and foster industrial growth in southern cities.

6. Ultimately, the most important part of Reconstruction was the push to secure rights for former slaves. Radical Republicans, aware that newly freed slaves would face subtle racism, passed a series of progressive laws and amendments in Congress that protected blacks' rights under federal and constitutional law.

7. Historians do agree that reconstruction changed the United States in several important ways. One of the most important changes was in the Constitution. Congress passed three historic amendments to the Constitution during this period. The first was the Thirteenth Amendment. It ended slavery in the United States. The next was the Fourteenth Amendment. It said all persons born or naturalized in the United States were citizens of the United States and of the state in which they lived. It said no state could limit the rights of these citizens. Finally, there was the Fifteenth Amendment. It said a citizen of the United States could not be prevented from voting because of his color. These laws alone, however, did not succeed in doing this. It would take another century —until Martin Luther King and other civil rights leaders —to make these rights a reality.

8. Reconstruction was a mixed success. Historians have tended to judge Reconstruction severely as a period of political conflict, corruption, and regression that failed to achieve its original goals. Slaves were granted freedom, but the North completely failed to satisfy their economic needs. The government was unable to provide former slaves with political and economic opportunity. Union military troops often could not even protect them from violence. Indeed, without economic resources of their own, many Southern African Americans were forced to become tenant farmers on land owned by their former masters, caught in a cycle of poverty that would continue well into the 20th century.

9. Reconstruction-era governments did make achievements in rebuilding Southern states devastated by the war, and in expanding public services, notably in establishing free public schools for African Americans and whites. However, the failure of Reconstruction meant that the struggle of African Americans for equality and freedom was postponed until the 20th century—when it would become a national, not just a Southern issue.

After You Read

Knowledge Focus

1. **Pair Work: Discuss the following questions with your partner.**
   (1) What is "Reconstruction"?
   (2) What was the situation of the South by the end of the Civil War?
   (3) What were the major aspects within Reconstruction?
   (4) What do you know about the Ten-Percent Plan President Abraham Lincoln mapped out?
   (5) What were the beliefs of the Radical Republicans?
   (6) How were the newly-freed slaves treated?
   (7) Why did historians consider Reconstruction as a "mixed success"?
   (8) Congress passed three historic amendments to the Constitution during this period. What were they?
   (9) Which amendment ended slavery in the United States?
   (10) How do you comment on the Reconstruction era? Was it a blessing or a curse?

2. **Solo Work: Tell whether the following are true or false according to the knowledge you have learned.**
   (1) American Civil War was known as the process of rebuilding the seceded States. ( )
   (2) By the end of the Civil War, the South was in a state of political upheaval, social disorder and economic decay. ( )
   (3) Restoration of the Union, transformation of southern society, and enactment of progressive laws favoring the rights of emancipated slaves were the three major

aspects of Reconstruction. ( )

(4) President Andrew Johnson mapped out his Ten-Percent Plan in hope of restoring the Union. ( )

(5) Both presidents and Congress agreed on one major point—that the southern states needed to abolish slavery in their new state constitutions before being readmitted to the Union. ( )

(6) The most important part of Reconstruction was the push to secure rights for former slaves. ( )

(7) The Congress passed four historic amendments to the Constitution during the period of Reconstruction. ( )

(8) The Fifteenth Amendment ended slavery in the United States. ( )

(9) Reconstruction-era governments did make achievements in rebuilding Southern states devastated by the war, and in expanding public services, notably in establishing free public schools for African Americans and the whites. ( )

(10) The failure of Reconstruction meant that the struggle of African Americans for equality and freedom was postponed until the 20th century—when it would become a national, not just a Southern issue. ( )

Language Focus

1. Fill in the blanks with the following words or expressions from the text.

upheaval	decay	emancipate	encompass
pardon	abolish	distribute	foster
map sth. out	in hope of		

(1) It would cause a tremendous _____ to install a different computer software.

(2) The old buildings had started to fall into _____.

(3) I think the cruel bullfighting should be _____.

(4) The grand ceremony is to _____ everything from music, theatre and ballet to literature, cinema and the visual arts.

(5) The 1920s turned out hundreds of _____ women.

(6) Large numbers of political prisoners have been _____ and released by the new president.

(7) I didn't phone till four o'clock _____ your complete accomplishment.

(8) Law-makers were discussing the best way to _____ democracy and prosperity in their country.

(9) The government has issued a new document _____ its policies on commerce.

(10) The company aims eventually at _____ its products throughout the United States.

2. Complete the following sentences with the proper forms of the words in the brackets.

(1) The _____ (restore) of the sculpture was costly; therefore, most representatives opposed it.

(2) The _____ (emancipate) of slaves encouraged them to strive for more rights.

(3) The members had conflicting points of view and even started wrestling in the meeting hall because of their _____ (agree).
(4) Nobody can sense the _____ (subtle) of his physical change.
(5) This program intends to familiarize students with the _____ (original) and customs of diversified western festivals.

3. **Find the appropriate prepositions or adverbs that collocate with the neighboring words.**
   (1) Reconstruction was known _____ the process of rebuilding the Southern states after the Civil War.
   (2) Thousands of southerners starved _____ death, and many who did not starve lost everything they owned: clothing, homes, land, and slaves.
   (3) President Abraham Lincoln mapped out his Ten-Percent Plan _____ hope of restoring the Union.
   (4) Under Ten-Percent Plan, each southern state would be readmitted _____ the Union after 10 percent of its voting population had pledged future loyalty to the United States.
   (5) The Radicals attempted to reshape the South _____ emancipating blacks.
   (6) As some northerners streamed _____ the South, southerners denounced them as traitors and falsely accused many _____ corruption.
   (7) The Fifteenth Amendment said a citizen of the United States could not be prevented _____ voting because of his color.
   (8) Reconstruction was a mixed success. Historians have tended to judge Reconstruction severely _____ a period of political conflict, corruption, and regression that failed to achieve its original goals.
   (9) Without economic resources of their own, many Southern African Americans were forced to become tenant farmers on land owned by their former masters, caught _____ a cycle of poverty that would continue well into the 20th century.
   (10) Reconstruction-era governments did make achievements _____ rebuilding Southern states devastated _____ the war.

Comprehensive Work
Group Work: Pros and Cons

Few topics in American history have triggered as much intellectual warfare as Reconstruction after the Civil War. Some regard Reconstruction as a kind of national disgrace, forced upon a defeated region by radical Republicans for their own interest. Others show more interest in the real problems of the black freedmen and admire the radical Republicans as real idealists rather than as self-seeking politicians.

How do you understand the Reconstruction period? Is it a blessing or a curse for the black?

It is a blessing because

_____

_____

It is a curse because

_____

_____

_____

Read More

Text B Education after the Civil War

Prior to the Civil War, slave states had laws forbidding literacy for the enslaved. Thus, by emancipation, only a small percentage of African Americans knew how to read and write. There was such motivation in the African American community and enough good will among white and black teachers that the majority of African Americans could read and write by the turn of the twentieth century. Many teachers commented that their classrooms were filled with both young and old, grandfathers with their children and grandchildren, all eager to learn.

Some emancipated slaves quickly fled from the neighborhood of their owners, while others became wage laborers for former owners. Most importantly, African Americans could make choices for themselves about where they labored and the type of work they performed.

Northern teachers, many of whom were white women, traveled into the South to provide education and training for the newly freed population. Schools from the elementary level through college provided a variety of opportunities, from the rudiments of reading and writing and various types of basic vocational training to classics, arts, and theology.

In May 1863, letters from teachers at St. Helena Island described their young students as "the prettiest little things you ever saw, with solemn little faces, and eyes like stars." Vacations seemed a hardship to these students, who were so anxious to improve their reading and writing that they begged not to "be punished so again." Voluntary contributions from various organizations aided fourteen hundred teachers in providing literacy and vocational education for 150,000 freedmen.

Questions for Discussion or Reflection

1. What was the most impressive picture in the classroom after the Civil War?
2. How do you account for "the hunger to learn" of those emancipated slaves?

3. Why were vacations regarded as hardships by the freed men?

Text C A Shattered Fairy Tale

Directions: Go through Text C quickly and finish the following multiple-choice questions.

1. When people speak of the antebellum South, they generally mean _____.
   A. the time when women wore hoop skirts
   B. the South after the Civil War
   C. the pre-Civil War South
   D. the South during the Civil War

2. Who called for a complete destruction of what could be used by the Confederacy?
   A. General Stonewall Jackson.　　B. General Grant.
   C. General Robert E. Lee.　　D. General William Sherman.

3. How many Southerners died in the Civil War?
   A. Over 500,000.　　B. Over 600,000.
   C. Almost 300,000.　　D. 50,500.

4. Why was slave labor so important to the Southern economy?
   A. Southerners were not used to working.
   B. Workers were needed for large-scale farming.
   C. Workers were needed for the many factories.
   D. Slave labor freed the upper class to work at their white collar jobs.

What happens when a fairy tale has an unhappy ending? For some people, the antebellum or pre-Civil War South was an American fairy tale. There were handsome princes, ladies fair, and a noble code of honor. The pace of life was serene and genteel. But in this fairy tale, no one was destined to live happily ever after.

Even before the Civil War, the South was not quite the place of enchantment it might have seemed. The agricultural economy relied heavily on slave labor. Thousands of black slaves were forced to work on the large plantations. They certainly did not lead storybook lives. Neither, for that matter, did poor whites. The fabled Southern culture may have been real only to the wealthy upper class.

In any case, nothing was the same for anyone after the war. By the time of Lee's surrender at Appomattox, the South lay in ruin. Cities, farms, and homes were burned and ravaged by cannon fire. Railroads and bridges were destroyed. Business and industry were nearly wiped out. Almost 300,000 men were dead.

In the midst of this shattered fairy tale, daily life followed a rocky path. Everything from food to fuel was in short supply, if it could be found at all. Families dug in burned and shell-studded fields for root crops or any kind of edible vegetation. Tents or ruined houses were shelter for many. Disease added to the huge death toll.

The Deep South lay in desolation. The rubble was a monument to General William T. Sherman's determined destruction of anything that could be used by the Confederacy. Rebuilding was a much lower priority than survival.

In the border states of Kentucky, Arkansas, and Missouri, prowling bands from both armies plundered homes and towns in "foraging" raids. Raiders took food, livestock, or whatever they could carry off. In some areas, these raids occurred regularly for weeks on end, even after the war was over.

Shortly after the cease-fire, Northern relief agencies came with food and other basic supplies for displaced slaves and poor whites. One way or another, most people made it through until the fields began to produce enough food to stave off starvation. The immediate crisis passed.

The federal government launched its rebuilding plans. Military governments and newly forming state agencies began to bring some order to the chaos. Life assumed a pattern that was not quite so desperate. But even for people not used to luxury, the war brought an existence totally different from what they had known.

The once-tranquil pace of the South was based on an agricultural lifestyle. With the loss of slave labor, large-scale farming could no longer be sustained. Federal control weakened the power of state governments. This change struck deep at the heart of Southern life. The Confederacy had gone to war to slay this dragon-sized threat. But the monster had defeated the hero, the castle was spoiled, and enchantment was no more.

The South moved into her post-war identity. Patterns of new life emerged. Blacks were no longer slaves. Some entered labor contracts with white employers; some became sharecroppers. Many looked to urban areas for their future, and the cities began to grow.

The stirrings of industrialization strengthened the economy. Relationships with Northern markets and investors were re-established. Slowly, railroads were recreated and goods moved to market. It became possible to do business and make a living. But the bitterness and destruction of ruined dreams shaped cultural landscapes.

Through institutionalized segregation, southern whites clung to their status as lords over the black man. Separation of blacks and whites became solidly established in everything from schools to public toilets. A distrust of Northerners and a deep, abiding grief over the loss of the antebellum South fixed themselves like thorns in the hearts of the people. The fairy tale was dead.

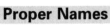

Proper Names

Abraham Lincoln 亚伯拉罕·林肯
Reconstruction (美国内战)战后重建
Ten-Percent Plan《百分之十计划》
the Amendment (宪法的)修正案

Notes

1. **The Freedmen's Bureau**: The Bureau of Refugees, Freedmen, and Abandoned Land, often referred to as the Freedmen's Bureau, was established in the War Department on March 3,1865. The Freedmen's Bureau offered education, employment and legal aid to freed slaves. The Bureau supervised all relief and educational activities relating to refugees and freedmen, including issuing rations, clothing and medicine. The Bureau also assumed custody of confiscated lands or property in the former Confederate States, border states, District of Columbia, and Indian Territory.

2. **The KKK (Ku Klux Klan)**: According to the Klan, the blood drop represents the blood shed by Jesus Christ as a sacrifice for the White Aryan Race. The KKK originated as a secret society organized in the South after the American Civil War to reassert white supremacy through terrorism and intimidation. The organization formed by Nathan Bedford Forrest to keep blacks under control was cruel and used "fear" as a weapon.

Books to Read

1. Eric Foner, *Reconstruction, America's Unfinished Revolution*

    This remarkably well-researched book gives probably the most thorough examination of Reconstruction to date.

2. William C. Harris, *With Charity for All: Lincoln and the Restoration of the Union*

    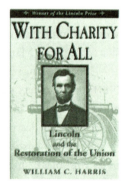

    This book is a must for all those interested in Abraham Lincoln, the Civil War and the Reconstruction period. Its theme is the "pre-history" of Reconstruction, dealing with the attempts by Lincoln, whilst the war was still in progress, to re-establish loyal governments in various southern states.

Movie to See

Twelve Years a Slave (2013)

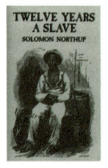

This movie is based on an incredible true story of one man's fight for survival and freedom. In the pre-Civil War United States, Solomon Northup, a free black man from upstate New York, is abducted and sold into slavery. Facing cruelty as well as unexpected kindnesses, Solomon struggles not only to stay alive, but to retain his dignity. In the twelfth year of his unforgettable odyssey, Solomon's chance meeting with a Canadian abolitionist (Brad Pitt) will forever alter his life.

Unit 7   Reconstruction

Song to Enjoy

The Battle Hymn of the Republic

lyrics by Julia Ward Howe

Mine eyes have seen the glory
Of the coming of the Lord;
He is trampling out the vintage
Where the grapes of wrath are stored;
He hath loosed the fateful lightning
Of His terrible swift sword;
His truth is marching on.

    Chorus

Glory! Glory! Hallelujah!
Glory! Glory! Hallelujah!
Glory! Glory! Hallelujah!
His truth is marching on.

I have seen Him in the watchfires
Of a hundred circling camps
They have builded Him an altar
In the evening dews and damps;
I can read His righteous sentence
By the dim and flaring lamps;
His day is marching on.

    Chorus

I have read a fiery gospel writ
In burnished rows of steel;
"As ye deal with My condemners,
So with you My grace shall deal";
Let the Hero born of woman
Crush the serpent with His heel,
Since God is marching on.

    Chorus

He has sounded forth the trumpet
That shall never call retreat;
He is sifting out the hearts of men
Before His judgment seat;
Oh, be swift, my soul, to answer Him;
Be jubilant, my feet;
Our God is marching on.

    Chorus

In the beauty of the lilies
Christ was born across the sea,
With a glory in His bosom
That transfigures you and me;
As He died to make men holy,
Let us die to make men free;
While God is marching on.

    Chorus

Unit 8
The Gilded Age

> So long as all the increased wealth which modern progress brings goes to build up great fortunes, to increase luxury and make sharper the contrast between the House of Have and the House of Want, progress is not real and cannot be permanent.
>
> —Henry George

Unit Goals

- To understand the significance of "the Gilded Age" as a transition period.
- To know the industrialization during this period.
- To learn the reasons for urbanization and mass immigration.
- To learn the useful words and expressions that describe "the Gilded Age".
- To improve English language skills.
- To develop critical thinking and intercultural communication skills.

Before You Read

1. Who coined the phrase "the Gilded Age"? What does the Gilded Age refer to?
2. Do you see any element of "the Gilded Age" in contemporary society?
3. List the impacts of the technological advances in the 19th century on society and business.

Technological Advances	Impacts

4. Form groups of three or four students. Try to find, on the Internet or in the library, more information about the Gilded Age which interests you most. Prepare a 5-minute classroom presentation.

Start to Read

Text A The Gilded Age

1. The term "Gilded Age" comes from a novel of the same name published in 1873 by Mark Twain, which, though fictional, is a critical examination of politics and corruption in the United States during the 19th century. By "Gilded Age," Mark Twain meant that the period was glittering on the surface but corrupt underneath.

2. The Gilded Age, a transition time from the late 19th century to the beginnings of the 20th century, witnessed industrialization, urbanization, mass immigration, the construction of great transcontinental railroads, innovations in science and technology, and the rise of big business. Afterward, the first years of the new century that followed were dominated by progressivism, a forward-looking political movement that attempted to redress some of the ills that had arisen during the Gilded Age. Progressives passed legislation to rein in big business, fight against corruption, free the government from special interests, and protect the rights of consumers, workers, immigrants, and the poor.

3. Some historians have called the presidents of the Gilded Age the "forgotten presidents," and indeed many Americans today have trouble remembering their names, what they did for the country, or even in which era they served. These six men—Ulysses S. Grant, Rutherford B. Hayes, James Garfield, Chester Arthur, Grover Cleveland, and Benjamin Harrison—had relatively unremarkable terms in office and faced

few, if any, major national crises during their presidencies. Some historians have suggested that these Gilded Age presidents were unexciting for a reason—because Americans wanted to avoid bold politicians who might ruin the delicate peace established after the Civil War.

4. This is not to say politics was unimportant in the Gilded Age. On the contrary, Americans paid more attention to politics and national elections during the post-Civil War period than at any other time in history, because each election had the potential to destroy the fragile balance and peace between North and South, Republican and Democrat. Voters turned out in record numbers for each presidential election in the late 19th century, with the number of voters sometimes reaching 80 percent or greater. The intensity of the elections also helps explain why Congress passed so little significant legislation after the Reconstruction era: control of the House of Representatives constantly changed hands between the Democrats and the Republicans with each election, making an agreement on any major issue nearly impossible.

Green Bay & Western locomotive, 1879

5. Driven by the North, which emerged from the Civil War an industrial powerhouse, the United States experienced unprecedented growth and industrialization during the Gilded Age, with a continent full of seemingly unlimited natural resources and driven by millions of immigrants ready to work. In fact, some historians have referred to this era as America's second Industrial Revolution, because it completely changed American society, politics, and economy. Mechanization and marketing were the keys to success in this age: companies that could mass-produce products and convince people to buy them accumulated enormous amounts of wealth, while companies that could not were forced out of business by fierce competition.

6. Railroads were vital in the new industrialized economy. The railroad industry enabled raw materials, finished products, food, and people to travel cross-country in a matter of days, as opposed to the months or years that it took just prior to the Civil War. By the end of the war, the United States boasted some 35,000 miles of track, mostly in the industrialized North. By the turn of the century, that number had jumped to almost 200,000 miles, linking the North, South, and West. With these railroads making travel easier, millions of rural Americans flocked to the cities, and by 1900, nearly 40 percent of the population lived in urban areas.

7. By the 20th century, the rise of big business and the large migration of Americans from the countryside to the cities caused a shift in political awareness, as elected officials saw the need to solve the growing economic and social problems that developed along with the urban boom, and so started the Progressive Movement. It was a movement at the turn of the 20th century which demanded government regulation of the economy and social conditions, spread quickly with the support of large number of people across the country. The Progressive Movement was not an organized campaign with clearly defined goals. Rather, it was a number of diverse efforts at political, social and economic reforms. Progressives believed that the government needed to take a strong and active role in the economy, regulating big business, immigration, and urban growth. These middle-class reformers hoped finally to regain control of the government from special interests like the railroads and trusts and pass effective legislation to protect consumers, organized labor, and minorities.

After You Read

Knowledge Focus

1. **Pair Work: Discuss the following questions with your partner.**
   (1) Why did Mark Twain describe the time as "the Gilded Age"?
   (2) Why was the Gilded Age considered a transition time in American history?
   (3) Why do many Americans have trouble remembering the names of presidents in the Gilded Age?
   (4) What was the situation in America after the Civil War?
   (5) Why was presidential election so important during the post-Civil War period in America?
   (6) How could companies survive during the Gilded Age?
   (7) What roles did railroads play at that time?
   (8) Did the urban boom cause any problems?
   (9) What was the government expected to do to solve the problems during the post-Civil War period?

2. **Solo Work**: Tell whether the following are true or false according to the knowledge you have learned.

   (1) The term "Gilded Age" comes from a novel of the same title published in 1873 by Mark Twain. (   )

   (2) Progressives passed legislation to rein in big business, fight against corruption, free the government from special interests, and protect the rights of consumers, workers, immigrants, and the poor. (   )

   (3) Ulysses S. Grant, Rutherford B. Hayes, James Garfield, Chester Arthur, Grover Cleveland, and Benjamin Harrison were the six presidents of the Gilded Age. (   )

   (4) Americans paid more attention to politics and national elections during the post-Civil War period than at any other time in history. (   )

   (5) Driven by the South, which emerged from the Civil War as an industrial powerhouse, the United States experienced exceptional growth and industrialization during the Gilded Age. (   )

   (6) Some historians have referred to the Gilded Age as America's first Industrial Revolution. (   )

   (7) Mechanization, marketing and railroads were the key elements in the new industrialized economy. (   )

   (8) The Progressive Movement was an organized campaign with clearly defined goals and was spread quickly with the support of large number of people across the country. (   )

   (9) The large migration of Americans from the countryside to the cities started the Progressive movement. (   )

   (10) Progressives finally freed the government from special interests like the railroads and trusts and pass effective legislation to protect consumers, organized labor, and minorities. (   )

Language Focus

1. **Fill in the blanks with the following words or expressions from the text.**

fierce	critical	accumulate	seemingly
effective	emerge	vital	redress
transition	relatively		

   (1) The _____ recent outbreak of street violence and protests largely reflect the frustration of young people unable to find jobs.

   (2) I just don't know how we've managed to _____ so much junk!

   (3) Regular exercise is _____ for your health.

   (4) The government has just published a highly _____ report on the state of the education system.

   (5) Congress has done little to _____ these injustices.

   (6) Swans are always _____ in defense of their young.

   (7) In my opinion, neither of these arguments is _____ in destroying its

opponent.
(8) Mid-1945 was an important period of _____ for him.
(9) Every year, in fact, _____ more celebrations, demonstrations and displays mark its passing.
(10) Hong Kong _____ as a dominant force in environmental and ecological protection.

2. **Complete the following sentences with the proper forms of the words in the brackets.**
   (1) A _____ (critical) is one who forms and expresses judgments of the merits, faults, value or truth of a matter.
   (2) The _____ (transition) sentence usually summarizes the previous paragraph and introduces the following topic.
   (3) Anyone who has creative thinking is always ready to present _____ (innovate) ideas to others.
   (4) In such an embarrassing situation, Johnson phrased the apology with _____ (delicate).
   (5) As a state official, he was entitled to live in a _____ (president) suite.
   (6) The _____ (intensity) sun of the tropics is barely tolerable to any of the visitors.
   (7) The past two decades witnessed _____ (precede) economic growth in south-east Asia.
   (8) As a career woman, she gives _____ (prior) to her business.
   (9) This program intends to raise the public _____ (aware) of animals in imminent danger.
   (10) Samantha's straight A's perfectly demonstrated she was both _____ (industry) and intelligent.

3. **Find the appropriate prepositions or adverbs that collocate with the neighboring words.**
   (1) By "Gilded Age," Mark Twain meant that the period was glittering _____ the surface but corrupt _____.
   (2) Voters turned _____ in record numbers for each presidential election in the late nineteenth century.
   (3) Progressives passed legislation to rein _____ big business, fight against corruption, free the government from special interests.
   (4) The control of the House of Representatives constantly changed hands between the Democrats and the Republicans with each election, making an agreement _____ any major issue nearly impossible.
   (5) Mechanization and marketing were the keys _____ success in this age: companies that could mass-produce products and convince people to buy them accumulated enormous amounts _____ wealth.
   (6) The railroad industry enabled raw materials, finished products, food, and people to travel cross-country _____ a matter of days, as opposed _____ the months or years that it took just prior to the Civil War.

(7) By the turn of the century, the number had jumped _____ almost 200,000 miles, linking the North, South, and West.

(8) With these railroads making travel easier, millions of rural Americans flocked _____ the cities.

(9) Progressives believed that the government needed to take a strong and active role _____ the economy, regulating big business, immigration, and urban growth.

Comprehensive Work

Team Work

American novelist Mark Twain coined the term the "The Gilded Age" in an effort to illustrate the outwardly showy, but inwardly corrupt nature of American society during the industrialization of the late 1800's.

You are a member of a film production studio that has recently been assigned to produce a documentary about the Gilded Age of American history. The documentary will need to highlight the many aspects of society that made up the Gilded Age, including technological innovation, big business, urbanization and immigration. You and your team will be responsible for producing one specific segment of the documentary. The details of each segment are as follows:

Documentary Segments		Required Content
Technology	Technology, and an abundance of natural resources, was the driving forces behind the Industrial Revolution in the United States. The telegraph, railroads, the telephone, and ultimately the use of electricity led to the shift from an agrarian to an industrial America.	**Industrial Revolution** **Use of Natural Resources** (Iron; Coal; Oil) **Transcontinental Railroad** **Inventors and their Inventions**
Big Business	Laissez-faire capitalism ruled the day during the beginning of the Industrial Revolution in the United States. In this atmosphere of unbridled money-making, numerous types of business organizations gave rise to Big Business. Were the leaders of these companies Captains of Industry or Robber Barons? While some used ruthless business practices to wipe out their competition and earn large profits, others gave enormous sums of money to charities and their communities.	**Laissez-Faire Capitalism** (Adam Smith's *The Wealth of Nations*) **Forms of Business Organization** (Monopoly; Conglomerate; Trust; Holding Company) **Entrepreneurs** (Andrew Carnegie; John D. Rockefeller; Pierpont Morgan; Henry Ford) **Conspicuous Consumption** **Philanthropy**

(Continued)

Urbanization	Urbanization was a direct result of the Industrial Revolution in the United States. Burgeoning factories were centralized in cities which offered a central location for resources and workers to fuel their production. Immigrants and displaced rural workers flooded cities in the hopes of finding employment. Throughout the Gilded Age there were several positive, as well as negative, effects that can be attributed to urbanization.	**Negative Effects** Housing (tenements, slums, etc.) Health (disease, sanitation, etc.) Working Conditions (child labor) **Positive Effects** New Technologies Cultural Benefits (museums, theaters, parks, libraries, education) Philosophies (Puritan Work Ethic; Social Darwinism)
Immigration	The United States has always been a nation of immigrants. During the Gilded Age, immigration to America increased tremendously. More people came to the United States than ever before, but they were also coming from different places, and in doing so they added to the culture of America. Was America becoming a "melting-pot" of different cultures?	**Periods of Immigration** **Reaction Against Immigration** (Nativism; Know-Nothing Party; Chinese Exclusion Act of 1882) **Theories of Immigration** (Melting-Pot Theory; Assimilation)

After completing this project, you will understand the major concepts and themes of the Gilded Age in American history. Check your understanding of these ideas by considering the following essential questions:

◇ What conditions existed in the United States which allowed the Industrial Revolution to take root and flourish in America?

◇ How did laissez-faire capitalism influence the development of business organization in the United States?

◇ Were the leaders of Big Business "robber barons," or in fact "captains of industry"?

◇ How did some philosophies serve to support class division during the Gilded Age?

◇ How did the Industrial Revolution cause urbanization and a dramatic increase in the number of immigrants to the United States?

◇ What effect did urbanization and immigration have on the United States?

◇ How did early reaction to the Gilded Age attempt to correct the abuses of the period?

Essay Writing

Urbanization refers to a process in which an increasing proportion of an entire population lives in urban areas or suburban areas. China is now witnessing urbanization. Some believe that urbanization could be the main engine of China's economic growth. However, urbanization gives rise to many social problems.

What's your view on urbanization? Write an essay within 300 words.

Read More

Text B Industrialization

Transcontinental Railroads

Gilded Age industrialization had its roots in the Civil War, which spurred Congress and the northern states to build more railroads and increased demand for a variety of manufactured goods. The forward-looking Congress of 1862 authorized construction of the first transcontinental railroad, connecting the Pacific and Atlantic lines. Originally because railroading was such an expensive enterprise at the time, the federal government provided subsidies by the mile to railroad companies in exchange for discounted rates. Congress also provided federal land grants to railroad companies so that they could lay down more track.

Early view of the Illinois Railroad

With this free land and tens of thousands of dollars per mile in subsidies, railroading became a highly profitable business venture. The Union Pacific Railroad company began construction on the transcontinental line in Nebraska during the Civil War and pushed westward, while Leland Stanford's Central Pacific Railroad pushed eastward from Sacramento. Tens of thousands of Irish and Chinese laborers laid the track, and the two lines finally met near Promontory, Utah, in 1869.

Captains of Industry

Big businessmen, not politicians, controlled the new industrialized America of the Gilded Age. Whereas past generations sent their best men into public service, in the last decades of the 1800s, young men were attracted by the private sector, where with a little persistence, hard work, and ruthlessness, one could get enormous profits. These so-called "captains of industry" were not regulated by the government and did whatever they could to make as much money as possible. These industrialists' business practices were sometimes so immoral that they were given the name "robber barons."

Rockefeller and Standard Oil

Oil was another lucrative business during the Gilded Age. Although there was very little need for oil prior to the Civil War, demand surged during the machine age of the 1880s, 1890s, and early 1900s. Seemingly everything required oil during this era: factory machines, ships, and, later, automobiles.

The biggest names in the oil industry were John D. Rockefeller and his Standard Oil Company—in fact, they were the only names in the industry. Whereas Carnegie employed vertical integration to create his steel empire, Rockefeller used horizontal integration, essentially buying out all the other oil companies so that he had no competition left. In doing so, Rockefeller created one of America's first monopolies, or trusts, that cornered the market of a single product.

Regulating Big Businesses

Without any form of government regulation, big business owners were able to create monopolies—companies that control all aspects of production for certain products. Economists agree that monopolies are rarely good for the market, as they often stifle competition, inflate prices, and hurt consumers.

In the late 1880s and early 1890s, the U.S. government stepped in and tried to start regulating the growing number of monopolies. In 1887, Congress passed the Interstate Commerce Act, which outlawed railroad discounts and kickbacks and also established the Interstate Commerce Commission to ensure that the railroad companies obeyed the new laws.

Questions for Discussion or Reflection

1. What did the government do to encourage the building of railroads?
2. What can we infer from the name "robber barons" about the so-called "captains of industry"?
3. What did Rockefeller do in order to avoid competition?
4. Why did the U.S. government start to regulate the monopolies?

Text C The Gilded Age Society

Urbanization

The Gilded Age saw the United States shift from an agricultural to an urban, industrial society, as millions of Americans flocked to cities in the post-Civil War era. Nearly 40 percent of Americans lived in urbanized areas by 1900, as opposed to 20 percent in 1860. Many young people left

the countryside in search of new wonders; cities were at the height of modernization for the time, with skyscrapers, electric trolleys, department stores, bridges, bicycles, indoor plumbing, telephones, and electric lamps. Industrialization and the rush to the cities led to the development of consumerism and a middle class.

Mass Immigration

In addition to this major shift from rural to urban areas, a new wave of immigration increased America's population significantly, especially in major cities. Immigrants came from war-torn regions of southern and eastern Europe, such as Italy, Greece, Poland, Russia, Croatia, and Czechoslovakia. This new group of immigrants was poorer and less educated than the Irish and German immigrants who had made the journey to the United States earlier in the century. By the early twentieth century, more than a million immigrants were entering eastern U.S. cities on a yearly basis. Many immigrants could barely make a living, working as unskilled laborers in factories or packinghouses for low wages.

Urban Slums

The sudden influx of millions of poor immigrants led to the formation of slums in U.S. cities. These new city dwellers lived in tenement buildings, often with entire families living together in tiny one-room apartments and sharing a single bathroom with other families on the floor. Tenements generally were dirty, poorly ventilated, and poorly lit, making them a hospitable environment for rats and disease.

Black Civil Rights

In 1896, the Supreme Court upheld the policy of segregation by legalizing "separate but equal" facilities for blacks and whites. In doing so, the court condemned blacks to more than another half century of second-class citizenship.

Despite the ruling, African-American leaders of the civil rights movement continued to press for equal rights. Booker T. Washington, president of the all-black Tuskegee Institute in Alabama, rather than press for immediate social equality, encouraged blacks to become economically self-sufficient so that they could challenge whites on social issues in the future. The Harvard-educated black historian and sociologist W. E. B. Du Bois, on the other hand, ridiculed Washington's beliefs and argued that blacks should fight for immediate and more social and economic equality. This dispute between Washington and Du Bois led to the divide in the civil rights movement at the end of the nineteenth century and the question as to how blacks could most effectively pursue equality—a debate that lasted well into the civil rights movement of the 1960s and continues today.

Questions for Discussion or Reflection

1. What made many young people in the U.S. move from rural areas to urban areas in the U.S. during the Gilded Age? Is this happening in China today?
2. Did the immigrants lead a comfortable life in the U.S.? What difficulties did they have to face?

3. What do you think is the most effective way for blacks to pursue equality?

Laissez faire 放任主义
Social Darwinism 社会达尔文主义
the Democrats 民主党人
the Gilded Age 镀金时代

the Progressive Movement 进步主义运动
the Progressivism 进步主义
the Republicans 共和党人
Trust 托拉斯

1. **Laissez faire**: It was an economic practice which stressed that the management of the economy should be left to the business men and the government should merely preserve the order and protect property.
2. **Mark Twain** (1835—1910): Mark Twain is the pseudonym of Samuel Langhorne Clemens. He was one of America's greatest nineteenth-century writers. Born in Hannibal, Missouri, he observed life along the Mississippi River and later incorporated these insights into his fiction. Clemens invested in several businesses but none prospered, and later in life he became more cynical about American society as he spoke throughout the country.
3. **Social Darwinism**: It adopted Darwin's theory of "survival of the fittest" to the business world, arguing competition is necessary to foster healthy economy.
4. **Trust**: It refers to the association of companies that illegally work together to reduce competition and control price.

Websites to Visit
1. **John D. Rockfeller and the Standard Oil Company**
   http://www.micheloud.com/FXM/so/index.htm
   This website helps to discover how Rockfeller came to dominate the oil industry for 50 years.
2. **Digital History**
   http://www.digitalhistory.uh.edu/modules/gilded_age/index.cfm
   This page introduces the information about the Gilded Age.

Books to Read

1. Ron Chernow, *Titan: The Life of John D. Rockefeller Sr.*

This is the best book about John D. Rockefeller ever written. The author carefully analyzes the man, his personality and the operation of his business. If you have only one book to read about Rockefeller, this is the one.

2. Mark Twain and Charles Dudley Warner, *The Gilded Age: A Tale of Today*

The novel satirized greed and political corruption in post-Civil War America. The novel mainly deals with the efforts of a poor Tennessee family to get rich by finding the right time to sell the 75,000 acres of unimproved land acquired by their patriarch, Silas Hawkins. After several adventures in Tennessee, the family fails to sell the land and Salis Hawkins dies. The rest of the Hawkins story line focuses on the beautiful adopted daughter, Laura. In the early 1870s, she travels to Washington, D.C. to become a lobbyist. With a Senator's help, she enters Society and attempts to persuade Congressmen to require the federal government to purchase the land.

Song to Enjoy

New ways of working and living transformed the American economy and American culture in the last decades of the 19th century. Heavy industry of manufacturing, iron and steel production, and railroad construction became the most important businesses in the country. A wave of revolutionary new inventions, including the telephone and the electric light bulb, changed the way people lived and worked, just as more and more people were leaving rural areas and moving to the city. By the end of the century, the U.S. had gone from being a country of small towns and farms to a country of big cities and factories. It had also become the wealthiest nation in the world.

Factory owners of the day could enjoy tremendous profits; however, many of their employees had to endure very harsh living and working conditions. In the 1870s and 1880s, hundreds of thousands of American workers joined unions or other labor organizations to bargain for better pay and greater workplace safety, sometimes striking.

Facing fierce opposition from the established mass media, labor leaders used many informal methods to spread the word, including popular song. Labor songs were used to raise awareness of the workers' plight to recruit new members to the cause, and to keep workers' morale up during a difficult strike or other labor action. As you read this song, you might ask yourself what the songwriter hoped to accomplish.

The Workers' Anvil

lyrics by Laura M. Griffing.

Strike, strike, the Workers anvil,   For the cause of Labor,

Strike for your homes and freedom,
For each friend and neighbor,
Ev'ry one.
For this great cause
And reform laws,
Now demand complete protection.
Strike, strike, the fire is glowing—
Heed ye not the minions,
Seeking to capture Labor,
And to clip the pinions
Of our clan.
Will you grant all
At the first call,
And submit to party factions.
Guard, guard the right, companions;
'Tis a phantom power,
From civic rule descending,
To despoil our dower.
Will you come?

Are you all strong,
To fight the wrong,
And advance the cause of labor.
Hail, hail, ye brother workmen,
Fierce and sharp the battle;
Make life a glorious triumph
Let the volleys rattle
Loud and deep.
Take a bold stand,
Throughout the land,
Thus to guard the rights of freemen.
Sound, sound the labor tocsin,
For our homes are cheerless;
Stay not, for Justice guides you
Be ye strong and fearless.
Guard your right!
If you dare, do!
And all be true—
You will gain a glorious victory.

Unit 9

America in World War I

> Every reform we have won will be lost if we go into this war.
> —President Wilson

Unit Goals

- To know the situation before the First World War.
- To learn about the U.S. neutrality and the reason of its entry into World War I.
- To learn the major consequences of the War.
- To learn the useful words and expressions that describe America in World War I.
- To improve English language skills.
- To develop critical thinking and intercultural communication skills.

Before You Read

1. World War I has often been described as an "unnecessary war." Do you agree?
2. What were the causes of the war?

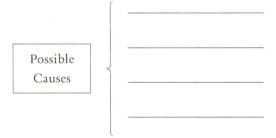

3. In what sense is World War I regarded as an ideological struggle?
4. Form groups of three or four students. Try to find, on the Internet or in the library, more information about America during World War I which interests you most. Prepare a 5-minute classroom presentation.

Text A The U.S.A. and World War I

1. A recent list of the hundred most important news stories of the 20th century ranked the onset of World War I as the 8th. This is a great error. Just about everything that happened in the remainder of the century was, in one way or another, a result of World War I, including the Bolshevik Revolution in Russia, World War II, the Holocaust, and the development of the atomic bomb. The Great Depression, the Cold War, and the collapse of European colonialism can also be traced, at least indirectly, to the First World War.

The Assassination of the Archduke

2. On June 28, 1914, a car carrying Archduke Franz Ferdinand made a wrong turn. As the car came to a halt and tried to turn around, a nervous teenager approached from a coffee house, pulled out a revolver, and shot twice. Within an hour, the Archduke and his wife were dead.

3. The assassination provoked outrage in Austro-Hungary. The assassination of the archduke triggered a series of events that would lead to the outbreak of World War I five weeks later. When the conflict was over, 11 million people had been killed, four powerful European empires had been overthrown, and the seeds of World War II and the Cold War had been planted.

U.S. Neutrality in World War I

4. President Wilson was reluctant to enter World War I. When the War began, Wilson declared U.S. neutrality and demanded that the belligerents respect American rights as a neutral party.

5. The United States hoped to stay out of the war because war was viewed as wasteful, irrational, and immoral. There was no reason for the U.S. to intervene with European affairs. In addition, America would largely profit from trading with both the Allies and Central Powers. Siding with Britain would cause the U.S. to lose trade with Germany.

6. In 1914, he had warned that entry into the conflict would bring an end to Progressive reform. "Every reform we have won will be lost if we go into this war," he said. In 1916, President Wilson narrowly won reelection after

campaigning on the slogan, "He kept us out of war."

U.S. Entry into World War I

7. Shortly after war erupted in Europe, President Wilson called on Americans to be "neutral in thought as well as deed." The United States, however, quickly began to lean toward Britain and France.

8. Convinced that wartime trade was necessary to fuel the growth of American trade, President Wilson refused to impose an embargo on trade with the belligerents. During the early years of the war, trade with the allies tripled. This volume of trade quickly exhausted the allies' cash reserves, forcing them to ask the United States for credit. In October 1915, President Wilson permitted loans to belligerents, a decision that greatly favored Britain and France. By 1917, American loans to the allies had soared to $2.25 billion.

9. In January 1917, Germany announced that it would resume unrestricted submarine warfare. This announcement gave rise to American entry into the conflict.

10. Then a fresh insult led Wilson to demand a declaration of war. In March 1917, newspapers published the Zimmerman Note, an intercepted telegram from the German Foreign Secretary Arthur Zimmerman to the German ambassador to Mexico. The telegram said that if Germany went to war with the United States, Germany promised to help Mexico recover the territory it had lost during the 1840s, including Texas, New Mexico, California, and Arizona. The Zimmerman telegram and German attacks on three U.S. ships in mid-March led Wilson to ask Congress for a declaration of war.

Treaty of Versailles

11. From the beginning of World War I, Wilson had hoped for a peace settlement promoting America's democratic ideals. President Wilson contributed greatly to an early end to the war by defining the war aims of the Allies, and by insisting that the struggle was being waged not against the German people but against their autocratic government. He wanted to end the

war through a liberal peace agreement.

12. On January 8, 1918, Wilson made his famous "Fourteen Points" address, introducing the idea of a League of Nations—a League that would guarantee all nations "fundamental rights, equal sovereignty, freedom from aggression, freedom of the seas, and eventual of disarmament." The League of Nations, he announced, would "insure peace and justice throughout the world."

13. In January 1919, diplomats gathered at the château of Versailles near Paris to negotiate a peace treaty to end the Great War. By the time work began, it was clear that the pre-war world map required drastic revision. The treaty formally placed the responsibility for the war on Germany and its allies and imposed on Germany the burden of the reparations payments.

14. When the *Treaty of Versailles* was signed on June 28th, 1919, almost all the points that Wilson had proposed were rejected. Only the League of Nations was established, which was replaced in 1946 by the United Nations.

Consequences of the War

15. American involvement in World War I lasted from the summer of 1917 to the armistice that ended the war in November 1918—just over one year. For America, the war was relatively brief, and the casualties, while large, could not be compared with those of the other major nations.

16. World War I killed more people (more than 9 million soldiers, sailors, and flyers and another 5 million civilians), involved more countries (28 nations), and cost more money ($186 billion in direct costs and another $151 billion in indirect costs), than any previous war in history. It was the first war to use airplanes, tanks, long-range artillery, submarines, and poison gas. It left at least 7 million men permanently disabled.

17. World War I probably had more far-reaching consequences than any other preceding war. Politically, it contributed to the Bolshevik rise to power in Russia in 1917 and the triumph of fascism in Italy in 1922. It ignited colonial revolts in the Middle East and in Southeast Asia.

18. Economically, the war severely disrupted the European economies and allowed the United States to become the world's leading creditor and industrial power. The war also brought vast social consequences, including the mass murder of Armenians in Turkey and an influenza epidemic that killed over 25 million people worldwide.

19. Few events better reveal the uttermost unpredictability of the future. At the dawn of the 20th century, most Europeans anticipated a future of peace and prosperity. Europe had not fought a major war for 100 years. But a belief in human progress was shattered by World War I, a war few wanted or expected. At any point during the five weeks leading up to the outbreak of fighting, the conflict might have been averted. World War I was a product of miscalculation, misunderstanding, and miscommunication.

20. No one expected a war of such magnitude or duration as World War I. At first, the armies relied on outdated methods of communication, such as carrier pigeons. The great powers mobilized more than a million horses. However, by the time the conflict was over, tanks, submarines, airplane-dropped bombs, machine guns, and poison gas had transformed the nature of modern warfare.

After You Read

Knowledge Focus

1. Pair Work: Discuss the following questions with your partner.
   (1) Why is it a great error to rank World War I the 8th in the news stories?
   (2) What was the result of the assassination of the archduke?
   (3) How do you account for the U.S. neutrality in World War I?
   (4) What did President Wilson's warning imply?
   (5) Who narrowly won reelection after campaigning on the slogan, "He kept us out of war"?
   (6) What events helped to involve the United States in the war?
   (7) What do you know about the Zimmerman Note?
   (8) What was the goal that the League of Nations intended to achieve?
   (9) What was the political contribution of World War I?
   (10) What were the impacts of World War I on this world?

2. Solo Work: Tell whether the following are true or false according to the knowledge you have learned.
   (1) The writer thought it was an error that the hundred most important news stories of the 20th century ranked the onset of World War I as the 8th. ( )
   (2) World War I caused the Bolshevik Revolution in Russia, World War II, the Holocaust, and the development of the atomic bomb. ( )
   (3) Only Archduke Franz Ferdinand died in the assassination. ( )
   (4) The assassination provoked outrage in Austria-Hungary. ( )
   (5) President Wilson was reluctant to enter World War I and declared the U.S. neutrality. He demanded that the belligerents respect American rights as a neutral party. ( )
   (6) In 1916, President Wilson achieved an overwhelming majority in the reelection after campaigning on the slogan, "He kept us out of war."( )
   (7) The Zimmerman telegram and German attacks on three U.S. ships in mid-March

led Wilson to ask the Congress for a declaration of war. ( )

(8) *Treaty of Versailles* was signed on June 28th, 1919. Almost all the points that Wilson had proposed were accepted. ( )

(9) World War I was the first war to use airplanes, tanks, long-range artillery, submarines, nuclear weapon, and poison gas. ( )

(10) No one expected a war of such magnitude or duration as World War I.

3. Solo Work

(1) Complete the table based on what you know about World War I.

Alliance	Countries in the Alliance
Triple Entente	
Triple Alliance	

(2) Complete the following text using the words in the box.

stolen	alliances	europe	Entente	alliance
austro-hungary		militarism	revenge	Britain

Europe was divided into two _____. These were called the Triple _____ and the Triple _____. Members of each alliance promised to fight for each other if they were attacked. It would only take a small incident to spark a war involving all of _____.

Germany had been trying to build up her navy and her empire. _____ was worried about this. Both countries raced each other to build the best navy. There was tension between both countries.

The area to the southeast of _____ was known as the Balkans. The area was very unstable. The European alliances had different ideas on how to deal with the problem.

France was keen for _____ on Germany. Germany had taken land from the French in 1871 and they wanted the land back. They said it had been _____ from them by Germany.

4. Pair Work

Directions: It was the assassination of the Austrian archduke, Franz Ferdinand that led to the outbreak of World War I in August 1914. However, the actual causes of the war were more complicated and not confined to a single cause. Learn the following words that can better explain the causes of World War I, and fill in the blanks with the words. Share your understanding of the key words with your partner.

World War I broke out in late Summer 1914. but tension had been building in Europe since 1900.

The Main Causes

M ilitarism
E mpire
A lliances
I mperialism
N ationalism

Glossary

Alliances	agreements or promises to defend and help another country
Imperialism	trying to build up an empire
Empire	where a powerful country controls several less powerful countries
Militarism	building up armed forces and getting ready for war
Nationalism	having pride in your country and being ready to defend it

Germany

Germany wanted to build up her empire. This is known as _____

Germany also built up her armed forces. This is known as _____

Britain

As Britain had the most powerful navy in the World, she was worried about other countries building up their armed forces. We could call this a worry about _____ . Britain, Germany and other countries were keen to have large empires.

Europe

European people were very proud of their countries and would defend their country as well as they could. This is called _____ .

Language Focus

1. **Fill in the blanks with the following words or expressions from the text.**

erupt	neutrality	reveal	provoke
bring an end to		trace	far-reaching
fuel	trigger	impose...on	

   (1) The practice of giving eggs at Easter can be _____ back to festivals in ancient China.
   (2) Test results _____ worries that the reactor could overheat.
   (3) Some people find that certain foods _____ their headaches.
   (4) The Queen has maintained political _____ throughout her reign.
   (5) This latest injury must surely have _____ her tennis career.

(6) Since the volcano last _____, many houses have been built in a dangerous position on its slopes.
(7) The prime minister's speech _____ speculation that she is about to resign.
(8) I don't want them to _____ their religious beliefs _____ my children.
(9) These new laws will have _____ benefits for all working mothers.
(10) He would not _____ where he had hidden her chocolate eggs.

2. Complete the following sentences with the proper forms of the words in the brackets.
    (1) Oil reserves were at _____ (depress) levels because of increasing industrial demands.
    (2) The facial expression of the chairman showed his _____ (reluctant) to be involved in such a political issue.
    (3) The runner in the Paralympic Games collapsed from _____ (exhaust).
    (4) Linda is obviously a(n) _____ (decide) manager, for she changes her mind very frequently.
    (5) In the _____ (precede) session, all the keynote speakers have presented their research findings to the committee members.

3. Find the appropriate prepositions or adverbs that collocate with the neighboring words.
    (1) A car carrying Archduke Franz Ferdinand came to a halt and tried to turn around. A nervous teenager approached _____ a coffee house, pulled _____ a revolver, and shot twice.
    (2) The assassination of the archduke triggered a series of events that would lead _____ the outbreak of World War I five weeks later.
    (3) The United States hoped to stay _____ of the war because war was viewed as wasteful, irrational, and immoral.
    (4) There was no reason for the U.S. to intervene _____ European affairs.
    (5) America would largely profit _____ trading with both the Allies and Central Powers. Siding _____ Britain would cause the U.S. to lose trade with Germany.
    (6) Convinced that wartime trade was necessary to fuel the growth of American trade, President Wilson refused to impose an embargo _____ trade _____ the belligerents.
    (7) American involvement _____ World War I lasted from the summer of 1917 to the armistice that ended the war in November 1918.
    (8) Politically, World War I contributed _____ the Bolshevik rise to power in Russia in 1917 and the triumph of fascism in Italy in 1922.
    (9) The event led _____ to the outbreak of fighting.
    (10) The army relied _____ outdated methods of communication such as carrier pigeons.

Comprehensive Work

Pair Work

1. World War I ended at 11 a.m. on 11th November 1918. In 1919, Lloyd George of England, Orlando of Italy, Clemenceau of France and Woodrow Wilson from the U.S. met to discuss how Germany was to be made to pay for the damage World War I had caused. Wilson had devised a 14-point plan that he believed would bring stability to Europe. Germany expected a treaty based on these 14 points. However, the French were not happy and wanted more from Germany. The Germans were not invited to the Paris Conference and had no say in the making of the peace treaty. Although Germany complained about the severity of the Treaty, it had no choice but to sign the document in the end.

Here is a British cartoon that appeared in a newspaper in 1919. Look at the cartoon and talk with your partner about what the various elements in the cartoon represent.

2. Look at the cartoon which illustrates the *Treaty of Versailles* and learn more about the treaty by yourself. Share with your partner what you have got from the cartoon.

Essay Writing

World War I exerted great impacts on both America and China. Write an essay of about 300 words, presenting your personal understanding of the impacts of the war on the two nations.

Read More

Text B Wilson's Declaration of Neutrality

By Woodrow Wilson

The effect of the war upon the United States will depend upon what American citizens say and do. Every man who really loves America will act and speak in the true spirit of neutrality, which is the spirit of impartiality and fairness and friendliness to all concerned. The spirit of the nation in this critical matter will be determined largely by what individuals and society and those gathered in public meetings do and say, upon what newspapers and magazines contain, upon what ministers utter in their pulpits, and men proclaim as their opinions upon the street.

The people of the United States are drawn from many nations, and chiefly from the nations now at war. It is natural and inevitable that there should be the utmost variety of sympathy and desire among them with regard to the issues and circumstances of the conflict. Some will wish one nation, others another, to succeed in the momentous struggle. It will be easy to excite passion and difficult to allay it. Those responsible for exciting it will assume a heavy responsibility, responsibility for no less a thing than that the people of the United States, whose love of their country and whose loyalty to its government should unite them as Americans all, bound in honor and affection to think first of her and her interests, may be divided in camps of hostile opinion, hot against each other, involved in the war itself in impulse and opinion if not in action.

Such divisions amongst us would be fatal to our peace of mind and might seriously stand in the way of the proper performance of our duty as the one great nation at peace, the one people holding itself ready to play a part of impartial mediation and speak the counsels of peace and accommodation, not as a partisan, but as a friend.

I venture, therefore, my fellow countrymen, to speak a solemn word of warning to you against that deepest, most subtle, most essential breach of neutrality which may spring out of partisanship, out of passionately taking sides. The United States must be neutral in fact, as well as in name, during these days that are to try men's souls. We must be impartial in thought, as well as action, must put a curb upon our sentiments, as well as upon every transaction that might be construed as a preference of one party to the struggle before another.

Questions for Discussion or Reflection
(1) How did President Wilson define the spirit of neutrality of Americans?
(2) What served as a natural and inevitable thing for Americans to behave in the war?
(3) How did the president warn the people of the fatal danger to their mind?

Text C U.S. Entry into World War I

On January 31, 1917, the German government resumed unrestricted submarine warfare. After five U.S. vessels were sunk, Wilson asked for a declaration of war on April 2, 1917. Congress quickly approved. The government rapidly mobilized military resources, industry, labor, and agriculture. By October 1918, a U.S. army of over 1,750,000 had been deployed in France on the eve of Allied victory.

In the summer of 1918, fresh American troops under the command of General John J. Pershing played a decisive role in stopping a last-ditch German offensive. That fall, Americans were key participants in the Meuse-Argonne offensive, which cracked Germany's vaunted Hindenburg Line.

President Wilson contributed greatly to an early end to the war by defining American war aims that characterized the struggle as being waged not against the German people but against their autocratic government. His Fourteen Points, submitted to the Senate in January 1918, called for: abandonment of secret international agreements, freedom of the seas, free trade between nations, reductions in national armaments, an adjustment of colonial claims in the interests of the inhabitants affected, self-rule for subjugated European nationalities, and, most importantly, the establishment of an association of nations to afford "mutual guarantees of political independence and territorial integrity to great and small states alike."

In October 1918, the German government, facing defeat, appealed to Wilson to negotiate on the basis of the Fourteen Points. After a month of secret negotiations that gave Germany no firm guarantees, an armistice (technically a truce, but actually a surrender) was concluded on November 11.

Questions for Discussion or Reflection
(1) What event made January 31, 1917 worthwhile to be commemorated?
(2) How did President Wilson contribute to the ending of the war?
(3) What was the main aim in Wilson's Fourteen Points?
(4) What happened in October 1918 in particular?

Proper Names

Archduke Franz Ferdinand 费迪南大公
Austro-Hungary 奥匈帝国
German militarism 德国军国主义
the League of Nations 国际联盟

The Treaty of Versailles 《凡尔赛条约》
the unrestricted submarine warfare 无限制潜水艇战
the Zimmerman Note 齐默尔曼电报

Notes

1. **The League of Nations**: It was an international organization established after World War I to encourage countries to work together and achieve international peace. It was replaced in 1946 by the United Nations.
2. **The *Treaty of Versailles***: It was a peace agreement made in 1919 at Versailles in France, following the defeat of Germany in World War I, between Germany and the allies. According to the treaty, Germany lost some of its land and had to agree to pay large amounts of money to the allies for damage caused by the war. The treaty also established the League of Nations.
3. **The unrestricted submarine warfare**: Submarines had been free to attack only armed targets of belligerent nations. By removing this restriction, submarines were free to attack any ship of any nation they encountered without concern for the cargo they carried, or the flag that they flew.

For Fun

Websites to Visit

1. BBC World War I

   http://www.bbc.co.uk/history/worldwars/wwone/

   This is a website which features the causes, events and people of World War I.

2. Wikipedia

   http://en.wikipedia.org/wiki/First_World_War

   It is a quick guide to World War I.

3. The Library of Congress

   http://memory.loc.gov/ammem/today/apr06.html

   This page focuses on America's entry into World War I.

Book to Read

Erich Maria Remarque, *All Quiet on the Western Front*

The book shows the war's horrors and also the deep detachment from German civilian life felt by many men returning from the front. The novel was first published in November and December 1928 in the German newspaper *Vossische Zeitung* and in book form in late January 1929. It sold 2.5 million copies in twenty-five languages in its first eighteen months in print. In 1930, the book was turned into an Oscar-winning movie of the same name, directed by Lewis Milestone.

Movies to See

1. *The Lost Battalion* (2001)

The Lost Battalion is a 2001 made-for-television film about the Lost Battalion of World War I. This fact-based war drama about an American battalion of over 500 men, which got trapped behind enemy, lined in the Argonne Forest in October 1918 France during the closing weeks of World War I. The film has received generally positive reviews, praised for its historical accuracy, cast, and intense action.

2. *Flyboys* (2006)

Flyboys is a 2006 British-American war drama film set during World War I. The film follows the enlistment, training, and combat experiences of a group of young Americans who volunteered to become fighter pilots in the Lafayette Escadrille. The squadron consisted of five French officers and 38 American volunteers who wanted to fly and fight in World War I during the main years of the conflict, 1914—1917, before the United States later joined the war against the Central Powers.

The film ends with an epilogue that relates each film character to the real-life Lafayette Escadrille figure on whom the movie was based.

Song to Enjoy
"You're a Grand Old Flag" by George M. Cohan

George M. Cohan was already a Broadway star in 1906, but sheet music made him a legend. As a performer and songwriter, he had been part of several successful shows and had written a number of hit songs, including "Give My Regards to Broadway." However, when he introduced an upbeat, patriotic song called "You're a Grand Old Rag" in his new musical George Washington, Jr., he became a nationwide sensation. The song's popularity quickly spread beyond New York and across the country, especially after he changed "Rag" to "Flag." Soon it was being sung in homes, social clubs, and taverns throughout the U.S. When the nation experienced a surge of patriotism on entering World War I in 1917, "You're a Grand Old Flag" surged with it and became the first song from a musical to sell over a million pieces of sheet music.

As you listen to this song, think about what makes the song successful, and decide if today's popular music might be any different if you had to play it or sing it all by yourself.

You're a Grand Old Flag

There's a feeling comes a stealing,
And it sets my brain a reeling,
When I'm listening to the music of a military band.
Any tune like "Yankee Doodle"
Simply sets me off my noodle,
It's that patriotic something that no one can understand.
"Way down South, in the land of cotton"
Melody untiring, ain't that inspiring?
Hurrah! Hurrah! We'll join the jubilee
And that's going some, for the Yankees, by gum!
Red, white and blue, I am for you!
Honest you're a grand old flag!
You're a grand old flag,
You're a high flying flag
And forever in peace may you wave.
You're the emblem of
The land I love.
The home of the free and the brave.
Ev'ry heart beats true
'neath the Red White and Blue,
Where there's never a boast or a brag.
Should auld acquaintance be forgot,
Keep your eye on the grand old flag.
You're a grand old flag,
You're a high flying flag
And forever in peace may you wave.
You're the emblem of
The land I love.
The home of the free and the brave.
Ev'ry heart beats true
'neath the Red White and Blue,
Where there's never a boast or a brag.
Should auld acquaintance be forgot,
Keep your eye on the grand old flag.

Unit 10
The Roaring Twenties

> The new generation of Americans was "dedicated more than the last to the fear of poverty and the worship of success; grown up to find all Gods dead, all wars fought, all faiths in man shaken."
>
> —F. Scott Fitzgerald

Unit Goals

- To get a whole picture of the Roaring Twenties.
- To learn about the American mass culture in the 1920s.
- To have a deep understanding of the American society in the 1920s.
- To learn the useful words and expressions that describe America in the 1920s.
- To improve English language skills.
- To develop critical thinking and intercultural communication skills.

Before You Read

1. What was the situation like in America in the 1910s?
2. Why is the 1920s depicted as "the Roaring Twenties"?
3. What lessons should be learned from the Great Depression?

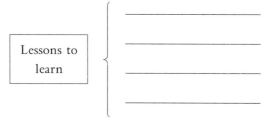

4. Form groups of three or four students. Try to find, on the Internet or in the library, more information about American life in the 1920s which interests you most. Prepare a 5-minute classroom presentation.

Start to Read

Text A　The Roaring Twenties

1. As the world bid farewell to the 1910s, it was introduced to a decade that would be unlike any other. Separating two world wars, the 1920s followed events such as the sinking of the Titanic (1912), the invention of stainless steel (1913), and the completion of the Panama Canal (1914). The Roaring Twenties would have their own share of excitement and wonder as well—the *Treaty of Versailles* ended World War I and penicillin was discovered. These events were and still are significant, but they reflect only a small portion of the full story. Unfortunately, this time period could not last forever. The 1930's soon led to the beginning of World War II.

2. In 1931, a journalist named Frederick Lewis Allen published a volume of informal history that did more to shape the popular image of the 1920s than any book ever written by a professional historian. The book, *Only Yesterday*, depicted the 1920s as an interlude between the Great War and the Great Depression. Allen argued that World War I shattered Americans' faith in reform and moral crusades, leading the younger generation to rebel against traditional beliefs while their elders engaged in an orgy of consumption and speculation.

3. The 1920s era went by such names as the Jazz Age, the Age of Intolerance and the Roaring Twenties. The popular image of the 1920s, as a decade of prosperity and riotous living and of bootleggers and gangsters, flappers and hot jazz, is indelible memory for the Americans. But this image is also profoundly misleading. The 1920s was a decade of deep cultural conflict. The decade witnessed a titanic struggle between an old and a new America. Immigration, race, alcohol, evolution, gender politics, and sexual morality—all became major cultural battlefields during the 1920s.

4. The decade was an extraordinary and confusing time, when hedonism coexisted with puritanical conservatism. It was the age of Prohibition: in 1920 a constitutional amendment outlawed the sale of alcoholic beverages. Yet drinkers cheerfully evaded the law in thousands of "speakeasies" (illegal bars), and gangsters made illicit fortunes in liquor.

5. For big business, the 1920s were golden years. The United States was now a consumer society, with booming markets for radios, home appliances, synthetic textiles and plastics. One of the most admired men of the decade was Henry Ford, who had introduced the assembly line into automobile factories. Ford could pay high wages and still earn enormous profits by mass-producing the Model T, the car that millions of buyers could afford.

6. The 1920s were a decade of profound social changes. The most obvious signs of change were the rise of a consumer-oriented economy and of mass entertainment, which helped to bring about a "revolution in morals and manners." Sexual mores, gender roles, hairstyles, and dress all changed profoundly during the 1920s. Many Americans regarded these changes as liberation from the country's past. But for others, morals seemed to be decaying, and the United States seemed to be changing in undesirable ways.

7. The 1920s were a period of deep social tensions, aggravated by high wartime inflation. Food prices more than doubled between 1915 and 1920; clothing costs more than tripled. A steel strike that began in Chicago in 1919 became much more than a simple dispute between labor and management. Organized labor had grown in strength during the course of the war. Many unions won recognition, and the 12-hour workday was abolished. An 8-hour day was instituted, and by 1919, half the country's workers had a 48-hour workweek.

8. With profits soaring and interest rate low, plenty of money was available for investment. Much of it, however, went into reckless speculation in the stock market. The bubble in the stock market burst in 1929, which triggered a worldwide depression. The Great Depression that followed after the crash was the most devastating economic blow that the nation had ever suffered. It lasted for ten years, dominating every aspect of American life during the 1930s. The

Depression loosened its grip on the nation only after the outbreak of World War II.

After You Read

Knowledge Focus

1. **Pair Work: Discuss the following questions with your partner.**
    (1) What significant events took place in the 1920s?
    (2) How were Americans influenced by World War I according to Frederick Lewis' book?
    (3) How does the writer of the text describe the image of the 1920s?
    (4) Can you find several adjectives to describe the 1920s?
    (5) Why was the 1920s confusing?
    (6) What was "Prohibition"? Was it effective?
    (7) Why was Henry Ford so successful in his business?
    (8) How do you define a "consumer-oriented" economy?
    (9) Why did some people think that the United States was changing in undesirable ways in the 1920s?
    (10) What caused the Great Depression?

2. **Tell whether the following are true or false according to the knowledge you have learned. Consider why.**
    (1) Among the significant events in the 1920s were the sinking of the Titanic, the invention of stainless steel, and the completion of the Panama Canal. (   )
    (2) The book *Only Yesterday* by Henry Ford is an interlude between the Great War and the Great Depression. (   )
    (3) The Jazz Age marked the Age of Intolerance and Roaring Twenties. And the images like gangsters, flappers and hot jazz, are unforgettable memory for Americans. (   )
    (4) In the 1920s, the United States is a consumer society with booming markets for radios, home appliances, synthetic textiles and plastics. (   )
    (5) All the Americans considered these changes like sexual mores, gender roles, hairstyles, and dress as liberation from the country's past. (   )
    (6) A worldwide depression was triggered in 1939 by the collapse of burst in the stock market. (   )
    (7) The Great Depression lasted for ten years, dominating almost all the aspects of the American life during the 1930s. (   )
    (8) A steel strike that began in Chicago in 1919 became much more than a simple dispute between labor and management. Many unions won recognition, and the 12-hour workday was abolished. An 8-hour day was instituted, and by 1919, half the country's workers had a 48-hour workweek. (   )

(9) In the 1920s, America witnessed high wartime inflation which led the country to a deep social tension. Food prices more than doubled between 1915 and 1920. Clothing costs more than tripled. ( )

Language Focus

1. Fill in the blanks with the following words or expressions from the text.

extraordinary	shatter	undesirable	crusade
misleading	abolish	coexist	consumption
devastating	illicit		

   (1) That would give them _____ power over the lives of other people.
   (2) Marijuana remains the most commonly used _____ drug in the United States.
   (3) Environmentalists claim that the development will have _____ effects on animal habitats in the area.
   (4) The unpopular tax was finally _____ some ten years ago.
   (5) These statistics give a _____ impression of what is happening to the economy.
   (6) All the windows in the farmhouse had been _____, and everything was in a mess.
   (7) Each approach has its advantages, and these and other options may _____ in the network.
   (8) He has begun a _____ against crime.
   (9) In 1980, the per capita _____ of cheese in the United States was 18 pounds. One-third was cottage cheese.
   (10) The fear of revolution and innovation can have a _____ effect on a developing nation.

2. Match the words in the left column with the corresponding explanations in the right column.

(1) farewell (2) dispute (3) mores (4) hedonism (5) speculation	A. engagement in risky business transactions on the chance of quick or considerable profit B. disagreement C. good-bye D. customs, social behavior or moral values of a particular group E. pursuit of happiness

3. Find the appropriate prepositions or adverbs that collocate with the neighbouring.
   (1) Henry Ford, who had introduced the assembly line _____ automobile factories, earned enormous profits by mass-producing the Model T.
   (2) The signing of the *Treaty of Versailles* and the discovery of penicillin reflected only a small portion _____ the advances in the period.
   (3) Allen argued that World War I led the young generation to rebel _____ the traditional beliefs.
   (4) The 1920s was a decade _____ deep cultural conflict.

(5) Many Americans regarded these changes _____ liberation from the country's past.
(6) It lasted _____ ten years, dominating every aspect of American life during the 1930s.
(7) The 1920s went by such names _____ the Jazz Age, the Age of Intolerance and the Roaring Twenties.
(8) The popular image of the 1920s, as a decade of prosperity and riotous living and of bootleggers and gangsters, flappers and hot jazz, is indelible memory _____ the Americans.
(9) The United States seemed to be changing _____ undesirable ways.
(10) Organized labor had grown _____ strength during the course of the war.

Comprehensive Work
Group Work
Directions: You are to create a magazine with the following components: Cover Page (Leading story, picture, title of magazine, editors, contributors, and date); Table of Contents; Four feature or news articles. Articles must be written as if they could be in your model magazine during the 1920s. Each group member is responsible for one. They can be about any significant event, trend or development in the 1920s. Your articles must correspond to the date of your magazine and have some perspective of time. For instance, if your magazine is written in 1927, you cannot write about the stock market crash of 1929, and any articles about Babe Ruth must either be about the glorious 1927 season or retrospectives about his still vibrant career.

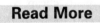

Text B   **Mass Entertainment in the 1920s**

Many of the defining features of modern American culture emerged during the 1920s. The record chart, the book club, the radio, the talking picture, and spectator sports—all became popular forms of mass entertainment. But the 1920s primarily stand out as one of the most important periods in American cultural history because the decade produced a generation of artists, musicians, and writers who were among the most innovative and creative in the country's history.

Of all the new appliances to enter the nation's homes during the 1920s, none had a more revolutionary impact than the radio. Sales of radios soared from $60 million in 1922 to $426 million in 1929. The first commercial radio station began broadcasting in 1919, and during the 1920s, the nation's airwaves were filled with musical variety shows and comedies.

Radio drew the nation together by bringing news, entertainment, and advertisements to more than 10 million households by 1929. Radio blunted regional differences and imposed similar tastes and lifestyles. No other media had the power to create heroes and villains so quickly. When Charles Lindbergh became the first person to fly nonstop across the Atlantic from New York to Paris in 1928, the radio brought this  incredible feat into American homes, transforming him into a celebrity overnight.

The phonograph was not far behind the radio in importance. The 1920s saw the record player enter American life in full force. Piano sales decreased as phonograph production rose from just 190,000 in 1923 to 5 million in 1929. The novelist F. Scott Fitzgerald called the 1920s the "Jazz Age"—and the decade was truly jazz's golden age. The blues craze erupted in 1920 when a black singer named Mamie Smith released a recording called "Crazy Blues." The record became a sensation, selling 75,000 copies in a month and a million copies in seven months. Recordings by Ma Rainey, the "Mother of the Blues," and Bessie Smith, the "Empress of the Blues," brought the blues, with their poignant and defiant reaction to life's sorrows, to a vast audience.

The single most significant new instrument of mass entertainment was the movies. Movie attendance soared from 50 million a week in 1920 to 90 million weekly in 1929. According to one estimate, Americans spent 83 cents of every entertainment dollar going to the movies, and three-fourths of the population went to a movie theater every week.

During the late teens and 1920s, the film industry took on its modern form. In cinema's earliest days, the film industry was based in the nation's theatrical center—New York. By the 1920s, the industry had relocated to Hollywood, drawn by its cheap land and labor, the varied scenery that was readily accessible, and a suitable climate ideal for year-round filming (some filmmakers moved to avoid lawsuits from individuals like Thomas Edison who owned patent rights over the filmmaking process). Each year, Hollywood released nearly 700 movies, dominating worldwide film production. By 1926, Hollywood had captured 95 percent of the British market and 70 percent of the French market. A small group of companies consolidated their control over the film industry and created the "studio system" that would dominate film production for the next 30 years. Paramount, 20th Century Fox, and other studios owned their own production facilities, ran their own worldwide distribution networks, and controlled theater chains committed to showing their companies' products. In addition, they kept the actors, directors, and screenwriters under contract.

Like radio, movies created a new popular culture with common speech, dress, behavior, and heroes. The radio, the electric phonograph, and the silver screen both molded and mirrored mass culture.

Spectator sports attracted vast audiences in the 1920s. The country yearned for heroes in an increasingly impersonal, bureaucratic society, and sports provided them. Prize fighters like Jack Dempsey became national idols. Team sports flourished, however,

Americans focused on individual superstars, people whose talents or personalities made them appear larger than life.

1. Questions for Discussion or Reflection
   (1) What were the most important features of the 1920s according to the writer?
   (2) What was the significance of radio in Americans' life?
   (3) Why did F. Scott Fitzgerald call the 1920s the "Jazz Age"?
   (4) Why did the movie industry become so popular in the 1920s?
   (5) Why were prize fighters like Jack Dempsey taken as national idols?

2. Multiple-Choice Questions
   (1) What American culture is NOT mentioned in detail in this text?
      A. The Radio.   B. Sports.
      C. The film industry.   D. The book club.
   (2) Which is NOT correct according to the text?
      A. Phonographs were not far behind the radios in importance.
      B. Sales of radios soared from $60 million in 1922 to $436 million in 1929.
      C. The single most significant new instrument of mass entertainment was the movies.
      D. Each year, Hollywood released nearly 700 movies, dominating worldwide film production.
   (3) Which is NOT the method for film makers to control their business?
      A. Running their own worldwide distribution networks.
      B. Keeping the actors, directors, and dramatist under contract.
      C. Controlling theater chains committed to showing their companies' products.
      D. Creating the studio system.

Text C   The Lost Generation

Directions: Go through Text C quickly, and find answers to the following questions.

1. Which city is the center for the lost generation?
   A. Paris.   B. New York.
   C. London.   D. Hollywood.
2. Which of the following is NOT the best-known literary artist concerning the Lost Generation?
   A. F. Scott Fitzgerald.   B. Ernest Hemingway.
   C. John Dos Passos.   D. Sherwood Anderson.
3. Which of the following statements is NOT proper?
   A. Hemingway was the Lost Generation's leader in the adaptation of the naturalistic technique.
   B. Hemingway volunteered to fight with the Italians in World War II.
   C. During the war, Hemingway was injured, but he saved one person's life.

D. Hemingway got some inspirations from his experience in the war.
4. Which of the following is NOT written by F. Scott Fitzgerald?
   A. *This Side of Paradise*.　　　　B. *The Great Gatsby*.
   C. *Tender Is the Night*.　　　　　D. *Manhattan Transfer*.

Seeking the bohemian lifestyle and rejecting the values of American materialism, a number of intellectuals, poets, artists and writers fled to France in the post World War I years. Paris was the center of it all.

American poet Gertrude Stein actually coined the expression "lost generation." Speaking to Ernest Hemingway, she said, "You are all a lost generation." The term stuck and the mystique surrounding these individuals continues to fascinate us.

Full of youthful idealism, these individuals sought the meaning of life, drank excessively, had love affairs and created some of the finest American literature to date.

There were many literary artists involved in the groups known as the Lost Generation. The three best known are F. Scott Fitzgerald, Ernest Hemingway and John Dos Passos. Others usually included Sherwood Anderson, Kay Boyle, Hart Crane, Ford Maddox Ford and Zelda Fitzgerald.

Ernest Hemingway was the Lost Generation's leader in the adaptation of the naturalistic technique in the novel. Hemingway volunteered to fight with the Italians in World War I and his Midwestern American ignorance was shattered during the resounding defeat of the Italians by the Central Powers at Caporetto. Newspapers of the time reported Hemingway, with dozens of pieces of shrapnel in his legs, had heroically carried another man out. That episode even made the newsreels in America. These wartime experiences laid the groundwork of his novel, *A Farewell to Arms* (1929). Another of his books, *The Sun Also Rises* (1926) was a naturalistic and shocking expression of post-war disillusionment.

John Dos Passos had also seen the brutality of the war and questioned the meaning of contemporary life. His novel *Manhattan Transfer* reveals the extent of his pessimism as he indicated the hopeless futility of life in an American city.

F. Scott Fitzgerald is remembered as the portrayer of the spirit of the Jazz age. Though not strictly speaking an expatriate, he roamed Europe and visited North Africa, but returned to the U.S. occasionally. Fitzgerald had at least two addresses in Paris between 1928 and 1930. He fulfilled the role of chronicler of the prohibition era.

His first novel, *This Side of Paradise* became a best-seller. But when first published, *The Great Gatsby*, on the other hand, sold only 25,000 copies. The free spirited Fitzgerald blew the publisher's advance money leasing a villa in Cannes. In the end, he owed his publishers, Scribers, money. Fitzgerald's Gatsby is the story of a somewhat refined and wealthy bootlegger whose morality is contrasted with the hypocritical attitude of most of his acquaintances. Many literary critics consider Gatsby his best work.

The impact of the war on the group of writers in the Lost Generation is aptly demonstrated by a passage from Fitzgerald's *Tender Is the Night* (1933):

> This land here cost twenty lives a foot that summer... See that little stream—we could walk to it in two minutes. It took the British a month to walk it —a whole empire walking very slowly, dying in front and pushing forward behind. And another empire walked very slowly backward a few inches a day, leaving the dead like a million bloody rugs. No Europeans will ever do that again in this generation.

The Lost Generation writers all gained prominence in 20th century literature. Their innovations challenged assumptions about writing and expression, and paved the way for subsequent generations of writers.

Questions for Discussion or Reflection

1. Who coined the expression "Lost Generation"? What is your understanding of the "Lost Generation"?
2. Scott Fitzgerald is remembered as the portrayer of the spirit of the Jazz Age. Have you ever read Fitzgerald's novel *The Great Gatsby*? What's your comment on Gatsby and his life?
3. What else do you know about the Lost Generation writers?

Proper Names

F. Scott Fitzgerald 弗朗西斯·斯科特·菲茨杰拉德 the Great Depression 经济大萧条
Hedonism 享乐主义   the Lost Generation 迷失的一代
Henry Ford 亨利·福特   the Panama Canal 巴拿马运河
Prohibition 禁酒令   the Roaring Twenties 喧嚣的 20 年代
Puritanical Conservatism 清教徒的保守主义   the *Treaty of Versailles*《凡尔赛条约》

Notes

1. **F. Scott Fitzgerald (1896—1940)**: He was the American writer who epitomized the Jazz Age. His best-known novels are *The Great Gatsby* (1925) and *Tender Is the Night* (1934).
2. **Hedonism**: It is a philosophy that pleasure is of ultimate importance. This is often used as a justification for evaluating actions in terms of how much pleasure and how little pain they produce. In very simple terms, a hedonist strives to maximize this net pleasure.
3. **The Jazz Age**: It was the period from 1918—1929, the years between the end of World War I and the start of the Roaring Twenties, ending with the rise of the Great Depression. The traditional values of this age saw great decline while the American stock market soared. The focus of the elements of this age, in some contrast with the Roaring Twenties, in historical and cultural studies, is somewhat different, with a greater emphasis on all Modernism. The age took its name from jazz music, which saw a tremendous surge in popularity among many segments of society. Among the

prominent concerns and trends of the period was the public embraces of technological developments—cars, air travel and the telephone—as well as new modernist trends in social behavior, the arts, and culture. Central developments included Art Deco design and architecture.

4. **Prohibition**: It was a sumptuary law which prohibits alcohol. Typically, the manufacture, transportation, import, export, and sale of alcoholic beverages were restricted or illegal. In the history of the United States, Prohibition is the period from 1920 to 1933, during which the sale, manufacture, and transportation of alcohol for consumption were banned nationally as mandated in the Eighteenth Amendment to the United States Constitution.

5. **The *Treaty of Versailles***: The *Treaty of Versailles* was signed on June 28, 1919, in the Hall of Mirrors at the Palace of Versailles, outside of Paris. The main points of the treaty were reparations and disarmament of Germany. Some historians point out that the treaty was more about punishing Germany than preventing another war.

6. **Henry Ford**: Ford was the founder of the Ford Motor Company and father of modern assembly lines used in mass production. His introduction of the Model T automobile revolutionized transportation and American industry. He was a prolific inventor and was awarded 161 U.S. patents. As owner of the Ford Company, he became one of the richest and best-known people in the world.

7. **The Sinking of Titanic**: On the night of 14 April 1912, during her maiden voyage, Titanic hit an iceberg. It sank two hours and forty minutes later, early on 15 April 1912. The sinking resulted in the deaths of 1,517 people, making it one of the most deadly peacetime maritime disasters in history. The Titanic used some of the most advanced technology available at the time and was, after the sinking, popularly believed to have been described as "unsinkable."

Books to Read

1. F. Scott Fitzgerald, *The Great Gatsby*

   The Great Gatsby symbolizes an era. It is both an indictment and a glorification of the "Jazz Age," and proves the most enduring novel to come out of America in the inter-war periods. Jay Gatsby, the hero of the story, represents all that is glorious and tarnished about the "Roaring Twenties." It was an age before the Great Depression when the economy was booming and conspicuous consumption was the order of the day.

2. Ernest Hemingway, *Farewell to Arms*

   Farewell to Arms is a semi-autobiographical novel. Much of the novel was written at the home of Hemingway's in-laws in Piggott, Arkansas. The novel is told through the point of view of Lieutenant Frederic Henry, an American serving as an ambulance driver in the Italian army during World War I. The title is taken from a poem by a 16th century English dramatist George Peele.

Movie to See

The Great Gatsby (2013)

The Great Gatsby is a film based on F. Scott Fitzgerald's 1925 novel of the same name. The film follows the life and times of millionaire Jay Gatsby and his neighbor Nick, who recounts his encounter with Gatsby at the height of the Roaring Twenties.

Poem to Enjoy

"Shadow" by R. Bruce Nugent

A great explosion of artistic creativity rocked the United States in the 1920s, and its center was in Harlem. Innovative young African American writers, painters, and musicians had been gathering in that upper Manhattan neighborhood since the beginning of the century, working together and developing new ideas. In the years after World War I, they gained national attention. Although they were all fiercely individualistic talents, these artists were soon identified as being part of a movement. The writers Langston Hughes, the composers Duke Ellington and Eubie Blake, and the painters Romare Bearden and Jacob Lawrence all became known as members of the Harlem Renaissance.

The writer and artist Richard Bruce Nugent played a key role in the Harlem Renaissance, even though his output was small. The poem was included in most of the African American anthologies of the time. Nugent himself never saw it as a poem about race, but about loneliness and being treated as someone different. As you read the poem, notice the ways the poet describes loneliness, and think about all the different things that could make a person feel like he or she stands out.

Shadow

Silhouette
On the face of the moon
Am I.
A dark shadow in the light.
A silhouette am I
On the face of the moon
Lacking color
Or vivid brightness
But defined all the clearer
Because

I am dark,
Black on the face of the moon.
A shadow am I
Growing in the light,
Not understood
As is the day,
But more easily seen
Because
I am a shadow in the light.

Unit 11

The Great Depression

> No one can possibly have lived through the Great Depression without being scarred by it. No amount of experience since the depression can convince someone who has lived through it that the world is safe economically.
>
> —Isaac Asimov

Unit Goals

- To know the causes and consequences of the Great Depression.
- To understand Roosevelt's New Deal policies.
- To learn the impact of the Depression on society.
- To learn the useful words and expressions that describe the Great Depression.
- To improve English language skills.
- To develop critical thinking and intercultural communication skills.

Before You Read

1. Would you rather have been a child during the 1920s or during the 1930s?
2. What's your impression of the Great Depression?
3. Form groups of three or four students. Try to find, on the Internet or in the library, more information about Great Depression which interests you most. Prepare a 5-minute classroom presentation.

Unit 11 The Great Depression

Start to Read

Text A The Great Depression in America

1. The Great Depression of 1929 was one of the worst time periods in American history. In October 1929, the booming stock market crashed, wiping out many investors. It aggravated fragile economy in Europe that had relied heavily on American loans. Over the next three years, an initial American recession became part of a worldwide depression. Business houses closed their doors, factories shut down, banks failed with the loss of savings. Farm income fell some 50 percent. By November 1932, approximately one of every five American workers was unemployed.

2. The impact of the Depression would be felt on economic reform, family structures and employment structures within the United States. The New Deal introduced by President Franklin Roosevelt would play a significant role in United States history. Although President Roosevelt managed to bring forth an economic recovery to the Great Depression of 1929, there were flaws in the new policies that irritated business owners and prohibited substantial growth for the common worker.

3. Economic and social hardship fell upon Americans like a dark blanket of total despair. Suddenly many workers were jobless in the market place. Companies had lower production demands and began to decrease wages to control financial burdens. As a result, there began a rise in child labor within the United States. Families were forced to rely on older children within the family to obtain jobs to help with the financial perils. Jobs included "newspaper carrier, baby sitter and store clerk." It is not surprising that the role of women changed within the family structure as they sought out employment to replace their husbands' previous earnings. To maintain the household while the mother was out seeking employment required that "the eldest child generally had greater responsibility in the household." Eventually the jobs for both women and children began to disappear in the major cities as production demands were met and economic purchasing power declined. To handle financial hardships, families sent children to other cities in hopes of finding employment.

4. With the crisis of the 1929 Great Depression, President Roosevelt implemented a New Deal policy to reform the United States. The intention of the New Deal was to put the purchasing power back in the hands of the general laborer and to create new jobs for renewed stable economic growth within the United States.

5. In 1933 the new president, Franklin D. Roosevelt, brought an air of confidence and optimism that quickly organized the people to the banner of his program, known as the New Deal. "The only thing we have to fear is fear itself," the president declared in his inaugural address to the nation.

6. In one sense, the New Deal merely introduced social and economic reforms familiar to many Europeans for more than a generation. Moreover, the New Deal represented a long-range trend toward abandoning "laissez-faire" capitalism, going back to the regulation of the railroads in the 1880s, and the flood of state and national reform legislation introduced in the Progressive era of Theodore Roosevelt and Woodrow Wilson.

7. What was truly novel about the New Deal, however, was the speed with which it accomplished what previously had taken generations. Many of its reforms were hastily drawn and weakly administered; some actually contradicted others. Moreover, it never succeeded in restoring prosperity. Yet its actions provided help for millions of Americans, laid the basis for a powerful new political coalition, and brought to the individual citizen a sharp revival of interest in government.

8. Roosevelt's New Deal policies were a short-term fix to the economic problems that faced both businesses and workers. A major trend emerged from the New Deal policies that manufacturers were forced to develop and use new technologies. The birth of a technological society resulted in less dependence on manual labor. "Thus when production levels were maintained or improved, workers suffered technological unemployment."

9. On the surface, it appeared that Roosevelt's New Deal was having a significant impact on restoring the economy and increasing production needs and consumption of products. As time progressed, Roosevelt was challenged because the "New Deal's failure to end the Depression or significantly reduce unemployment."

10. The Great Depression of 1929 was a major turning point within United States history. Some believe the Great Depression was strictly the result of the stock market crash in 1929 while others believe that under-consumption led to

the fall of the economy during that time period. Out of the Great Depression rose a new attitude among youth who were forced to join the labor force and even migrate to other communities to assist in financially supporting their families. Eventually, through the New Deal policies manufacturers developed new technologies to depend less upon the manual labor and the labor force requirements greatly changed. Even though the New Deal reform policies was

originally established to rebuild the working force and lessen financial burdens on the common laborer, President Roosevelt had not anticipated the resistance that he faced by businesses. Unfortunately, the negative effects of the depression would continue to be felt by Americans until the emergence of World War II.

After You Read

Knowledge Focus
1. **Pair Work: Discuss the following questions with your partner.**
   (1) When did the Great Depression start in America?
   (2) Who introduced the New Deal? What do you know about the New Deal?
   (3) What were the social and economic impacts that the Great Depression had?
   (4) How did the role of women change in the Great Depression?
   (5) What was the intention of the New Deal put forward by President Roosevelt?
   (6) How do you understand the quotation "the only thing we have to fear is fear itself"?
   (7) How do you comment on the New Deal?
   (8) Why was the Great Depression considered a major turning point in U.S. history?
   (9) What were the negative effects of the Depression?

2. **Solo Work: Tell whether the following are true or false according to the knowledge you have learned. Consider why.**
   (1) The crashed stock market worsened the fragile economy in Europe that had relied heavily on American loans. ( )
   (2) The American recession had led business houses to close their doors, factories to shut down, and banks to fail with the loss of savings. ( )
   (3) The New Deal introduced by President Franklin Roosevelt played a significant role in United States history. ( )
   (4) The New Deal comforted business owners but prohibited substantial growth for

common workers. ( )

(5) In order to control financial burdens, families forced all their children to find jobs to help with the financial perils. ( )

(6) It is surprising that the role of women changed within the family structure as they sought out employment to replace their husbands' previous earnings. ( )

(7) The intention of the New Deal was to put the purchasing power back in the hands of the general laborer and to create new jobs for renewed stable economic growth within the United States. ( )

(8) President Franklin Roosevelt delivered his inaugural address to the nation in 1929. ( )

(9) The New Deal only represented a long-range trend toward abandoning "laissez-faire" capitalism. ( )

(10) Roosevelt's New Deal policies were a long-term fix to the economic problems faced by both businesses and workers. ( )

(11) In fact, the New Deal did not solve the Depression problems totally or reduce unemployment significantly. ( )

3. Match the American Presidents in the left column with the events in the right column.

  (1) George Washington   A. Watergate Scandal
  (2) Abraham Lincoln   B. the first black president
  (3) Franklin D. Roosevelt   C. the first president
  (4) Richard Nixon   D. the Civil War
  (5) Bill Clinton   E. the bombing of Pearl Harbor
  (6) George W. Bush   F. the Iraq war
  (7) Barack Obama   G. the sex Scandal

Language Focus

1. Fill in the blanks with the following words or expressions from the text.

booming	aggravate	fragile	flaw
bring forth	peril	novel (a.)	succeed in
revival	assist in		

(1) In this position, you will _____ training new employees.
(2) The Web browser is nice, but it also has its _____.
(3) Scientists claim that they have _____ finding a cure for cancer.
(4) The disorder was _____ by the economic depression of the 1930s.
(5) Elizabeth continued reading her latest library book and did not notice my possible _____.
(6) We are happy to report that business is _____ this year.
(7) Tonight's TV news will be presented in a _____ format.
(8) Relations between the two countries are in a _____ state.
(9) Traditional English food seems to be enjoying a _____ at the moment.
(10) A tragic love affair could only _____ painful life after marriage.

2. **Find the appropriate prepositions or adverbs that collocate with the neighboring words.**
    (1) The New Deal introduced by President Franklin Roosevelt would play a significant role _____ the United States history.
    (2) Economic and social hardship fell _____ Americans like a dark blanket of total despair.
    (3) Families were forced to rely _____ older children within the family to obtain jobs to help with the financial perils.
    (4) It is not surprising that the role of women changed within the family structure as they sought _____ employment to replace their husbands' previous earnings.
    (5) To handle financial hardships, families sent children to other cities in hopes _____ finding employment.
    (6) The intention of the New Deal was to put the purchasing power back _____ the hands of the general laborer.
    (7) The New Deal merely introduced social and economic reforms familiar _____ many Europeans for more than a generation.
    (8) The New Deal never succeeded _____ restoring prosperity.
    (9) A major trend emerged _____ the New Deal policies that manufacturers were forced to develop and use new technologies.
    (10) Roosevelt's New Deal had a significant impact _____ restoring the economy and increasing production needs and consumption of products.

3. **Fill in the blanks with the proper form of the words in the brackets.**
    (1) The Great Depression of 1929 was one of the _____ (bad) time periods in American history.
    (2) It aggravated fragile _____ (economic) in Europe that had relied heavily on American loans.
    (3) The economic recession makes many workers _____ (job) in the market place.
    (4) The _____ (intend) of the New Deal was to resume the economic growth and create new jobs.
    (5) Franklin D. Roosevelt brought an air of _____ (confident) and optimism that quickly organized the people to the banner of his program, known as the New Deal.
    (6) Many of its reforms were _____ (hasty) drawn and weakly administered; some actually contradicted others.
    (7) The birth of a _____ (technology) society resulted in less dependence on manual labor.
    (8) The New Deal was having a significant impact on restoring the economy and increasing production needs and _____ (consume) of products.
    (9) The New Deal reform policies were _____ (origin) established to rebuild the working force and lessen financial burdens on the common laborer.

Comprehensive Work

Pair Work: Have a look at the following two pictures by Grant Wood (*Appraisal* and *Lilies of the Alley*), and then discuss the questions with your partner.

Grant Wood, *Appraisal*, 1931

Grant Wood, *Lilies of the Alley*, 1925

(1) What is going on in the picture? (*Appraisal*)
(2) How does this piece of art relate to what we know about the Great Depression?
(3) What do you think the women are saying to each other in this picture? (*Appraisal*)
(4) If you could fast-forward through the frozen moment of this picture, predict what would happen next. (*Appraisal*)
(5) Why do you think Grant Wood chose these objects for this piece of art? (*Lilies of the Alley*)
(6) Do you think this art is "beautiful" to people in Iowa during the Great Depression? Why or why not? (*Lilies of the Alley*)

Solo Work

Compare and contrast the causes premises and consequences of the following 3 events. The first one took place in the beginning of the 20th century and the second one took place at the end of the 20th century:

1. The United States is experiencing an economic boom in which industrialists and the capitalists who back them are amassing great wealth. The boom ends abruptly with the stock market crash of 1929.

2. The United States has just experienced an economic boom in which high-tech entrepreneurs and those who invested in their ventures became wealthy very quickly. The year 2000 marks the beginning of the end, as stock markets retreat significantly for consecutive years, wiping out the wealth of some, and adversely affecting most companies and investors.

Read More

Text B Iowa in the 1920s and the 1930s

The First World War ended in 1918. Iowans cheered home the soldiers who had fought in Europe to defeat Germany. Most people hoped that there would be a time with few problems, but that did not happen. The war brought changes that lasted even after the fighting had ended.

Farmers were some of the first to have trouble. During the war, they had worked hard to produce more corn and livestock. The extra food helped to feed the American armies and our allies in Great Britain and France. When the war ended, farms in Europe began to produce food again. There was not as much need for American food.

Soon there was more corn, cattle, and hogs than people wanted to buy. The prices for farm produce fell and farmers received less money. Many farmers had borrowed money from banks to buy new tractors and farm equipment. Some had bought more land.

When prices fell, many farmers could not repay their loans to the banks. Without those repayments, the banks could not continue. In the early 1920s, many banks in small Iowa towns had to close. People who had savings accounts in those banks lost the money they had invested.

In 1928, the United States elected Herbert Hoover to be president. Hoover was born in West Branch, Iowa, the only Iowan to be elected president. When Hoover was still a boy, his parents died and he moved away to live with his relatives. After World War I, many people in Europe were starving because they had no food. Hoover worked hard to get food to these people, and he was highly respected in Europe. By 1930 and throughout the next few years, farm prices dropped even lower. In some places, farmers burned corn in their stoves rather than coal because corn was so cheap. Factories closed when people could not buy the products they produced. The people who worked at the factories lost their jobs. A depression is when many people are out of work and have little money. Things were so bad in the 1920s and 1930s that it is called the Great Depression.

The government in Washington stepped in to try to help things. The government hired people to work on projects like building highways, schools, and bridges. It gave money to farmers who promised to produce smaller crops. While things got better for some people, many people in the 1930s had a hard time making a living.

There were some good things for farmers, however. An Iowan named Henry Wallace began experimenting with corn. He discovered how to grow a better kind of corn seed. It is called "hybrid" corn. When farmers planted it, they got more corn out of each field. In the 1920s and 1930s, farmers began using more hybrid corn. Henry Wallace became Vice President of the United States in 1940.

Some other good things happened during this time. Many more families bought automobiles. They took vacations to near and distant places. More Iowa children attended high school than ever before. Iowa built many miles of highways to make travel easier.

By the end of the 1930s, some brave Iowans were even making trips in airplanes. Trucks were hauling goods from farms to towns and from towns to cities. Sports became popular. Radios and newspapers carried reports of football and basketball games. In 1939, Nile Kinnick, a football player at the University of Iowa, won the Heisman Trophy, the nation's highest award in college football. The twenty years after WWI were years of tremendous change. On Iowa farms and in Iowa towns and cities, people adjusted to the new ways as best they could.

Questions for Discussion or Reflection
(1) What were the good things that happened in the 1920s and 1930s in the eyes of Iowans?
(2) What do you know about President Herbert Hoover?

Text C　Franklin D. Roosevelt

In June 1932, Franklin D. Roosevelt received the Democratic presidential nomination. At first glance, he did not look like a man who could relate to other peoples' suffering—Roosevelt had spent his entire life in the lap of luxury.

Born in 1882 to one of New York's wealthiest families, Roosevelt enjoyed a privileged youth. He attended Groton, an exclusive private school, and then went to Harvard University and Columbia Law School. After three years in the New York state senate, Roosevelt was tapped by President Wilson to serve as assistant secretary of the navy in 1913. His status as the rising star of the Democratic Party was confirmed when James Cox chose Roosevelt as his running mate in the presidential election of 1920.

Handsome and outgoing, Roosevelt seemed to have a bright political future. Then disaster struck. In 1921, he was stricken with polio. The disease left him paralyzed from the waist down and confined to a wheelchair for the rest of his life. Instead of retiring, however, Roosevelt labored diligently to return to public life. "If you had spent two years in bed trying to wiggle your toe," he later declared, "after that anything would seem easy."

Buoyed by an exuberant optimism and devoted political allies, Roosevelt won the governorship of New York in 1928—one of the few Democrats to survive the Republican landslide. Surrounding himself with able advisors, Roosevelt labored to convert New York into a laboratory for reform, involving conservation, old-age pensions, public works projects, and unemployment insurance.

In his acceptance speech before the Democratic convention in Chicago, Roosevelt promised "a New Deal for the American people." Although his speech contained few concrete proposals, Roosevelt radiated confidence, giving many desperate voters hope. He even managed during the campaign to turn his lack of a blueprint into an asset, offering instead a policy of experimentation. "It is common sense to take a method and try it," he declared, "if it fails, admit it frankly and try another."

Questions for Discussion or Reflection

1. What qualities of President Roosevelt impress you most?
2. "It is common sense to take a method and try it. If it fails, admit it frankly and try another." Comment on this quotation.

Proper Names

Franklin D. Roosevelt 富兰克林·D. 罗斯福　　the New Deal 新政
Iowa 爱荷华州　　Woodrow Wilson 伍德罗·威尔逊
the Great Depression 经济大萧条

Notes

1. **Woodrow Wilson**: He was son of a Presbyterian minister. He was born in Staunton, Virginia, in 1856. Educated at Princeton, the University of Virginia and Johns Hopkins University, he became a professor at Princeton. He also published the book, *History of the American People*. In 1912, he was elected as the twenty-eighth president of the United States.
2. **Laissez-faire**: Laissez-faire is a term used to describe a policy of allowing events to take their own course. The term is a French phrase literally meaning "let do" ("allow to do"). The term is often used to refer to various economic philosophies and political philosophies which seek to minimize or eliminate government intervention in most or all aspects of society.

For Fun

Book to Read

Christopher Paul Curtis, *Bud, not Buddy*

　　This fictional story of a boy's search for his father in 1936 presents glimpses of life in Michigan during the Great Depression.

Movies to See

1. ***Paper Moon*** (1973)

　　Paper Moon, a 1973 American comedy-drama film, was set in Kansas and Missouri during the Great Depression. Con man Moses Pray meets 9-year-old Addie Loggins at Addie's mother's graveside service, where the neighbors suspect he is Addie's father. He denies this, but agrees to deliver the orphaned Addie to her aunt's home in St. Joseph, Missouri.

2. Of Mice and Men (1992)

Based on John Steinbeck's 1937 classic tale of two travelling companions, George and Lennie, who wander the country during the Depression, dreaming of a better life for themselves. Then, just as heaven is within their grasp, it is inevitably yanked away. The film follows Steinbeck's novel closely, exploring questions of strength, weakness, usefulness, reality and utopia, bringing Steinbeck's California vividly to life.

Song to Enjoy

Brother, Can You Spare a Dime?

lyrics by Yip Harburg, music by Jay Gorney

Once I built a railroad, made it run
made it race against time
once I built a railroad, now it's done
brother can you spare a dime?
Once I built a tower to the sun
brick and rivet and lime
once I built a tower, now it's done
brother can you spare a dime?

Once in khaki suits
gee, we looked swell
full of that Yankee doodle de dum
half a million boots went slogging through hell
I was the kid with the drum
say don't you remember, they called me al
it was al all the time
say don't you remember, I'm your pal!
Buddy can you spare a dime?

Once I built a railroad, made it run
made it race against time
once I built a railroad, now it's done
brother can you spare a dime?
Once I built a tower to the sun
brick and rivet and lime
once I built a tower, now it's done
brother can you spare a dime?

Once in khaki suits
gee, we looked swell
full of that Yankee doodle de dum
half a million boots went slogging through hell
I was the kid with the drum
say don't you remember, they called me al
it was al all the time
say don't you remember, I'm your pal!
Buddy can you spare a dime?

Unit 12

America in World War II

> The structure of world peace cannot be the work of one man, or one party, or one nation. It must be a peace which rests on the cooperative effort of the whole world.
>
> —President Roosevelt (1945)

Unit Goals

- To have a general idea of America in World War II.
- To know the cause and progress of the war.
- To know the aftermath of the war and its impact on America.
- To learn the important words and expressions that describe America in World War II.
- To improve English language skills.
- To develop critical thinking and intercultural communication skills.

Before You Read

1. The Second World War was not unfamiliar to most of us. What do you know about the war? Can you name one or two important figures or battles during the war? Share what you know with your classmates.
2. What was the trigger that brought America into the war?
3. How was the world affected by the war? Some say that wars are not simply destructive forces, and wars bring about advances in many fields. Do you agree?
4. Form groups of three or four students. Try to find, on the Internet or in the library, more information about America during World War II which interests you most. Prepare a 5-minute classroom presentation.

Start to Read

Text A World War II

1. World War II began on September 1, 1939, when Germany, without a declaration of war, invaded Poland. Britain and France declared war on Germany on September 3, and all the members of the Commonwealth of Nations, except Ireland, rapidly followed suit. The fighting in Poland was brief. The German blitzkrieg, or lightning war, with its use of new techniques of mechanized and air warfare, crushed the Polish defenses, and the conquest was almost complete when Soviet forces entered Poland on September 17.

2. Again neutrality was the initial American response to the outbreak of war in Europe. But the bombing of Pearl Harbor naval base in Hawaii by the Japanese in December 1941 brought the United States into the war, first against Japan and then against its allies, Germany and Italy.

The Cause of the War

3. The source of the war in Europe came from Germany. The country had not been destroyed completely and the German people were very unhappy with the unfair *Treaty of Versailles*. Thus, they kept demanding that it be revised. And it was indeed revised a little during the 1920s. But the world-wide depression caused the failure of the democratic German government.

4. Consequently, a new German nationalist movement arose, led by Adolf Hitler and the Nazi (National Socialist) Party. Hitler was a fascist dictator. He conceived a scheme in which Germany would conquer all of Europe and the world. He advocated that the Germanic race was superior and the Jews and the Slavic people were inferior. He looked on them as the enemies of Germany, and took whatever means necessary to wipe them out of the earth.

5. Hitler and the Nazis broke the *Treaty of Versailles* when they began to reorganize the German war industry. They also developed a highly efficient army trained in blitzkrieg, a type of a military maneuver.

6. Japan, the fascist nation in Asia, launched war on China in 1931. And within a very short time, Japan occupied the Northeast of China. On July 7th, 1937, Japan began an all-out attack on China. Then Japan joined together with the Axis powers, Germany and Italy. Finally on December 7th 1941, Japan's planes from carriers at sea made a swift and sudden raid on the United States' naval base at Pearl Harbor. Submarines also participated in the "sneak attack." This attack gave a heavy blow to the United States navy. The incident of the attack on Pearl Harbor shook the whole country of the United States. The next day heard a short address by President Roosevelt, and Congress declared war on Japan. Then the whole world was drawn into the war.

Progress of the War

7. In 1939, Germany launched a lightning attack on Poland, and both England and France then declared war on Germany for Poland was an ally of the two countries. Throughout the winter, however, the British and French armies remained immobile. So Germany went on invading Denmark, Norway, the Netherlands, Belgium and Luxemburg. Then in June 1940, Germany attacked France, and Italy declared war in support of Germany.

8. Britain, under the leadership of Winston Churchill, defeated Germany's attempt to destroy its air force and air defenses in the Battle of Britain and escaped invasion. Then Germany began to look eastward towards the Soviet Union. In June, 1941, Nazi forces made an overall sudden attack upon the Soviet Union. The Soviet army and people, headed by Stalin, rose to resist. Neither side could thoroughly defeat the other until the decisive Battle of Stalingrad in 1943, which marked the turning point of the Second World War.

9. After the Pacific War broke out, there were two war arenas in the world. One was the European arena; the other was the Pacific arena. In the European arena, the war on land was proceeding on mainly between Germany and the Soviet Union, together with the African arena. While in the Pacific arena, the war went on between Japan and the U.S.A., Britain, China and some other countries. The Japanese captured a large part of China and rapidly overran the Philippines, Malaya, Singapore, Burma, Indonesia and many of the British islands. It was not until June 1942 that their advance was checked when the main force of the Japanese United Fleet was destroyed in the Midway Island Battle, which was the turning point of the Pacific War.

10. After the Battle of Midway Island and the Battle of Stalingrad, the armies of the Allies began their large offensive operations. At last, the Nazi troops began to be driven back. The British attacked the Germans in North Africa. The Chinese, French and the people in other occupied countries carried on active guerilla warfare against the enemy. The Americans began to take the offensive in the Pacific. The Russians, after having liberated their own territory, pursued the Germans across Eastern Europe. In 1944, the second European battlefield was opened. The Allied armies of Britain and the U.S. landed on the beaches of Normandy. Then the Allied armies began to move across France and into Germany. The Soviet counter-offensive was under way, thus the German troops were caught in a pincer movement from both East and West. On May 8th, Germany surrendered. Hitler and some members of his government committed suicide.

11. The Japanese, however, still fought, refusing to surrender. On August 6th and 9th, 1945, the U.S. dropped two atomic bombs on the cities of Hiroshima and Nagasaki, killing over 200,000 Japanese people. On August 8th in the same year, the Soviet Union declared war on Japan. More than one million Soviet troops entered the Northeast of China by four routes, destroying the main force of the Japanese army there, while all the Chinese armed forces began an all-out counter attack. Japan had to surrender unconditionally on August 14th, 1945. The Second World War thus came to an end.

Aftermath of the War

12. World War II was very destructive. It claimed more than 36 million lives. It killed more people, cost more money, damaged more property, affected more people, and caused more far-reaching changes in nearly every country than any other war in history. More than 50 countries took part in the war, and the whole world felt its effects. Men fought in almost every part of the world, on every continent except Antarctica. Chief battlegrounds included Asia, Europe, North Africa, the Atlantic and Pacific oceans, and the Mediterranean Sea.

13. The number of people killed, wounded, or missing between September 1939 and September 1945 can never be calculated, but it is estimated that more than 55 million people perished. Eastern Europe and East Asia suffered the heaviest losses.

14. World War II was the most expensive war in history. It has been estimated that the cost of the war totaled between $1 and $2 trillion, and the property damage amounted to more than $239 billion.

15. The Allies were determined not to repeat the mistakes of World War I, in which Allies had failed to set up an organization to enforce the peace until after World War I ended. In June 1941, nine European governments-in-exile joined with Great Britain and the Commonwealth countries in signing the Inter-Allied Declaration, which called for nations to cooperate and work for lasting peace. In 1944, an idea emerged to create a postwar international organization. As the war was nearing its end, on April 25, 1945, representatives of 50 nations met at San Francisco to erect the framework for the United Nations and to draft its constitution. China was granted membership of the Security Council as one of the five permanent member states.

16. The conferences attended by the United States and the Soviet Union to solve the postwar issues at the close of World War II ended on an apparent note of harmony. Beneath the surface, however, the bitter antagonism of the Cold War was already festering. The United States and the Soviet Union, each distrustful of the other, were preparing for a long and bitter confrontation. A cold war between the two major world powers ensued right after the end of World War II.

After You Read

Knowledge Focus

1. **Pair Work: Discuss the following questions with your partner.**
    (1) How did the U.S. respond to the outbreak of World War II?
    (2) What was the major cause of World War II?
    (3) What do you know about the attack on Pearl Harbor?
    (4) What countries were invaded by Germany by 1940?
    (5) How did Britain escape the invasion by Germany?
    (6) What was the turning point of the Second World War?
    (7) What do you know about the two war arenas in the world after the Pacific War broke out?
    (8) What caused the surrender of Germany on May 8th, 1945?
    (9) How did the Second World War come to an end?
    (10) What lessons do you think we should learn from this war?

2. **Solo Work: Tell whether the following are true or false according to the knowledge you have learned. Consider why.**
    (1) Germany's invasion of Poland without a declaration preluded the World War II.
     (   )
    (2) It took a long time for Germany to conquer Poland though lots of new techniques

of mechanized and air warfare used. ( )

(3) The America's initial response to the outbreak of war in Europe was neutrality. But after the bombing of the Pearl Harbor, their attitude changed. ( )

(4) In June, 1941, Nazi forces made an overall sudden attack upon France and Italy. ( )

(5) There were all together two war arenas in the world. One was the Pacific arenas, and the other was the African arenas. ( )

(6) After Germany surrendered, Japanese still refused to surrender until August 6th and 9th, 1945. ( )

(7) The whole world can feel the effects of World War II, and men fought on every continent. ( )

(8) Europe and Asia suffered the heaviest losses during World War I. ( )

(9) The effect of the Inter-Allied Declaration was to call for nations to cooperate and work for lasting peace. ( )

(10) The United States and the Soviet Union attended conferences to solve the postwar issues at the close of World War II. ( )

3. Finish the multiple-choice questions based on what you have read in Text A.

(1) Which of the following was NOT the cause of the war?
   A. German people did not agree with the unfair *Treaty of Versailles*.
   B. A new German nationalist movement arose.
   C. Japan launched war in China and raid on the United States' naval base at Pearl Harbor.
   D. America adopted neutrality attitude towards the war.

(2) Which of the following countries escaped the invasion of Germany?
   A. Denmark.   B. France.   C. Belgium.   D. Britain.

(3) The turning point of the Pacific War was _____.
   A. the Japanese United Fleet was destroyed in the Midway Island Battle
   B. the Japanese captured a large part of China and rapidly overran the Philippines, and other countries
   C. the Nazi troops began to be driven back
   D. the Chinese, the French and the people in other occupied countries carried on active guerilla warfare against their enemies

(4) Which is NOT the immediate cause of Japanese surrender?
   A. The U.S. dropped two atom bombs on the cities of Hiroshima and Nagasaki.
   B. Soviet Union declared war on Japan.
   C. All the Chinese armed forces began an all-out counter attack.
   D. Germany defeated France.

Language Focus

1. **Fill in the blanks with the following words or expressions from the text.**

perish	under way	confrontation	enforce
distrustful	offensive	emerge	far-reaching
decisive	surrender		

   (1) A national announcement has been made to _____ military discipline.
   (2) He was convicted of carrying a(n) _____ weapon and got a 28-day suspended sentence and £200 fine.
   (3) Plans are well _____ for a new shopping centre.
   (4) The inspector made _____ remarks after listening to the official's report.
   (5) However well you try to equip yourself, qualifications are unlikely to be the _____ factor.
   (6) Poor countries fear that _____ will upset their relations with the West.
   (7) The court's decision will have _____ implications for the health care industry.
   (8) Everyone aboard the ship _____ when it sank off the coast of Maine.
   (9) All three gunmen _____ by the end of the day.
   (10) At the airport, people stood behind a metal fence, waiting for passengers to _____ from customs.

2. **Find the appropriate prepositions or adverbs that collocate with the neighboring words.**
   (1) The bombing of Pearl Harbor naval base _____ Hawaii by the Japanese in December 1941 brought the United States into the war, first _____ Japan and then against its allies, Germany and Italy.
   (2) The country had not been destroyed completely and the German people were very unhappy _____ the unfair *Treaty of Versailles*.
   (3) He looked on them as the enemies of Germany, and took whatever means necessary to wipe them _____.
   (4) The war on land was proceeding _____ mainly between Germany and the Soviet Union, together with the African arena.
   (5) The Chinese, the French and the people in other occupied countries carried _____ active guerilla warfare _____ the enemy.
   (6) The Allied armies began to move _____ France and into Germany at the end of World War II.
   (7) The United States and the Soviet Union, each distrustful _____ the other, were preparing for a long and bitter confrontation.
   (8) _____ the surface, the bitter antagonism of the Cold War was already festering.
   (9) Allies had failed to set _____ an organization to enforce the peace until after World War I ended.
   (10) The property damage amounted _____ more than $239 billion.

Comprehensive Work

Group Work

Was the dropping of the atomic bombs justified?

Supporters believe that the atomic bombs helped to end the war more quickly. They argue that, without the atomic bombs, the armed forces of the United States would have had to enter the home islands of Japan, resulting in hundreds of thousands of additional American and Japanese casualties. Opponents argue that Japan would have surrendered without the use of an atomic bomb on a civilian target. They say that Japan was a beaten nation in August of 1945 and was only looking for a way to surrender while preserving the role of their emperor.

You are expected to join one of four teams. Each team will research the decision to drop the bomb from a different perspective. These are the four perspectives: 1) a scientist involved with the Manhattan Project; 2) a senior civilian diplomatic/political/military advisor to President Truman; 3) a senior U.S. military leader; and 4) a Japanese survivor of the bombing.

You are supposed to write a short individual report to answer the question. The individual report is a short persuasive essay that must incorporate both pro and con arguments.

Essay Writing

How was the world affected by World War II? Some say that wars are not simply destructive forces, and wars bring about advances in many fields. What's your opinion on wars? Write an essay of about 300 words to illustrate your point.

Read More

Text B The Origins of World War II

America and Isolationism

When events began happening in Europe that would eventually lead to World War II, many Americans took an increasingly hard line towards getting involved. The events of World War I had fed into America's natural desire to isolationism, and this was reflected by the passage of *Neutrality Acts* along with the general hands off approach to the events that unfolded on the world stage.

Increasing tensions

While America was wallowing in neutrality and isolationism, events were occurring in Europe and Asia that were causing increasing tension across the regions. These events included:

- Totalitarianism as a form of government in Italy (Benito Mussolini), Germany

(Adolf Hitler), and Spain (Francisco Franco).
- A move towards fascism in Japan.
- The creation of "Manchukuo," Japan's puppet government in Northeast China, beginning the war in China.
- The conquest of Ethiopia by Mussolini.
- Revolution in Spain led by Francisco Franco.
- Germany's continuing expansion including taking the Rhineland.
- The worldwide Great Depression.
- World War I allies with large debts, many of which were not paying them off.

America passed the *Neutrality Acts* in 1935—1937. These created an embargo on all war item shipments. Americas were not allowed to travel on belligerent ships and no belligerents were allowed loans in the United States.

The Road to War

The actual war in Europe itself began with a series of events:
- Germany took Austria (1938) and the Sudtenland (1938)
- *The Munich Pact* was created (1938) with England and France agreeing to allow Hitler to keep the Sudtenland as long as no further expansion occurred.
- Hitler and Mussolini created the Rome-Berlin Axis military alliance to last 10 years (1939)
- Japan entered an alliance with Germany and Italy (1939)
- The Moscow-Berlin Pact occurred promising nonaggression between the two powers (1939)
- Hitler invaded Poland (1939)
- England and France declared war on Germany (September 30, 1939).

The Changing American Attitude

At this time despite Franklin Roosevelt's desire to help the "allies" (France and Great Britain), the only concession America made was to allow the sale of arms on a "cash and carry" basis. Hitler continued to expand taking Denmark, Norway, the Netherlands, and Belgium. In June, 1940, France fell to Germany. Obviously, this quick expansion got America nervous and the military began to be built up.

The final break in isolationism began with the *Lend Lease Act* (1941) whereby America was allowed to "sell, transfer title to, exchange, lease, lend, or otherwise dispose of, to any such government... any defense article." Great Britain promised not to export any of the lend lease materials. After this, America built a base on Greenland and then issued the *Atlantic Charter* (August 14, 1941)—a joint declaration between Great Britain and the U.S. about the purposes of war against fascism. The Battle of the Atlantic began with German U-Boats wreaking havoc. This battle would last throughout the war.

The real event that changed America into a nation actively at war was the attack on Pearl Harbor. This was precipitated in July 1939 when FDR announced that the U.S. would no longer trade items such as gasoline and iron to Japan who needed it for their war with China. In July 1941, the Rome-Berlin-Tokyo Axis was created. The Japanese began occupying French Indonesia and the Philippines. All Japanese assets were frozen in the U.S. On December 7, 1941, the Japanese attacked Pearl Harbor killing over 2,000 people and damaging or destroying 8 battleships greatly harming the Pacific fleet. America officially entered the war and now had to fight on two fronts: Europe and the Pacific.

1. Questions for Discussion or Reflection
   (1) Why did Americans take an attitude of not getting involved in the world events?
   (2) What were the *Neutrality Acts* about?
   (3) How did America feel about German expansion in Europe?
   (4) What move did America make to break isolationism?
   (5) What is the casualty of the attack on Pearl Harbor?

2. Multiple-Choice Questions
   (1) The events that occurred in Europe and Asia and caused increasing tension across the regions do NOT include _____.
       A. the worldwide economic recession
       B. revolution in Spain led by Francisco Franco
       C. the continuing expansion of Germany
       D. the surrender of Japan in China
   (2) The war in Europe began with a series of events which included ____.
       A. declaration of war by England and France on Japan
       B. Japan's entry into the Fascism alliance with Germany and Italy
       C. German occupation of Austria and the Sudtenland
       D. the Moscow-Berlin Pact
   (3) Which of the following descriptions is NOT attributable to the change of the American attitude?
       A. America sold arms based on a "cash and carry" policy.
       B. The *Lend Lease Act* finally broke the isolationism.
       C. Great Britain built a base on Greenland and then issued the Atlantic Charter.
       D. The attack on Pearl Harbor turned America into a nation active in the war.

Text C American Domestic Situation During World War II

Americans at home sacrificed while soldiers fought overseas. By the end of the war, more than 12 million American soldiers had joined or were drafted into the military. Widespread rationing occurred. For example, to purchase sugar, families were given coupons based on size. They could not buy more than their coupons would allow. However, rationing covered more than just food—it also included goods such as shoes and gasoline.

Some items were just not available in America. Silk stockings made in Japan were not available—the new synthetic nylon stockings replaced them. No automobiles were produced from February 1943 until the end of the war to move the manufacturing to war specific items.

Many women entered the workforce to help make munitions and implements of war. These women were nicknamed "Rosie the Riveter" and were a central part of America's success in war.

Wartime restrictions were imposed on civil liberties. A real black mark on the American home front was the Executive Order No. 9066 signed by Roosevelt in 1942. This ordered those of Japanese-American descent to be removed to "Relocation Camps." This law eventually forced close to 120,000 Japanese-Americans in the western part of the United States to leave their homes and move to one of ten "relocation" centers or to other facilities across the nation. Most of those relocated were American citizens by birth. They were forced to sell their homes, most for next to nothing, and take only what they could carry. In 1988, President Ronald Reagan signed the Civil Liberties Act that provided redress for Japanese-Americans. Each living survivor was paid $20,000 for the forced incarceration. In 1989, President George H. W. Bush issued a formal apology. However, nothing can make up for the pain and humiliation that this group of individuals had to face for nothing more than their ethnicity.

In the end, America came together to successfully defeat fascism abroad. The end of the war would send the U.S. into a Cold War due to concessions made to the Russians in exchange for their aid in defeating the Japanese.

Questions for Discussion or Reflection
1. What sacrifices did Americans at home make while soldiers were fighting overseas?
2. What role did American women play in the war?

Proper Names

Adolf Hitler 阿道夫·希特勒
Bataan Peninsula 巴丹半岛
Blitzkrieg 闪电战
Fascism 法西斯主义
Guadalcanal 瓜达康纳尔岛
Guerilla Warfare 游击战
Hiroshima 广岛
Holocaust (第二次世界大战时纳粹对犹太人的)大屠杀
Isolationism 政治或经济上的孤立主义
Nagasaki 长崎
Neutrality Acts《中立法》
Pearl Harbor 珍珠港

the Atlantic Charter《大西洋宪章》
the Battle of Stalingrad 斯大林格勒战役
the Commonwealth of Nations 英联邦
the Coral Sea 珊瑚海
the Inter-Allied Declaration《同盟国宣言》
the Jews and the Slavic people 犹太和斯拉夫人
the Lend Lease Act《租借法》
the Midway Island Battle 中途岛战役
the Munich Pact《慕尼黑公约》
the Nazi 纳粹
the Security Council (联合国)安理会
Winston Churchill 温斯顿·丘吉尔

Notes

1. **The Commonwealth of Nations**: It is usually known as the Commonwealth, a voluntary association of 53 independent sovereign states, most of which are former British colonies, or dependencies of these colonies (the exceptions being the United Kingdom itself and Mozambique). No single government in the Commonwealth, British or otherwise, exercises power over the others, as in a political union. Rather, the relationship is one of an international organization through which countries with diverse social, political, and economic backgrounds are regarded as equal in status, and co-operate within a framework of common values and goals.

2. **The Inter-Allied Declaration**: It is a declaration "to work together with other free peoples, both in war and in peace." It was signed in London on 12 June 1941, as the first step towards the establishment of the United Nations.

3. **The Midway Island Battle**: The Battle of Midway was a major naval battle in the Pacific Theater of World War II. The battle permanently weakened the Imperial Japanese Navy (IJN), in particular through the loss of four fleet carriers and over 200 irreplaceable experienced naval aviators. The Midway operation, like the attack on Pearl Harbor, was not part of a campaign for the conquest of the United States, but was aimed at its elimination as a strategic Pacific power, thereby giving Japan a free hand in establishing its Greater East Asia Co-Prosperity Sphere.

4. **The Neutrality Acts**: They were the acts to limit U.S. involvement in future wars. They were based on the widespread disillusionment with World War I in the early 1930s and the belief that the United States had been drawn into the war through loans and trade with the Allies.

5. **The Atlantic Charter**: It was drafted at the Atlantic Conference (codenamed Riviera) by British Prime Minister Winston Churchill and U.S. President Franklin D. Roosevelt, and was the essential blue-print for the Post War world and is the foundation for many of the international treaties and organizations that currently shape the world.

6. **The Cold War**: It was the state of conflict, tension and competition that existed between the United States and the Soviet Union and their respective allies from the mid-1940s to the early 1990s. Throughout this period, rivalry between the two superpowers was expressed through military coalitions, propaganda, espionage, weapons development, industrial advances, and competitive technological development, which included the space race.

For Fun

Movie to See

Pearl Harbor (2001)

On the morning of December 7, 1941, Imperial Japanese forces made a surprise attack on the American forces based at Pearl Harbor, Hawaii. In an instant, war began for America. In exclusive interviews, survivors of the battle share their memories, recalling the terror, confusion and bravery of those who suddenly found the peaceful Hawaiian paradise shattered by bombs and bullets wreaking death and devastation all around them.

Books to Read

1. Alex Kershaw, *The Bedford Boys*

    It is an astonishing true story of 21 young men killed during the first horrifying minutes of D-Day and the friends and families they left behind in the small town of Bedford. Twenty-one sons killed—no other town in America suffered a greater loss in one day. It is an unforgettable story of triumph, courage, and tragedy based on extensive interviews with survivors and relatives as well as diaries and letters.

2. Donovan Webster, *The Burma Road*

    The Burma Road vividly re-creates the sprawling, sometimes hilarious, often harrowing, and still largely unknown stories of one of the greatest chapters of World War II.

Websites to Visit

1. http://www.academicinfo.net/usmodwar.html

    The website focuses on America in World War II.

2. http://www.historycentral.com/WW2/Index.html

    The comprehensive web page is about the battles and major events in World War II.

Poem to Read

"Textile Life" was discovered in 1938 when a Writers' Project field worker visited a North Carolina textile mill village. At the time, the village's textile workers were suffering greatly under the effects of the Depression, and they sent the field worker to Mary Branch, a longtime mill employee who had written a poem that "put down on paper what the rest of us feel."

Branch's poem is direct and very personal, and provides a vivid, authentic portrait of a community struggling to survive. As you read it, think about why the author might have written down and shared this poem with her neighbors.

Textile Life

The life of a textile worker
is trouble and worry and fears.
We can never get through what we are expected to do
If we work at it ninety-nine years.
There are lots and scores of people
Don't seem to understand
That when God made man, he made him out of sand
And he only gave him two hands.
With these two hands he said labor,
And that we are willing to do.
But he gave us six days to do our work,
And not try to do it all in two.
We have the stretch-out system
And it spreads throughout the mill
Two-thirds of the people it has sent to hospitals
And the other one-third it has killed.
We have what is called a production
And it hurts us in many ways,
If we can't reach that we must get our hat
And stay out a couple of days.
We get our pay envelope,
and oh how ugly it looks
It is mashed so flat until it looks Just like
it was stamped by an elephant's foot.
Our troubles and trials are many
Our dollars and cents are few
The Butcher, the Doctor, the Merchant we owe
And sometimes the undertaker too.
There is one little word called unearned
And that causes us evil to think
It appears on the face of our pay envelope
And its surely put there with red ink.
Sometimes the snow is fast falling
And we don't even have wood or coal
This is only part of a textile life
But the half can never be told.

Unit 13
Postwar American Society

> Being a Negro in America means trying to smile when you want to cry. It means trying to hold on to physical life amid psychological death. It means the pain of watching your children grow up with clouds of inferiority in their mental skies. It means having their legs off, and then being condemned for being a cripple.
> —Martin Luther King, Jr. 1967

Unit Goals

- To have a bird's-eye view of American society in the 1950s.
- To know the origins of the Civil Rights Movement.
- To learn the important words and expressions that describe America after World War II.
- To improve English language skills.
- To develop critical thinking and intercultural communication skills.

Before You Read

1. You must have heard of the singer Elvis Presley. He was somehow revolutionary. How did his song reflect the change of culture in those days?
2. What kind of civil rights do you enjoy?

   The Civil Rights Enjoyed {
   _____
   _____
   _____
   _____
   }

3. What do you know about the Civil Rights Movement in the history of the U.S.?

4. Form groups of three or four students. Try to find, on the Internet or in the library, more information about America in the post-war period which interests you most. Prepare a 5-minute classroom presentation.

Start to Read

Text A   American Society in the 1950s

1. During the 1950s, many cultural commentators argued that a sense of uniformity pervaded American society. Though men and women had been forced into new employment patterns during World War II, traditional roles were reaffirmed once the war was over. Men expected to be the breadwinners in each family; women, even when they worked, assumed their proper place was at home. In his influential book, *The Lonely Crowd*, sociologist David Riesman called this new society "other-directed," characterized by conformity, but also by stability. Television, still very limited in the choices it gave its viewers, contributed to the cultural trend by providing young and old with a shared experience reflecting accepted social patterns.

2. Yet beneath this seemingly peaceful surface, important segments of American society were filled with rebellion. A number of writers, collectively known as the "beat generation," went out of their way to challenge the patterns of respectability and shock the rest of the culture.

3. The literary work of the beats displayed their sense of alienation and quest for self-realization. Jack Kerouac typed his best selling novel *On the Road* on a 75-meter roll of paper. Lacking traditional punctuation and paragraph structure, the book glorified the possibilities of the free life. Poet Allen Ginsberg gained similar notoriety for his poem "Howl," a critique of modern, mechanized civilization. When police charged that it was obscene and seized the published version, Ginsberg successfully challenged the ruling in court.

4. Musicians and artists rebelled as well. Tennessee singer Elvis Presley was the most successful of several white performers who popularized a sensual style of African-American music, which began to be called "rock and roll." At first, he outraged middle-class Americans with his ducktail haircut and undulating hips. Similarly, it was in

the 1950s that painters like Jackson Pollock discarded easels and laid out gigantic canvases on the floor, then applied paint, sand, and other materials in wild splashes of color. All of these artists and authors, whatever the medium, provided models for the wider and more deeply felt social revolution of the 1960s.

The Civil Rights Movement

5. African Americans became increasingly restive in the postwar years. During the war, they had challenged discrimination in the military services and in the work force, and they had made limited gains. Millions of African Americans had left Southern farms for Northern cities, where they hoped to find better jobs. They found instead crowded conditions in urban slums. Now, African-American servicemen returned home, with many intent on rejecting second-class citizenship.

6. Jackie Robinson dramatized the racial question in 1947 when he broke baseball's color line and began playing in the major leagues. As a member of the Brooklyn Dodgers, he often faced trouble with opponents and teammates as well. But the outstanding first season led to his acceptance and eased the way for other African-American players, who now left the Negro leagues to which they had been confined.

7. Government officials, and many other Americans, discovered the connection between racial problems and Cold War politics. As the leader of the free world, the United States sought support in Africa and Asia. Discrimination at home impeded the effort to win friends in other parts of the world.

8. Harry Truman supported the early civil rights movement. He personally believed in political equality, though not in social equality, and recognized the growing importance of the African-American urban vote. When informed in 1946 of anti-black violence in the South, he appointed a committee on civil rights to investigate discrimination. Its report, *To Secure These Rights*, issued the next year, documented African Americans' second-class status in American life and recommended numerous federal measures to secure the rights guaranteed to all citizens.

9. A number of the angriest, led by Governor Strom Thurmond of South Carolina, opposed the president in 1948. Truman thereupon issued an executive order barring discrimination in federal employment, ordered equal treatment in the armed forces, and appointed a committee to work toward an end to military segregation, which was largely ended during the Korean War.

10. African Americans in the South in the 1950s still enjoyed few, if any, civil and political rights. In general, they could not vote. Those who tried to register faced the likelihood of beatings, loss of job, or loss of their land. Occasional lynchings still occurred. Jim Crow laws enforced segregation of the races in streetcars, trains, hotels, restaurants, hospitals, recreational facilities, and employment.

After You Read

Knowledge Focus

1. Pair Work: Discuss the following questions with your partner.
   (1) What were the traditional roles that men and women play in American families?
   (2) What do you know about the "beat generation"?
   (3) Can you name several literary works of the beats? What common features do they share?
   (4) How did the musicians and painters revolutionize their forms of arts?
   (5) How did African Americans change in the postwar years?
   (6) What was the situation before the Civil Rights Movement?
   (7) What do you know about Jackie Robinson?
   (8) What was the significance of the report *To Secure These Rights*?
   (9) What was the attitude of Harry Truman towards the early Civil Rights Movement?
   (10) What was the situation of African Americans in the South in the 1950s?

2. Solo Work: Tell whether the following are true or false according to the knowledge you have learned. Consider why.
   (1) After World War II, men and women shouldered equal responsibility on maintaining families. (　)
   (2) Beneath the seemingly peaceful surface, the American society in the 1950s was filled with rebellion. (　)
   (3) The representative literary work of the beats showed their sense of alienation and quest for self-realization. (　)
   (4) Elvis Presley popularized a sensual style of African-American music, which began to be called "rock and roll". (　)
   (5) Millions of African Americans had left Northern farms for Southern cities, where they hoped to find better jobs. (　)
   (6) The "beat generation" refers to those people born after World War Ⅱ. It witnessed a sudden increase in population (　)
   (7) Martin Luther King supported the early civil rights movement, and personally believed in political equality. (　)
   (8) After the 1950s, African Americans in the South enjoyed the same civil and

political rights as those whites. ( )
(9) The angriest, led by Governor Strom Thurmond of South Carolina, opposed the president in 1948. ( )
(10) President Truman issued an executive order in favor of discrimination in federal government. ( )

Language Focus
1. Fill in the blanks with the following words from the text.

| pervade | notoriety | quest | obscene | gigantic |
| intent | numerous | appoint | guarantee | glorify |

(1) Your descriptions have _____ an average house into a mansion.
(2) The president _____ her chief operating officer of the company.
(3) The law enacted last week helped to _____ freedom of speech.
(4) The recently-published novel dramatized the _____ for the Holy Grail.
(5) The young man, fresh out of graduate school, was _____ upon being recognized by the academic circle.
(6) His unexpected marriage added to his _____.
(7) Microsoft, the leading company in software industry, is a _____ corporation.
(8) As soon as the monitor cracked a joke, laughter _____ the whole meeting hall.
(9) "The way he writes about the disease that killed her is simply _____." (Michael Korda)
(10) Before the opening ceremony, _____ athletes assembled and headed for the stadium.

2. Fill in the blanks with the proper prepositions or adverbs that collocate with the neighboring words.
(1) They appointed a committee to work _____ an end to military segregation, which was largely ended during the Korean War.
(2) Men and women had been forced _____ new employment patterns during World War II.
(3) The Beat Generation went _____ of their way to challenge the patterns of respectability and shock the rest of the culture.
(4) The literary work of the beats displayed their sense of alienation and quest _____ self-realization.
(5) Jackson Pollock discarded easels, laid _____ gigantic canvases on the floor, and then applied paint, sand, and other materials in wild splashes of color.
(6) All of these artists and authors, whatever the medium, provided models _____ the wider and more deeply felt social revolution of the 1960s.
(7) Millions of African Americans went to Northern cities, where they hoped to find better jobs. They found _____ crowded conditions in urban slums.
(8) _____ a member of the Brooklyn Dodgers, he often faced trouble with

opponents and teammates as well.

(9) A number of the angriest, led _____ Governor of South Carolina, opposed the president in 1948.

(10) The new society is characterized _____ conformity.

3. **Fill in the blanks with the proper form of the words in the brackets.**

(1) During the 1950s, many cultural commentators argued that a sense of _____ (uniform) pervaded American society.

(2) In his _____ (influence) book, *The Lonely Crowd*, sociologist David Riesman called this new society "other-directed."

(3) Beneath this seemingly _____ (peace) surface, important segments of American society were filled with rebellion.

(4) Poet Allen Ginsberg gained similar _____ (notorious) for his poem "Howl," a critique of modern, mechanized civilization.

(5) Elvis Presley _____ (popular) a sensual style of African-American music, which began to be called "rock and roll."

(6) _____ (similar), it was in the 1950s that painters like Jackson Pollock discarded easels and laid out gigantic canvases on the floor.

(7) Jackie Robinson _____ (drama) the racial question in 1947 when he broke baseball's color line and began playing in the major leagues.

(8) The outstanding first season led to his _____ (accept) and eased the way for other African-American players.

(9) Harry Truman _____ (person) believed in political equality, though not in social equality, and recognized the growing importance of the African-American urban vote.

(10) Government officials and many other Americans discovered the _____ (connect) between racial problems and Cold War politics.

Comprehensive Work
Group Work
Directions: In 1983, the Congress of the United States set aside the third Monday in January as a federal holiday to honor the life of Martin Luther King, Jr. This date falls near his birthday, January 15. It is a day for remembering and rededication to the principles for which he stood—freedom, justice, and equal rights for all, achieved through peaceful means. Form a group of five to six students and do a research on Martin Luther King, Jr. and then finish the following tasks with your team members.

1. Please define prejudice and explain what it means. Talk about the reasons why people might be prejudiced (fear, ignorance, echoing parents' sentiments, etc.). Discuss how people can overcome their prejudices—learning about others, discussing fears, cooperating with others, etc.

2. Discuss Dr. King's speech—"I Have a Dream." If time permits, read the speech to your class or listen to the recording. Discuss how to keep Dr. King's dreams alive.

Essay Writing

Consider the following questions. Write an essay of about 300 words to illustrate your points.

(1) When, if ever, is it best to remain colorblind to race and ethnicity? When, if ever, is it best to celebrate multicultural differences? Do the goals of colorblindness and multiculturalism conflict with each other?

(2) What do you think the most difficult aspect is of being a racial, ethnic, or religious minority member? What is the most difficult aspect of being a majority group member?

Read More

Text B The Postwar Economy: 1945—1960

In a decade and a half after World War II, the United States experienced phenomenal economic growth and secured its position as the world's richest country. Gross national product (GNP), a measure of all goods and services produced in the United States, jumped from about $200,000 million in 1940 to $300,000 million in 1950 to more than $500,000 million in 1960. More and more Americans now considered themselves part of the middle class.

The growth had different sources. The economic stimulus provided by large-scale public spending for World War II helped get it started. Two basic middle-class needs did much to keep it going. The number of automobiles produced annually quadrupled between 1946 and 1955. A housing boom, stimulated in part by easily affordable mortgages for returning servicemen, fueled the expansion. The rise in defense spending as the Cold War escalated also played a part.

After 1945, the major corporations in America grew even larger. There had been earlier waves of mergers in the 1890s and in the 1920s; in the 1950s another wave occurred. Franchise operations like McDonald's fast-food restaurants allowed small entrepreneurs to make themselves part of large, efficient enterprises. Big American corporations also developed holdings overseas, where labor costs were often lower.

Workers found their own lives changing as industrial America changed. Fewer workers produced goods; more provided services. As early as 1956, a majority of employees held white-collar jobs, working as managers, teachers, salespersons, and office operatives. Some firms granted a guaranteed annual wage, long-term employment contracts, and other benefits. With such changes, labor militancy was undermined and some class distinctions began to fade.

Farmers—at least those with small operations—faced tough times. Gains in productivity led to agricultural consolidation, and farming became a big business. More and more family farmers left the land.

Other Americans moved too. The West and the Southwest grew with increasing rapidity, a trend that would continue through the end of the century. Sun Belt cities like Houston, Texas; Miami, Florida; Albuquerque, New Mexico; and Phoenix, Arizona, expanded rapidly. Los Angeles, California, moved ahead of Philadelphia, Pennsylvania, as the third largest U.S. city and then surpassed Chicago, metropolis of the Midwest. The 1970 census showed that California had displaced New York as the nation's largest state. By 2000, Texas had moved ahead of New York into second place.

An even more important form of movement led Americans out of inner cities into new suburbs, where they hoped to find affordable housing for the larger families spawned by the postwar baby boom. Developers like William J. Levitt built new communities—with homes that all looked alike—using the techniques of mass production. Levitt's houses were prefabricated—partly assembled in a factory rather than on the final location—and modest, but Levitt's methods cut costs and allowed new owners to possess a part of the American dream.

As suburbs grew, businesses moved into the new areas. Large shopping centers containing a great variety of stores changed consumer patterns. The number of these centers rose from eight at the end of World War II to 3,840 in 1960. With easy parking and convenient evening hours, customers could avoid city shopping entirely. An unfortunate by-product was the "hollowing-out" of formerly busy urban cores.

New highways created better access to the suburbs and its shops. *The Highway Act* of 1956 provided $26,000-million, the largest public works expenditure in U.S. history, to build more than 64,000 kilometers of limited access interstate highways to link the country together.

Television, too, had a powerful impact on social and economic patterns. Developed in the 1930s, it was not widely marketed until after the war. In 1946, the country had fewer than 17,000 television sets. Three years later consumers were buying 250,000 sets a month, and by 1960 three-quarters of all families owned at least one set. In the middle of the decade, the average family watched television four to five hours a day. Popular shows for children included *Howdy Doody Time* and *The Mickey Mouse Club*; older viewers preferred situation comedies like *I Love Lucy* and *Father Knows Best*. Americans of all ages became exposed to increasingly sophisticated advertisements for products said to be necessary for the good life.

1. Questions for Discussion or Reflection
   (1) What was the general tendency of economic development in the U.S. after World War II?
   (2) How did the lives of workers and farmers change after World War II?
   (3) What was the transformation of cities and suburbs like at that time with the economic boom?
   (4) What changes did American enterprises undergo? Give one example in detail.
   (5) What changes did American workers experience after 1945? What kind of jobs did they do most?

2. **True or False**
   (1) After World War II, the economic growth in the U.S. secured its position as the world's richest country. (　)
   (2) Major corporations in America grew even larger, and franchise operations began to take shape. (　)
   (3) After 1945, big American corporations established their subsidiary companies overseas. (　)
   (4) The West and the Southwest grew with increasing rapidity. (　)
   (5) The postwar baby boom led Americans out of suburbs into inner cities. (　)

Text C　　Desegregation

The National Association for the Advancement of Colored People (NAACP) took the lead in efforts to overturn the judicial doctrine, established in the Supreme Court case Plessy v. Ferguson in 1896, that segregation of African-American and white students was constitutional if facilities were "separate but equal". That decree had been used for decades to sanction rigid segregation in all aspects of Southern life, where facilities were seldom, if ever, equal.

African Americans achieved their goal of overturning Plessy in 1954 when the Supreme Court—presided over by an Eisenhower appointee, Chief Justice Earl Warren—handed down its Brown v. Board of Education ruling. The Court declared unanimously that "separate facilities are inherently unequal," and decreed that the "separate but equal" doctrine could no longer be used in public schools. A year later, the Supreme Court demanded that local school boards move "with all deliberate speed" to implement the decision.

Eisenhower, although sympathetic to the needs of the South as it faced a major transition, nonetheless acted to see that the law was upheld in the face of massive resistance from much of the South. He faced a major crisis in Little Rock, Arkansas, in 1957, when Governor Orval Faubus attempted to block a desegregation plan calling for the admission of nine black students to the city's previously all-white Central High School. After futile efforts at negotiation, the president sent federal troops to Little Rock to enforce the plan.

Governor Faubus responded by ordering the Little Rock high schools closed down for the 1958—1959 school year. However, a federal court ordered them reopened the following year. They did so in a tense atmosphere with a tiny number of African-American students. Thus, school desegregation proceeded at a slow and uncertain pace throughout much of the South.

Another milestone in the Civil Rights movement occurred in 1955 in Montgomery, Alabama. Rosa Parks, a 42-year-old African-American seamstress who was also secretary of the state chapter of the NAACP, sat down in the front of a bus in a section reserved by law and custom for whites. Ordered to move to the back, she refused. Police came and arrested her for violating the segregation statutes. African-American leaders, who had been waiting for just such a case, organized a boycott of the bus system.

Martin Luther King Jr., a young minister of the Baptist church where the African Americans met, became a spokesman for the protest. "There comes a time," he said, "when people get tired...of being kicked about by the brutal feet of oppression." King was arrested, as he would be again and again; a bomb damaged the front of his house. But African Americans in Montgomery sustained the boycott. About a year later, the Supreme Court affirmed that bus segregation, like school segregation, was unconstitutional. The boycott ended. The Civil Rights Movement had won an important victory—and discovered its most powerful, thoughtful, and eloquent leader in Martin Luther King Jr.

African Americans also sought to secure their voting rights. Although the 15th Amendment to the U.S. Constitution guaranteed the right to vote, many states had found ways to circumvent the law. The states would impose a poll ("head") tax or a literacy test—typically much more stringently interpreted for African Americans—to prevent poor African Americans with little education from voting.

Eisenhower, working with Senate majority leader Lyndon B. Johnson, lent his support to a congressional effort to guarantee the vote. *The Civil Rights Act* of 1957, the first such measure in 82 years, marked a step forward, as it authorized federal intervention in cases where African Americans were denied the chance to vote. Yet loopholes remained, and so activists pushed successfully for the Civil Rights Act of 1960, which provided stiffer penalties for interfering with voting, but still stopped short of authorizing federal officials to register African Americans.

Relying on the efforts of African Americans themselves, the civil rights movement gained momentum in the postwar years. Working through the Supreme Court and through Congress, civil rights supporters had created the groundwork for a dramatic yet peaceful "revolution" in American race relations in the 1960s.

The picture on the right shows that Rosa Parks sits in one of the front seats of a city bus following the successful boycott of the bus system in 1955—1956 by African-American citizens of Montgomery, Alabama. The boycott was organized to protest the practice of segregation in which African Americans were forced to sit in the back of the bus. The Supreme Court agreed that this practice was a constitutional violation a year after the boycott began. The great leader of the Civil Rights Movement in America, Martin Luther King Jr., gained national prominence through the Montgomery bus boycott.

Questions for Discussion or Reflection

1. What was the situation of African Americans like after the Second World War? How did their living conditions and political rights change with the advancement of the Civil Rights Movement?
2. What were the milestones of the Civil Rights Movement that occurred in 1955? Discuss with your partners and present your views.

Proper Names

Allen Ginsberg 艾伦·金斯堡
David Riesman 大卫·雷斯曼
Elvis Presley 埃尔维斯·普雷斯利
gross national product (GNP) 国民生产总值
Harry Truman 哈里·杜鲁门
Jack Kerouac 杰克·凯鲁亚克

Jackie Robinson 杰基·罗宾森
Jackson Pollock 杰克森·波洛克
Martin Luther King, Jr. 马丁·路德·金(小)
The Beat Generation 垮掉的一代
the Brooklyn Dodgers 布鲁克林道奇棒球队

Notes

1. **Allen Ginsberg**: He is an American poet. Ginsberg is best known for the poem "Howl" (1956), celebrating his friends of the Beat Generation and attacking what he saw as the destructive forces of materialism and conformity in the United States at the time.

2. **The Beat Generation**: It is a term used to describe both a group of American writers who came to prominence in the late 1950s and the early 1960s and the cultural phenomena that they wrote about and inspired. "Beat" writers like Allen Ginsberg, Gregory Corso, Peter Orlovsky, Jack Kerouac, and William S. Burroughs wrote poetry and novels that were marked by spontaneity, open emotion. They described gritty worldly experiences, including frank depictions of sexuality and drug use. The language and topics (drug use, sexuality and aberrant behavior) pushed the boundaries of acceptability in the conformist 1950s.

3. **David Riesman**: He was an American sociologist, best known for his influential study of post-World War II American society, *The Lonely Crowd*. He died on May 10 in Binghamton, NY. For almost 20 years, he taught a popular undergraduate course, "American Character and Social Structure," and, through his voluminous correspondence, continued to exert an influence on many of his students long after they had left Harvard.

4. **Elvis Presley**: He was an American singer, musician and actor. A cultural icon, he is commonly referred to by his first name, and as the "The King of Rock'n' Roll" or "The King."

5. **Jack Kerouac**: He was an American novelist and poet, leading figure and spokesman of the Beat Generation. Kerouac's search for spiritual liberation produced his best known work, the autobiographical novel *On the Road* (1957). The first beat novel was based on Kerouac's travels across America with his friend Neal Cassidy. Its importance was compared to Hemingway's novel *The Sun Also Rises*, generally seen as the testament of the "Lost Generation" of the 1920s.

6. **Jackson Pollock**: He was an influential American painter and a major force in the abstract expressionist movement. He was married to noted abstract painter Lee

Krasner.

7. **Martin Luther King, Jr.**: He was an American clergyman, activist and prominent leader in the African-American civil rights movement. His main legacy was to secure progress on civil rights in the United States and he is frequently referenced as a human rights icon today.

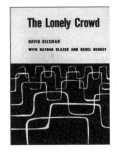

Books to Read

1. David Riesman, *The Lonely Crowd*

   This book was a 1950 sociological analysis by David Riesman, Nathan Glazer, and Reuel Denney. It is considered—along with *White Collar: The American Middle Classes* written by Riesman's friend and colleague C. Wright Mills—to be a landmark study of American character.

2. Jack Kerouac, *On the Road*

   It is largely an autobiographical work based on the spontaneous road trips of Kerouac and his friends across mid-century America. It is often considered a defining work of the postwar Beat Generation that was inspired by jazz, poetry, and drug experiences. While many of the names and details of Kerouac's experiences are changed for the novel, hundreds of references in *On the Road* have real-world counterparts.

Movie to See

The Beat Generation: An American Dream (1987)

Steve Allen narrates this documentary by Janet Forman concerning the influential writers of the beat generation. Film archives are used to familiarize the viewers with the late Jack Kerouac, Neal Cassidy, and jazz great Thelonius Monk. Allen recalls providing piano accompaniment to Kerouac as he reads from his own writing in a recording session. Interviews with surviving members of the movement such as William Burroughs, Gregory Corso, Lawrence Ferlinghetti, along with 1960s political activist Abbie Hoffman and acid guru Timothy Leary underscore the influence the beat generation has affected the future generations beyond the 1950s.

Song to Enjoy

"We Shall Overcome"

   "We Shall Overcome" has it roots in African American hymns from the early 20th century, and was first used as a protest song in 1945, when striking tobacco workers in Charleston, S. C., sang it on their picket line. By the 1950s, the song had been discovered by the young activists of the African American civil rights movement, and it quickly became the movement's unofficial anthem. Its verses were sung on protest marches and in sit-ins, through clouds of tear gas and under rows of police batons, and it brought courage and comfort to bruised, frightened activists as they waited in jail cells, wondering if they would survive the night. When the long years of struggle ended and President Lyndon Johnson vowed to fight for voting rights for all Americans, he included a final promise: "We shall overcome."

In the decades since, the song has circled the globe and has been embraced by civil rights and pro-democracy movements in dozens of nations worldwide. From Northern Ireland to Eastern Europe, and from South Africa to South America, its message of solidarity and hope has been sung in dozens of languages, in presidential palaces and in dark prisons, and it continues to lend its strength to all people struggling to be free.

As you listen to "We Shall Overcome," think about the reasons it has brought strength and support to so many people for so many years. And remember that someone, somewhere, is singing it right now.

We Shall Overcome

By Mahalia Jackson

We shall overcome, we shall overcome,
We shall overcome someday;
Oh, deep in my heart, I do believe,
We shall overcome someday.

The Lord will see us through, The Lord will see us through,
The Lord will see us through someday;
Oh, deep in my heart, I do believe,
We shall overcome someday.

We're on to victory, We're on to victory,
We're on to victory someday;
Oh, deep in my heart, I do believe,
We're on to victory someday.

We'll walk hand in hand, we'll walk hand in hand,
We'll walk hand in hand someday;
Oh, deep in my heart, I do believe,
We'll walk hand in hand someday.

We are not afraid, we are not afraid,
We are not afraid today;
Oh, deep in my heart, I do believe,
We are not afraid today.

The truth shall set us free, the truth shall set us free,
The truth shall set us free someday;
Oh, deep in my heart, I do believe,
The truth shall set us free someday.

We shall live in peace, we shall live in peace,
We shall live in peace someday;
Oh, deep in my heart, I do believe,
We shall live in peace someday.

Unit 14
America in Transition

> I have always believed that there was some divine plan that placed this great continent between two oceans to be sought out by those who were possessed of an abiding love of freedom and a special kind of courage.
>
> —California Governor Ronald Reagan, 1974

Unit Goals

- To be familiar with the major changes of America in the 1960s.
- To know the significant events and people in the 1970s.
- To learn the historical terms that describe the Women's Liberation Movement, Cuba Missile Crisis and the Space Race.
- To learn the important words and expressions that describe America in the 1960s and the 1970s.
- To improve English language skills.
- To develop critical thinking and intercultural communication skills.

Before You Read

1. Examine each of the following items and decide whether it can be associated with America in the 1960s. If yes, put a tick "√" right to the item. Discuss and define these items with your partner.

Items	YES/ NO	Your Definition
Sit-ins		
Baby Boom		
Martin Luther King		
John F. Kennedy		
The Cuban Missile Crisis		
Hippies		
The Beatles		

2. The 1964 *Civil Rights Act* outlawed gender discrimination. At the time, few Americans understood the significance of that small provision of the landmark law or foresaw the ways in which a massive, grassroots women's movement would transform women's roles and rights in the last few years of the twentieth century. Discuss the following questions with your partner and summarize your points in phrases.

   (1) If women's choices have expanded, have the pressures on women also grown greater?

   _____

   _____

   (2) What inequalities between women and men remain?

   _____

   _____

   (3) How does race affect women's lives?

   _____

   _____

   (4) How has the women's movement changed men's lives?

   _____

   _____

3. Form groups of three or four students. Try to find, on the Internet or in the library, more information about America from the 1960s to the 1970s which interests you most. Prepare a 5-minute classroom presentation.

Start to Read

Text A　　America in the 1960s

1. The sixties were the age of youth, as 70 million children from the post-war baby boom became teenagers and young adults. The movement away from the conservative fifties continued and eventually resulted in revolutionary ways of thinking and real change in the cultural fabric of American life. No longer content to be images of the generation ahead of them, young people wanted change. The changes affected education, values, lifestyles, laws, and entertainment. Many of the revolutionary ideas which began in the sixties are continuing to evolve today.

2. The Civil Rights movement made great changes in society in the 1960s. The movement began peacefully, with Martin Luther King and Stokely Carmichael leading sit-ins and peaceful protests, joined by whites, particularly Jews. In 1965, the Watts riots broke out in Los Angeles. This large-scale race riot lasted 6 days in the Watts neighborhood of Los Angeles, California, in August 1965. By the time the riot subsided, 34 people had been killed, 1,032 injured, and 3,952 arrested.

3. The term "blacks" became socially acceptable, replacing "Negroes." The number of Hispanic Americans tripled during the decade and became recognized as an oppressed minority. American Indians, facing unemployment rates of 50% and a life expectancy only two-thirds that of whites, began to assert themselves in the courts and in violent protests.

4. *The Civil Rights Act* of 1964 was amended to include gender. The birth control pill became widely available and abortion for cause was legalized in Colorado in 1967. In 1967, both abortion and artificial insemination became legal in some states.

5. As the 1960s progressed, respect for authority declined among the youth, and crime rates soared to nine times the rate of the 1950s. Marijuana use soared. The hippie movement endorsed drugs, rock music, mystic religions and sexual freedom. They opposed violence. The Woodstock Festival at which 400,000 young people gathered in a spirit of love and

sharing, represents the pinnacle of the hippie movement.

6. When Fidel Castro, soon after overtaking Cuba, declared that he was a communist, the United States broke off diplomatic relations with Cuba. Castro seized American property. The CIA attacked Cuba in an ill-fated mission at the Bay of Pigs. In 1962, a spy plane identified long range missiles in Cuba. President John F. Kennedy readied troops to invade Cuba, and the Soviet Union prepared to fire at U.S. cities if Americans made a move.

7. John F. Kennedy was young and charismatic, and his brief reign as president was often called "Camelot." He was assassinated in 1963. His Vice President, Lyndon B. Johnson became president, and was reelected the following year. To prevent communist North Vietnam from overtaking South Vietnam, the United States sent military advisors and then soldiers. It was largely a secret war until 1965, when massive troop buildups were ordered to put an end to the conflict. The draft was accelerated and anti-war sentiment grew in the U.S. College. Students organized anti-war protests, draft dodgers fled to Canada, and there were reports of soldiers that reflected the growing disrespect for authority, shooting their officers rather than follow orders. Johnson, blamed by many for the war and the racial unrest in the country, did not run for reelection in 1968. John Kennedy's brother, Robert campaigned for the nomination for President and he, too was killed.

8. The Space Race, begun by the Soviets in 1957, was highlighted by Alan Shepard, the first American in space in 1961. Neil Armstrong and Buzz Aldrin, in Apollo XI, were the first men to walk on the moon in 1969. The surgeon general determined that smoking was a health hazard, and in 1965 required cigarette manufacturers to place warnings on all packages and in all advertisements. Dr. Denton Cooley implanted the first artificial heart in a human, and it kept the patient alive for three days until a human heart could be transplanted.

Text B America in the 1970s

The chaotic events of the 1960s, including war and social change, seemed destined to continue in the 1970s. Major trends included a growing disillusionment of government, advances in civil rights, increased influence of the women's movement, a heightened concern for the environment, and increased space exploration. Many of the "radical" ideas of the 1960s gained wider acceptance in the new decade, and were mainstreamed into American life and culture.

During the 1970s the United States underwent some profound changes. The Vietnam War continued to divide the country even after the *Paris Peace Accords* in January 1973 put an end to U.S. military participation in the war. Crime increased despite Nixon's pledge to make law and order a top priority of his presidency. People from Third World countries came to this country in search of economic improvement or to escape political repression.

Women and minorities increasingly demanded full legal equality and privileges in society. Women expanded their involvement in politics. The proportion of women in state legislatures tripled. Women surpassed men in college enrollment in 1979. However, the rising divorce rate left an increasing number of women as sole breadwinners and forced more and more of them into poverty. African-Americans also made their presence felt as the number of black members in Congress increased, and cities such as Los Angeles, Detroit, and Atlanta elected their first African-American mayors.

Technology advanced at amazing speed in the 1970s. The floppy disc appeared in the 1970s, and the next year Intel introduced the microprocessor, the "computer on a chip."

Apollo 17, the last manned craft to the moon, brought back 250 samples of rock and soil. The videocassette recorder (VCR) changed home entertainment forever. Jumbo jets revolutionized commercial flight, doubling passenger capacity and increasing flight range to 6,000 miles. The neutron bomb, which destroys living beings but leaves buildings intact, was developed. In medicine, ultrasound diagnostic techniques were developed. The first test tube baby, Louise Brown, was born, developed from an artificially inseminated egg implanted in the mother's womb. Other noteworthy developments of the 1970s included these inventions or innovations: email (1971), first retail barcode scanned (1974), the laser printer (1975), MRI scanner (1977), and the first space lab (USA Skylab, 1973).

After You Read

Knowledge Focus

1. **Pair Work: Discuss the following questions with your partner.**
   (1) Why was the 1960s called "the age of youth"?
   (2) What do you know with regard to the Civil Rights Movement?
   (3) What was Martin Luther King famous for?
   (4) What do you know about Hispanic Americans? What was the situation of Hispanic Americans in the 1960s?
   (5) Can you list a few key figures in Women's Liberation? What do you know about the Women's Lib?
   (6) Why did the United States wage the Vietnam War?

(7) What was the public response to the Vietnam War?
(8) Who were the first men to walk on the moon in 1969?
(9) Can you name the major trends of America in the 1970s?
(10) What were the technological advances in the 1970s' America?

2. Solo Work: Tell whether the following are true or false according to the knowledge you have learned. Consider why.
   (1) Comparatively speaking, the 1950s was revolutionary, whereas the 1960s was conservative. ( )
   (2) American young people in the 1960s were ready to embrace revolutionary changes in education, values, lifestyles, laws, and entertainment. ( )
   (3) In the 1960s, the term "blacks" became socially acceptable and was replaced by "Negroes." ( )
   (4) American Indians faced unemployment rates of 50% and a life expectancy only two-thirds that of the whites, and they resigned themselves to life. ( )
   (5) The artificial insemination and abortion was never legalized in America. ( )
   (6) Compared with the situation in the 1950s, the crime rate of America in the 1960s decreased dramatically. ( )
   (7) The hippies were opponents of drugs, rock music, mystic religions and sexual freedom. ( )
   (8) Both the Soviet Union and the United States were involved in Cuba Missile Crisis. ( )
   (9) In 1979, women and men had equal enrollment in college for the first time. ( )
   (10) The floppy disc, VCR, neutron bomb and the first test tube baby all appeared in the 1970s. ( )

Language Focus

1. Solo Work: Fill in the blanks with the following words from the texts.

   | fabric | evolve | subside | assert | legalize |
   | artificial | pinnacle | overtake | hazard | surpass |

   (1) On the table was a vase filled with _____ flowers.
   (2) Brook's original idea has _____ into an official NASA program.
   (3) Television soon _____ the cinema as the most popular form of entertainment.
   (4) He _____ that nuclear power was a safe and non-polluting energy source.
   (5) In several years, this nation is likely to _____ the U.S. as the world's largest export market.
   (6) Gambling has recently been _____ in three towns in Colorado.
   (7) For international traders, changes in the exchange rate are an unavoidable _____.
   (8) The pains in his head had _____, but he still felt dizzy and sick.
   (9) The bank was at the _____ of England's financial system then.

(10) Man-made _____ such as polyester are easy to wash and iron.

2. Pair Work: Choose the appropriate word to complete each of the following sentences. Check your answers with your partner.
   (1) The restaurant slowly _____ (evolves/revolves), giving excellent views of the city.
   (2) They built and financed a whole new suburb, and they did it without a public _____ (subside/subsidy).
   (3) He had long ago _____ (repressed/oppressed) the painful memories of his childhood.
   (4) _____ (Insert/Assert) the correct coins, select the drink you want and then press the button.
   (5) Tony was always in trouble with the police when he was young, but now he is a _____ (respectful/respectable) married man.
   (6) Carla seems pretty much content _____ (in/with) her life.
   (7) An exact _____ (diagnose/diagnosis) can only be made by obtaining a blood sample.
   (8) Many rock stars have pledged _____ (to support/supporting) the campaign to save the rainforests.

Comprehensive Work

Solo Work: Ready, Set—The Space Race Begins

Directions: Some words are missing in the following passage about the Space Race. Fill in the blanks with the words that best complete the passage.

pounds	satellites	force	battle	scientists
Wernher	scientist	country	determined	satellite
possible	half	shocked	contenders	radiation
powerful	rock			

For thousands of years, man has looked out into the sky in wonder. What was out there beyond their home? Were there warriors out there who had died bravely in (1) _____? Were there dragons and monsters? What were the stars made of? How hot is the sun? Is there life on other planets? Who is the man in the moon? It was not until the mid 1950s that scientists developed the technology needed to explore the mysteries of space.

Scientists can be very competitive, just like athletes. It was understood in the scientific world that the first country to conquer space would become the most (2) _____ (3) _____ on earth. The Soviet Union and the United States became the top (4) _____ in this space race. Think of some of the problems connected to exploring space. The next time you are in an open field, pick up a rock and throw it as high and as hard as you can. What happens to the (5) _____? It will go a short distance and then fall back to earth. How then, can (6) _____ propel a heavy object into the sky and have it stay there for long periods of time? Years of research and study had to go into this problem. Scientists knew that (7) _____ were (8) _____. The moon is a (9) _____. It travels around the earth at all times. Earth's gravity keeps it from floating out into deep space. Centrifugal (10) _____ keeps it from crashing into the earth.

Scientists wanted to develop an artificial satellite that would have the same characteristics. In October 1957, the Soviet Union (11) _____ the entire world. They launched a satellite they had named Sputnik. It was about the size of a basketball. It weighed about 183 (12) _____. It took about 98 minutes to make one trip, orbit, around the earth. The race was now officially on. The winner would be determined by who could put a human being on the moon first. About three and a (13) _____ months later, in January of 1958, the United States successfully launched their first satellite. (14) _____ von Braun, a famous German (15) _____ who had moved to the United States, and his team of scientists launched Explorer I. This satellite was built for research. Equipment on Explorer I discovered that there is a magnetic (16) _____ belt around Earth. Scientists named this discovery the Van Allen Belt after the man who led the research. In July of 1958, the United States Congress passed a bill which created the National Aeronautics and Space Administration which you probably know as NASA. The United States was bound and (17) _____ that they would not lose the Space Race. They may have gotten behind when Sputnik headed into space, but the scientists were going to do their best to win the long race.

Essay Writing

Among the many important dates in American history is May 25, 1961, where President John F. Kennedy announced to America that we would put a man on the moon by the end of the decade. The 1960s was an age of space race. The Space Race has affected our everyday lives. In a mere forty years, we have had more technological advances than the Industrial Revolution. With the technology gained from the Space Race, we can perform medical tasks that only existed in the dreams of surgeons; we can communicate with another person on the other side of the world in seconds, not days or months. Without the Space Race, we would not have the technological advances that exist today.

What's your view on space race? Write an essay of about 300 words to illustrate your point.

Read More

Text C   The Cuban Missile Crisis

The Cuban Missile Crisis was the closest the world ever came to nuclear war. The United States armed forces were at their highest state of readiness ever and Soviet field commanders in Cuba were prepared to use battlefield nuclear weapons to defend the island if it was invaded. Luckily, thanks to the bravery of two men, President John F. Kennedy and Premier Nikita Khrushchev, war was averted.

In 1962, the Soviet Union was desperately behind the United States in the arms race. Soviet missiles were only powerful enough to be launched against Europe but U.S. missiles were capable of striking the entire Soviet Union. In late April 1962, Soviet Premier Nikita Khrushchev conceived the idea of placing intermediate-range missiles in  Cuba. A deployment in Cuba would double the Soviet strategic arsenal and provide a real deterrent to a potential U.S. attack against the Soviet Union.

Meanwhile, Fidel Castro was looking for a way to defend his island nation from an attack by the U.S. Ever since the failed Bay of Pigs invasion in 1961, Castro felt a second attack was inevitable. Consequently, he approved of Khrushchev's plan to place missiles on the island. In the summer of 1962, the Soviet Union worked quickly and secretly to build its missile installations in Cuba.

For the United States, the crisis began on October 15, 1962 when photographs revealed Soviet missiles under construction in Cuba. Early the next day, President John Kennedy was informed of the missile installations. Kennedy immediately organized the EX-COMM, a group of his twelve most important advisors to handle the crisis. After seven days of guarded and intense debate, Kennedy concluded to impose a naval quarantine around Cuba. He wished to prevent the arrival of more Soviet offensive weapons on the island. On October 22, Kennedy announced the discovery of the missile installations to the public and his decision to quarantine the island. He also proclaimed that any nuclear missile launched from Cuba would be regarded as an attack on the United States by the Soviet Union and demanded that the Soviets remove all of their offensive weapons from Cuba.

During the public phase of the Crisis, tensions began to build on both sides. Kennedy eventually ordered low-level reconnaissance missions once every two hours. On the 25th, Kennedy pulled the quarantine line back and raised military readiness to DEFCON 2. (DEFCON—The Defense readiness Condition is a measure of the activation and readiness level of the United States Armed Forces.) Then on the 26th, EX-COMM heard from Khrushchev in an impassioned letter. He proposed removing Soviet missiles and personnel if the U.S. would guarantee not to invade Cuba. October 27 was the worst day of the crisis. A U-2 was shot down over Cuba and EX-COMM received a second letter from Khrushchev demanding the removal of U.S. missiles in Turkey in exchange for Soviet missiles in Cuba. Attorney General Robert Kennedy suggested ignoring the second letter and contacted Soviet Ambassador Anatoly Dobrynin to tell him of the U.S. agreement with the first.

Tensions finally began to ease on October 28 when Khrushchev announced that he would dismantle the installations and return the missiles to the Soviet Union, expressing his trust that the United States would not invade Cuba. Further negotiations were held to implement the October 28 agreement, including a United States demand that Soviet light bombers be removed from Cuba, and specifying the exact form and conditions of United States assurances not to invade Cuba.

Unit 14　America in Transition

1. **Reading Comprehension**

   Scan the passage and figure out the answers to the following questions.

   (1) When did the Cuban Missile Crisis occur?
   　　A. November 1963.　　　　　　B. April 1961.
   　　C. October 1962.　　　　　　　D. September 1959.

   (2) Who was the Soviet Premier at the time of the crisis?
   　　A. Stalin.　　　　　　　　　　B. Khrushchev.
   　　C. Lenin.　　　　　　　　　　 D. Brezhnev.

   (3) Who was the American President during the crisis?
   　　A. Carter.　　　　　　　　　　B. Nixon.
   　　C. Johnson.　　　　　　　　　 D. Kennedy.

   (4) Who was the leader in power in Cuba at the time of the crisis?
   　　A. Batista.　　　　　　　　　 B. Castro.
   　　C. Peron.　　　　　　　　　　 D. Noriega.

2. **Questions for Discussion or Reflection**

   (1) How was the Soviet Union involved in the Cuban Missile Crisis?

   (2) What countries and political leaders were involved during the Cuban Missile Crisis?

   (3) Why was the Cuban Missile Crisis a major turning point in the Cold War?

Proper Names

Alan Shepard 艾伦·谢泼德(美国第一位进入太空的宇航员)
Buzz Aldrin 巴兹·奥尔德林(第二位登上月球的宇航员)
Fidel Castro 菲德尔·卡斯特罗
Martin Luther King 马丁·路德·金
Neil Armstrong 尼尔·阿姆斯特朗(第一位登上月球的宇航员)
Stokely Carmichael 斯托克利·卡迈克尔(黑人民权领袖)
the Bay of Pigs invasion 猪湾事件
The Civil Rights Act 《美国民权法案》
the Paris Peace Accords 《巴黎和平协议》
the Space Race 太空竞赛
the Vietnam War 越南战争
the Woodstock Festival 伍德斯托克音乐节

Notes

1. **The Bay of Pigs Invasion**: It is an unsuccessful attempt by United States-backed Cuban exiles to overthrow the government of Fidel Castro. Increasing friction between the U.S. government and Castro's administration led President Dwight D. Eisenhower to break off diplomatic relations with Cuba in January 1961. Even before that, however, the Central Intelligence Agency had been training anti-revolutionary Cuban exiles for a possible invasion of the island. The invasion plan was approved by Eisenhower's

successor, John F. Kennedy.

2. **The Civil Rights Act (1964)**: This act, signed into law by President Lyndon Johnson on July 2, 1964, prohibited discrimination in public places, provided for the integration of schools and other public facilities, and made employment discrimination illegal. This document was the most sweeping civil rights legislation since Reconstruction.

3. **Hippies**: The hippie subculture was originally a youth movement that began in the United States during the early 1960s and spread around the world. These people inherited the countercultural values of the Beat Generation, created their own communities, listened to psychedelic rock, embraced the sexual revolution, and used drugs to explore alternative states of consciousness.

4. **Hispanic Americans**: Hispanic and Latino Americans are Americans of origins in Hispanic countries of Latin America or in Spain. The group encompasses distinct subgroups by national origin and race, and there is much diversity of race and ancestry within national origin groups as well. Hispanic and Latino Americans are the largest ethnic minority in the United States; African Americans, in turn, are the largest racial minority after white Americans in general.

5. **The Woodstock Festival**: Woodstock is a music festival. The festival exemplified the counterculture of the late 1960s to early 1970s and the "hippie era." Thirty-two of the best-known musicians of the day appeared during the sometimes rainy weekend in front of nearly half a million concertgoers. Although attempts have been made over the years to emulate the festival, the original event has proven to be unique and legendary. It is widely regarded as one of the greatest moments in popular music history and was listed on "Rolling Stone's 50 Moments That Changed the History of Rock and Roll."

6. **Stokely Carmichael**: He is an American black activist active in the 1960s American Civil Rights Movement. He rose to prominence first as a leader of the Student Nonviolent Coordinating Committee (SNCC).

Books to Read

1. Sharon Monteith, *American Culture in the 1960s*

   This book charts the changing complexion of American culture in one of the most culturally vibrant of twentieth-century decades. It provides a vivid account of the major cultural forms of the 1960s America as well as influential texts, trends and figures of the decade.

2. Thomas Parker, *Day by Day: The Sixties*

It introduces what happened in politics, science and culture each day for the entire decade. It gives a closer look at current events during this turbulent decade.

Movies to See

1. *Dazed and Confused* (1993)

Dazed and Confused is a 1993 coming-of-age comedy film. The plot follows various groups of Texas teenagers during the last day of school in 1976. Featuring an excellent ensemble cast, a precise feel for the 1970s, and a killer soundtrack, *Dazed and Confused* is a funny, affectionate, and clear-eyed look at high school life. From the music to the clothes and the hairstyles, this movie captured what the 1970s were all about.

2. *Forrest Gump* (1994)

Forrest Gump is a 1994 American epic romantic-comedy-drama film based on the 1986 novel of the same name by Winston Groom. The story depicts several decades in the life of Forrest Gump, a slow-witted and naïve, but good-hearted and athletically prodigious man from Alabama who witnesses, and in some cases influences, some of the defining events of the latter half of the 20th century in the United States; more specifically, the period between Forrest's birth in 1944 and 1982. The film differs substantially from Winston Groom's novel, including Gump's personality and several events that were depicted.

Websites to Visit

1. http://www.bbhq.com/sixties2.php?caller=kclibrary

   The website includes an interesting quiz on happenings from 1960 to 1969.

2. http://www.sixtiescity.com/index.shtm

   It is a comprehensive introduction to culture, music, history and everything of the 1960s.

3. http://www.virtualstampclub.com/century8.html

   The website features a collection of U.S. Postal Service's stamps honoring the culture of the 1970s.

Song to Enjoy

The Sound of Silence

lyrics by P. Simon

Hello darkness, my old friend
I've come to talk with you again
Because a vision softly creeping
Left its seeds while I was sleeping

And the vision that was planted in my brain
Still remains
Within the sound of silence

In restless dreams I walked alone
Narrow streets of cobblestone
'Neath the halo of a street lamp
I turn my collar to the cold and damp
When my eyes were stabbed by the flash of a neon light
That split the night
And touched the sound of silence

And in the naked light I saw
Ten thousand people maybe more
People talking without speaking
People hearing without listening
People writing songs that voices never shared
No one dared
Disturb the sound of silence

"Fools," said I, "you do not know
Silence like a cancer grows
Hear my words that I might teach you
Take my arms that I might reach you"
But my words like silent raindrops fell
And echoed in the wells of silence

And the people bowed and prayed
To the neon god they made
And the sign flashed out its warning
In the words that it was forming
And the sign said "The words of the prophets are written on the subway walls
And tenement halls"
And whispered in the sound of silence

Unit 15

Toward a New Century

> Change will not come if we wait for some other person or some other time. We are the ones we've been waiting for. We are the change that we seek.
>
> —Barack Obama

Unit Goals

- To be familiar with the important events in the 1980s.
- To gain a general understanding of the American culture in the 1990s.
- To learn the important words and expressions that describe U.S.-Soviet Relations and the Gulf War.
- To improve English language skills.
- To develop critical thinking and intercultural communication skills.

Before You Read

1. Make lists of major events and trends in America in the 1970s, 1980s and 1990s respectively. Put your answers in the following boxes. If you find it hard to accomplish the task, please start reading Text A.

1970s	1980s	1990s

2. Form groups of three or four students. Try to find, on the Internet or in the library, more information about America today which interests you most. Prepare a 5-minute classroom presentation.

Start to Read

Text A America Entering a New Century

1. For the United States, the 20th century ended on a note of triumph. As the 21st century began, the United States was without a doubt the strongest, wealthiest, most powerful nation on earth. It possessed the world's most productive economy and the mightiest armed forces; it dominated global manufacturing and trade; it held an unchallenged lead in invention, science, and technology. Its popular culture was dominant across much of the globe.

2. Few would have imagined the United States' success decades ago. The United States confronted a new and unsettling set of cultural challenges: the youth revolt, the sexual revolution, women's liberation, the civil rights struggles of African Americans, and the environmental and consumer movements.

3. During the 1970s, the country faced a severe crisis of confidence deepened by a sense of economic and military decline and political scandal. Watergate, economic stagnation, mounting inflation, energy crisis, foreign competition and the loss of industrial jobs, the defeat in Vietnam—all contributed to a sense of national decline.

4. By 1980, the sense of American pre-eminence had faded. Other countries saved more, invested more, worked harder, and increased the productivity of their industries faster than did America—a shocking recognition that American economic competitiveness had declined. In the U.S., real wages had fallen since 1973; families required two incomes, instead of one, to maintain a middle class standard of living.

5. Economic decline was accompanied by a deep sense of social decay. There was a mounting recognition that the United States' level of crime and violence

was the highest in the industrialized world. Not even the presidency was untouched by this epidemic of violence. Between 1963 and 1981, four presidents were the targets of assassins' bullets.

6. But as a result of the longest post-war economic boom, the upsurge in stock prices, falling energy prices, a dramatic decline in unemployment, and the proliferation of new communication and computer technologies, Americans came to see themselves once again standing astride the world like a colossus.

7. Science and technology made terrific strides in the eighties. Large numbers of Americans began using personal computers in their homes, offices, and schools. Columbia, America's first reusable spacecraft was launched in 1981. A sad day in world history was January 28, 1986, when space shuttle Challenger exploded 74 seconds after liftoff killing all seven astronauts. Research money allowed for studies and new treatments for heart, cancer, and other diseases. Major advances in genetics research led to the 1988 funding of the Human Genome Project. This project will locate the estimated 80,000 genes contained in human DNA.

8. Families changed drastically during these years. The 1980s continued the trends of the 1960s and 1970s—more divorces, more unmarried people living together, more single parent families. The two-earner family was even more common than in previous decades, more women earned college and advanced degrees, married, and had fewer children.

9. In the 1990s, the United States played the role of world policeman, sometimes alone but more often in alliances. The decade began with Sadam Husein's invasion of Kuwait and the resultant Gulf War. By September, 1994, the U.S. was once again sending troops to a foreign country to overthrow a military dictatorship, this time in Haiti. In 1996, about 20,000 American troops were deployed to Bosnia as part of a NATO peace keeping force. In late March 1999, the U.S. joined NATO in air strikes against Yugoslavia in an effort to halt the Yugoslavian government's policy of ethnic cleansing in its province of Kosovo. The decade was to end much as it began with U.S. forces deployed in many countries, and the U.S. playing arbitrator, enforcer, and peace keeper throughout the world.

10. On the domestic front of the 1990s, some big issues were health care, social security reform, and gun control—unresolved and debated during the whole decade. Violence and sex scandals dominated the media. President Clinton kept the gossip flowing as several women accused him of sexual misconduct.

The ten years ended with this president narrowly surviving a trial to remove him from office for obstruction of justice. The polls were reporting that 70% of the American people were saying that they were "tired of the Clintons."

11. From its origins as a set of obscure colonies hugging the Atlantic coast, the United States has undergone a remarkable transformation into what political analyst Ben Wattenberg has called "the first universal nation," a population of almost 300 million people representing virtually every nationality and ethnic group on the globe. It is also a nation where the pace and extent of change—economic, technological, cultural, demographic, and social—is unceasing. The United States is often the pioneer of the modernization and change in an increasingly interdependent, interconnected world.

After You Read

Knowledge Focus

1. **Pair Work: Discuss the following questions with your partner.**
    (1) What were the cultural challenges that America confronted in the 1960s?
    (2) Why do we say the country faced a national decline during the 1970s?
    (3) Between 1963 and 1981, four presidents were the targets of assassins' bullets. Can you figure out who they are?
    (4) Can you name some scientific and technological breakthroughs in the 1980s?
    (5) Why was two-earner family more common in the 1980s than in previous decades?
    (6) Why was the U.S. considered world police by the international community?
    (7) Can you name several wars that America was engaged in the 1990s?
    (8) How do you comment on the role that America played as a world policeman? Share your views with your partner.
    (9) What were the big issues on the domestic front?
    (10) How do you understand "the first universal nation" that political analyst Ben Wattenberg has mentioned?

2. **Solo Work: Tell whether the following are true or false according to the knowledge you have learned. Consider why.**
    (1) Watergate, mounting inflation, energy crisis, the loss of industrial jobs, and the defeat in Vietnam were all events in the 1980s that led to a sense of national decline. ( )
    (2) It is generally believed that American economic competitiveness had declined by the 1980s. ( )
    (3) Challenger, America's first reusable spacecraft was launched in 1981. ( )
    (4) Space shuttle Challenger exploded 74 seconds after its liftoff, killing all seven astronauts in 1986. ( )

(5) The 1980s did not follow the trends of the 1960s and the 1970s—more divorces, more unmarried people living together, more single parent families. ( )
(6) More women earned college and advanced degrees, married, and had fewer children in the 1980s. ( )
(7) By September, 1994, the U.S. was once again sending troops to a foreign country to overthrow a government. ( )
(8) In late March 1999, the U.S. joined NATO in air strikes against Yugoslavia. ( )

Language Focus

1. **Solo Work**: Fill in the blanks with the following words from the text.

| mighty | eminence | epidemic | assassin | upsurge |
| stride | proliferation | colossus | launch | cleanse |

  (1) The sponsor itself is the _____ transnational corporation.
  (2) The seminar focuses on the topic of the _____ of global media networks.
  (3) Doctors warn that a flu _____ may be on the way.
  (4) The organization has _____ a campaign to raise $350,000.
  (5) His government blames the _____ of violence on the record inflow of immigrants this year.
  (6) The mayor was elected on a promise to _____ the city government of corruption.
  (7) Although the _____ were never caught, it is commonly believed that they were working for the government.
  (8) The merged bank will be a _____.
  (9) Anyone can quote the names of a few specialists who have attained local or even national _____.
  (10) The government has made great _____ in reducing poverty.

2. **Pair Work**: Choose the appropriate word to complete each of the following sentences. Check your answers with your partner.
  (1) The team seems to have lost its _____ (competition/competitive) edge recently.
  (2) Managers are always looking for ways to increase worker _____ (product/productivity).
  (3) President Lincoln was _____ (assassin/assassinated) by John Wilkes Booth.
  (4) An old portrait shows her sitting _____ (stride/astride) a horse.
  (5) There was an upsurge _____ (in/on) violence during June and July.
  (6) New _____ (gene/genetic) tests for other dread diseases are appearing almost every day.
  (7) Advances _____ (in/on) medical science may make it possible for people to live for 150 years.
  (8) The _____ (consultant/resultant) changes in regional species composition have many consequences for human health.
  (9) Employers cannot discriminate on the basis of racial or _____ (ethic/ethnic)

background.

(10) The style of these paintings can be traced _____ (in/to) early medieval influences.

Comprehensive Work

Pair Work

Pirections: When we recollect the history of America, some names cannot be forgotten. Please identify the faces of the most admired American presidents carved by Gutzon Borglum into the southeast face of Mount Rushmore in South Dakota. Can you briefly retell their contributions to the United States?

George Washington: _____ ;
Thomas Jefferson: _____ ;
Theodore Roosevelt: _____ ;
Abraham Lincoln: _____ ;

Team Work:

Directions: The study of history cannot help us foresee the future. But it can remind us how far we have come and how far we have to go. It can also help us understand that change is inevitable and the future is not preordained. History reminds us that we have got where we are, not through a chain of inevitabilities, but through a sequence of choices, actions, and struggles. History can never come to its end.

What is the use of learning American history or history in general? What is the benefit of learning history? Summarize your points and share with your team members.

Learning history can _____ .
Learning history can _____ .
Learning history can _____ .

Essay Writing

Which American president impressed you most? And what quality in him is worthy to be cherished? Write an essay within 300 words to describe the most memorable American president and his qualities and personalities that are worth learning.

Read More

Text B　　The Gulf War

The excitement caused by the drawing down of the Cold War was dramatically overshadowed by the August 2, 1990, invasion of the small nation of Kuwait by Iraq. Iraq, under Saddam Hussein, and Iran, had emerged as the two major military powers in the oil-rich Persian Gulf area. The two countries had fought a long war in the 1980s. Less hostile to the United States than Iran, Iraq had won some support from the Reagan and Bush administrations. The occupation of Kuwait, posing a threat to Saudi Arabia, changed the diplomatic calculation overnight.

President Bush strongly condemned the Iraqi action, called for Iraq's unconditional withdrawal, and sent a major deployment of U.S. troops to the Middle East. He assembled one of the most extraordinary military and political coalitions of modern times, with military forces from Asia, Europe, and Africa, as well as the Middle East.

In the days and weeks following the invasion, the U.N. Security Council passed 12 resolutions condemning the Iraqi invasion and imposing economic sanctions on Iraq. On November 29, it approved the use of force if Iraq did not withdraw from Kuwait by January 15, 1991. Gorbachev's Soviet Union, once Iraq's major arms supplier, made no effort to protect its former client.

Bush also confronted a major constitutional issue. The U.S. Constitution gives the legislative branch the power to declare war. Yet in the second half of the 20th century, the United States had become involved in Korea and Vietnam without an official declaration of war and with only legislative authorization. On January 12, 1991, three days before the U.N. deadline, Congress granted President Bush the authority of war-making power.

The United States, in coalition with Great Britain, France, Italy, Saudi Arabia, Kuwait, and other countries, succeeded in liberating Kuwait with a U.S.-led air campaign that lasted slightly more than a month. With the superior speed, mobility, and firepower, the allied forces overwhelmed the Iraqi forces in a land campaign lasting only 100 hours.

The victory, however, was incomplete and unsatisfying. The U.N. resolution called only for the expulsion of Iraq from Kuwait. Saddam Hussein remained in power, savagely repressing the Kurds in the north and the Shiites in the south, both of whom the United States had encouraged to rebel. Hundreds of oil-well fires, deliberately set in Kuwait by the Iraqis, took until November 1991 to extinguish. Saddam's regime also apparently prevented U.N. inspectors who worked to locate and destroy Iraq's weapons of mass destruction, including nuclear facilities more advanced than had previously been suspected and huge stocks of chemical weapons.

The Gulf War enabled the United States to persuade the Arab states, Israel, and a

Palestinian delegation to begin direct negotiations aimed at resolving the complex and interlocked issues that could eventually lead to a lasting peace in the region. The talks began in Madrid, Spain, on October 30, 1991. In turn, they set the stage for the secret negotiations in Norway that led to what at the time seemed a historic agreement between Israel and the Palestine Liberation Organization, signed at the White House on September 13, 1993.

Questions for Discussion or Reflection
(1) What was the major cause of the Gulf War?
(2) What was the major constitutional issue that Bush confronted?
(3) What else do you know about the Gulf War? Discuss the significance and the impact of the war with your partner.

Text C No Ordinary Day

It should have been just an ordinary day at the office for Noel Sepulveda. Sepulveda was an Air Force Master Sergeant. Usually, he worked at Kirtland Air Force Base in New Mexico. In September of 2001, he was helping out in Washington, D. C. He was heading up a reserve program for the Air Force Strategies Office at the Pentagon.

Sepulveda was born in Puerto Rico. He came to the U. S. as a child and joined the Air Force in 1969 at the age of 19. During his six years of active duty, Sepulveda may not have had many ordinary days. In 1972, he was in Vietnam serving as a medic with a helicopter crew. On a mission to rescue a downed American soldier, the chopper flew low over a group of people huddled around a stretcher on the ground. Sepulveda, looking down, saw some things that made him wary. "I don't like what I'm seeing here," Sepulveda said to the pilot.

Suddenly, the "patient" pulled a weapon from beneath his body. From the brush, mortar shells exploded. The helicopter's tail rudder took a hit. Sepulveda was standing in the open door of the aircraft at the time. He'd neglected to fasten his safety harness. When the mortar hit, he was jolted from the helicopter.

Trees and brush broke his fall. Still, one hand, one leg, and part of Sepulveda's ribcage were smashed up in his plunge from the sky. As it turned out, he was the lucky one. Just as Sepulveda fell, the chopper blew up. The medic who fell from the aircraft was the only one of the crew who lived.

Another helicopter in the squadron rescued Sepulveda. It took a year in various hospitals before he was back on duty again. He served another four years on active duty. His medical skills were called upon again during Operation Desert Storm. In all, Sepulveda had 26 years of service behind him when he was called to work in Washington.

On this particular morning in September, Sepulveda was hurrying to the Pentagon. He was late for a 9:30 appointment. As he sprinted toward the building, he phoned ahead. A secretary told him that everything had been cancelled due to the drama going on in New York. It was suspected that the events in New York were part of a terrorist attack. The Pentagon was locked down on red alert, she told him.

Then Sepulveda noticed a plane coming in over the area. It came low over the top of a hotel, not following the usual flight pattern. As he watched, the plane dropped even lower. Electrical poles snapped like toothpicks as the plane blasted through them and veered toward the Pentagon. Frozen in place, the sergeant saw the plane crash into the building, burying the fuselage up past the wings. A second later, it exploded in flames. The blast picked Sepulveda up and slammed him back against a light pole.

Before he could think, the medic inside took over. Sepulveda dashed to the nearest opening in the ravaged building. Flames and smoke were boiling out of the wreckage. "Is anybody in here?" he shouted, searching frantically for those who might need help. People were screaming and staggering about, trying to get out. A man stumbled toward him, his clothes hanging in rags, his face and chest badly burned. Sepulveda pulled him out. He found others and led them out, too.

A Pentagon policeman joined in the task. The men worked together to drag the dazed and injured people to safety. At one point, the policeman handed Sepulveda an armful of dirty rags. When he held it, Sepulveda realized there was a baby inside. The little body was way too still. Quickly, the medic began CPR as he raced to hand the child to paramedics. With great relief, Sepulveda finally heard the infant cough and begin to cry. He placed the battered bundle into the waiting arms of a paramedic and went back to bring out the baby's young mother.

Later, Sepulveda seized a spot in a nearby tunnel. He set up a triage area like he had in combat zones. To make it easier to treat the injured he used a color system, ranking the injuries according to their urgency. Still, the chaos around him was overwhelming. Sepulveda grabbed a bullhorn and leaped up to the edge of a street above the scene. He calmed the crowd and began directing medical efforts.

He was gathering people with medical skills from the crowd when a voice behind him demanded to know what he was doing. Sepulveda realized he was being questioned by no less than the Air Force Surgeon General. "Great!" the General boomed as the sergeant finished explaining his plan. "You're my onsite medical commander. You will coordinate military efforts with the civilian health care system."

Before Sepulveda could say "Yes, Sir!" the General was gone. The medic who had become a commander went on with what had to be done to get people to treatment. It was days before he slowed down enough to be aware of his own injuries. When he was examined later, it was found that Sepulveda had taken such a blow to the back of his head that blood was pooling inside. In spite of his own injuries, Sepulveda stayed at his command post for the next couple of weeks.

Six months after the tragedy, the Air Force recognized Sepulveda's great contribution. The Surgeon General commented, "Master Sergeant Sepulveda is one of the real heroes of 9/11. He did exactly what he needed to do at exactly the right moment. He created order out of chaos. He behaved as all airmen are trained to behave, as a real leader, making all of us proud."

Many heroes emerged from the tragedy of 9/11. Other people were recognized for

their efforts as well. But Sepulveda's instant and selfless response to those in need saved many lives on that day. Sepulveda was the only person awarded the Airman's Medal, the highest honor that can be given in a non-combat situation. He was also given a Purple Heart. These days, Sepulveda runs an Air Force fitness clinic. The Pentagon is still his office, but perhaps, every once in a while, he enjoys having just an ordinary day.

Reading Comprehension

(1) Describe the skills and duties of a combat medic.
   _____
   _____

(2) Puerto Rico is _____.
   A. a territory of the United States   B. a Spanish colony
   C. a province of Mexico   D. a part of Cuba

(3) Sepulveda honed his medical skills serving in two different conflicts. They were _____.
   A. the Viet Nam War and Operation Desert Storm
   B. the Viet Nam War and the Iraq War
   C. the Korean War and the Vietnam War
   D. World War II and the Korean War

(4) Explain why Sepulveda spent a year in hospitals in his early twenties.
   _____

(5) How did Sepulveda learn about the 9/11 terrorist attack in New York City?
   _____

(6) In a triage area, medical personnel would _____.
   A. evaluate patients according to the urgency of their need for care
   B. perform emergency surgery
   C. prepare patients for surgery
   D. scrub up for surgery

Proper Names

Human Genome Project 人类基因组计划
Intermediate Range Nuclear Forces (INF) Treaty《中程核武器条约》
Kosovo 科索沃
Mikhail Gorbachev 米凯尔·戈尔巴乔夫
NATO (North Atlantic Treaty Organization) 北大西洋公约组织
Sadam Husein 萨达姆·侯赛因
SDI (Strategic Defense Initiative) 战略防御计划(星球大战计划)
the Gulf War 海湾战争
the Palestine Liberation Organization 巴勒斯坦解放组织
USSR (Union of Soviet Socialist Republics) 苏联
Watergate 水门事件
Yugoslavia 南斯拉夫

Notes

1. **The Cuban Revolution**: It was a revolution that led to the overthrow of the dictatorial government of Cuban President General Fulgencio Batista on January 1, 1959 by the 26th of July movement and other revolutionary organizations. The Cuban Revolution also refers to the ongoing implementation of social and economic programs by the new government since the overthrow of the Batista dictatorship, including the implementation of Marxist policies.
2. **The Watergate scandals**: It was a series of American political scandals during the presidency of Richard Nixon that resulted in the indictment of several of Nixon's closest advisors, and ultimately his resignation on August 9, 1974. The scandals began with the arrest of five men for breaking and entering into the Democratic National Committee headquarters at the Watergate Office complex in Washington, D.C. on June 17, 1972.

For Fun

Books to Read

1. Carl Bernstein & Bob Woodward, *All the President's Men*

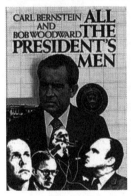

This is the book that changed America. Published just months before President Nixon's resignation, *All the President's Men* revealed the full scope of the scandal and introduced for the first time the mysterious "Deep Throat." Beginning with the story of a simple burglary at Democratic headquarters and then continuing through headline after headline, Bernstein and Woodward deliver a riveting firsthand account of their reporting. Their explosive reports won a Pulitzer Prize for *The Washington Post*, toppled the president, and have since inspired generations of reporters.

2. George Moss, *America Since 1900*

This book is a comprehensive study of America in the 20th century. Written to provide a strong understanding of America since the beginning of the 20th century, this comprehensive survey covers topics and personalities from the late 19th through the beginning of the 21st century. Broad in scope and written in a lively narrative style, *America Since 1900* emphasizes social history and multicultural experiences of the American people in addition to political, diplomatic and military history.

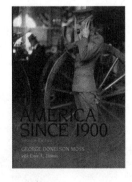

Movies to See

1. ***Good Morning, Vietnam***

    It was a 1987 comedy-drama film set in Saigon during the Vietnam War. Robin Williams played the leading role and he was nominated for the Academy Award for Best Actor. This film is No. 36 on Bravo's "100 Funniest Movies."

2. ***Fahrenheit 9/11***

    It was an award-winning 2004 documentary film by American filmmaker Michael Moore. The film takes a critical look at the presidency of George W. Bush, the War on Terrorism, and its coverage in the American news media. The film holds the record for highest box office receipts by a general release political film.

Websites to Visit

1. http://www.afn.org/~afn30091/80songs.html

    It has a collection of songs popular in the 1980s.

2. http://www.thepeoplehistory.com/1990s.html

    This website features the 1990s' homes, cars, food, clothes, electrical, furniture and history.

3. http://www.fashion-era.com/the_1990s.htm

    It is a website which provides a bird's-eye view of the fashion in the 1990s.

Song to Enjoy

Take Me Home, Country Roads
lyrics by John Denver

Almost heaven, West Virginia,
Blue Ridge Mountains, Shenandoah River.
Life is old there, older than the trees,
Younger than the mountains, growin' like a breeze.
Country Roads, take me home,
To the place I belong:
West Virginia, mountain momma,
Take me home, country roads.

All my mem'ries, gather' round her,
Miner's lady, stranger to blue water.
Dark and dusty, painted on the sky,
Misty taste of moonshine, teardrop in my eye.

Country Roads, take me home,
To the place I belong:
West Virginia, mountain momma,

Take me home, country roads.
I hear her voice, in the mornin' hours she calls me,
The radio reminds me of my home far away.
And drivin' down the road,
I get a feelin' that I should have been home yesterday,
Yesterday.

Country Roads, take me home,
To the place I belong:
West Virginia, mountain momma,
Take me home, country roads.

Take me home, country roads.
Take me home, down country roads.

Appendixes

Appendix 1 States, Their Entry into Union & Their Settlement

State	Entered Union	Year settled
1. Delaware	Dec. 7, 1787	1638
2. Pennsylvania	Dec. 12, 1787	1682
3. New Jersey	Dec. 18, 1787	1660
4. Georgia	Jan. 2, 1788	1733
5. Connecticut	Jan. 9, 1788	1634
6. Massachusetts	Feb. 6, 1788	1620
7. Maryland	Apr. 28, 1788	1634
8. South Carolina	May 23, 1788	1670
9. New Hampshire	June 21, 1788	1623
10. Virginia	June 25, 1788	1607
11. New York	July 26, 1788	1614
12. North Carolina	Nov. 21, 1789	1660
13. Rhode Island	May 29, 1790	1636
14. Vermont	Mar. 4, 1791	1724
15. Kentucky	June 1, 1792	1774
16. Tennessee	June 1, 1796	1769
17. Ohio	Mar. 1, 1803	1788
18. Louisiana	Apr. 30, 1812	1699
19. Indiana	Dec. 11, 1816	1733
20. Mississippi	Dec. 10, 1817	1699
21. Illinois	Dec. 3, 1818	1720
22. Alabama	Dec. 14, 1819	1702
23. Maine	Mar. 15, 1820	1624
24. Missouri	Aug. 10, 1821	1735
25. Arkansas	June 15, 1836	1686
26. Michigan	Jan. 26, 1837	1668
27. Florida	Mar. 3, 1845	1565
28. Texas	Dec. 29, 1845	1682
29. Iowa	Dec. 28, 1846	1788

(Continued)

State	Entered Union	Year settled
30. Wisconsin	May 29, 1848	1766
31. California	Sept. 9, 1850	1769
32. Minnesota	May 11, 1858	1805
33. Oregon	Feb. 14, 1859	1811
34. Kansas	Jan. 29, 1861	1727
35. West Virginia	June 20, 1863	1727
36. Nevada	Oct. 31, 1864	1849
37. Nebraska	Mar. 1, 1867	1823
38. Colorado	Aug. 1, 1876	1858
39. North Dakota	Nov. 2, 1889	1812
40. South Dakota	Nov. 2, 1889	1859
41. Montana	Nov. 8, 1889	1809
42. Washington	Nov. 11, 1889	1811
43. Idaho	July 3, 1890	1842
44. Wyoming	July 10, 1890	1834
45. Utah	Jan. 4, 1896	1847
46. Oklahoma	Nov. 16, 1907	1889
47. New Mexico	Jan. 6, 1912	1610
48. Arizona	Feb. 14, 1912	1776
49. Alaska	Jan. 3, 1959	1784
50. Hawaii	Aug. 21, 1959	1820

Appendix 2 Presidents & Vice Presidents of the U.S.

President	Place of Birth	Party	Term as President	Vice-President
1. George Washington (1732—1799)	Westmoreland County, Virginia	None, Federalist	1789—1797	John Adams
2. John Adams (1735—1826)	Braintree, Norfolk, Massachusetts	Federalist	1797—1801	Thomas Jefferson
3. Thomas Jefferson (1743—1826)	Albermarle County, Virginia	Democratic-Republican	1801—1809	Aaron Burr, George Clinton
4. James Madison (1751—1836)	Port Conway, Virginia	Democratic-Republican	1809—1817	George Clinton, Elbridge Gerry
5. James Monroe (1758—1831)	Westmoreland County, Virginia	Democratic-Republican	1817—1825	Daniel Tompkins
6. John Quincy Adams (1767—1848)	Braintree, Norfolk, Massachusetts	Democratic-Republican	1825—1829	John Calhoun
7. Andrew Jackson (1767—1845)	Waxhaw, South Carolina	Democrat	1829—1837	John Calhoun, Martin van Buren
8. Martin van Buren (1782—1862)	Kinderhook, New York	Democrat	1837—1841	Richard Johnson
9. William H. Harrison (1773—1841)	Berkeley, Virginia	Whig	1841	John Tyler
10. John Tyler (1790—1862)	Charles City County, Virginia	Whig	1841—1845	none
11. James K. Polk (1795—1849)	Mecklenburg County, North Carolina	Democrat	1845—1849	George Dallas
12. Zachary Taylor (1784—1850)	Orange County, Virginia	Whig	1849—1850	Millard Fillmore
13. Millard Fillmore (1800—1874)	Cayuga County, New York	Whig	1850—1853	none
14. Franklin Pierce (1804—1869)	Hillsboro, New Hampshire	Democrat	1853—1857	William King
15. James Buchanan (1791—1868)	Cove Gap, Pennsylvania	Democrat	1857—1861	John Breckinridge

(Continued)

President	Place of Birth	Party	Term as President	Vice-President
16. Abraham Lincoln (1809—1865)	Hodgenville, Hardin County, Kentucky	Republican	1861—1865	Hannibal Hamlin, Andrew Johnson
17. Andrew Johnson (1808—1875)	Raleigh, North Carolina	National Union	1865—1869	none
18. Ulysses S. Grant (1822—1885)	Point Pleasant, Ohio	Republican	1869—1877	Schuyler Colfax
19. Rutherford Hayes (1822—1893)	Delaware, Ohio	Republican	1877—1881	William Wheeler
20. James Garfield (1831—1881)	Orange, Cuyahoga County, Ohio	Republican	1881	Chester Arthur
21. Chester Arthur (1829—1886)	Fairfield, Vermont	Republican	1881—1885	none
22. Grover Cleveland (1837—1908)	Caldwell, New Jersey	Democrat	1885—1889	Thomas Hendriks
23. Benjamin Harrison (1833—1901)	North Bend, Ohio	Republican	1889—1893	Levi Morton
24. Grover Cleveland (1837—1908)	Caldwell, New Jersey	Democrat	1893—1897	Adlai Stevenson
25. William McKinley (1843—1901)	Niles, Ohio	Republican	1897—1901	Garret Hobart, Theodore Roosevelt
26. Theodore Roosevelt (1858—1919)	New York City	Republican	1901—1909	Charles Fairbanks
27. William Taft (1857—1930)	Cincinnati, Ohio	Republican	1909—1913	James Sherman
28. Woodrow Wilson (1856—1924)	Staunton, Virginia	Democrat	1913—1921	Thomas Marshall
29. Warren Harding (1865—1923)	Blooming Grove, Ohio	Republican	1921—1923	Calvin Coolidge
30. Calvin Coolidge (1872—1933)	Plymouth, Vermont	Republican	1923—1929	Charles Dawes

(Continued)

President	Place of Birth	Party	Term as President	Vice-President
31. Herbert C. Hoover (1874—1964)	West Branch, Iowa	Republican	1929—1933	Charles Curtis
32. Franklin Delano Roosevelt (1882—1945)	Hyde Park, New York	Democrat	1933—1945	John Garner, Henry Wallace, Harry S. Truman
33. Harry S. Truman (1884—1972)	Lamar, Missouri	Democrat	1945—1953	Alben Barkley
34. Dwight David Eisenhower (1890—1969)	Denison, Texas	Republican	1953—1961	Richard Milhous Nixon
35. John Fitzgerald Kennedy (1917—1963)	Brookline, Massachusetts	Democrat	1961—1963	Lyndon Johnson
36. Lyndon Baines Johnson (1908—1973)	near Stonewall, Texas	Democrat	1963—1969	Hubert Humphrey
37. Richard Milhous Nixon (1913—1994)	Yorba Linda, California	Republican	1969—1974	Spiro Agnew, Gerald R. Ford
38. Gerald R. Ford (1913— 2006)	Omaha, Nebraska	Republican	1974—1977	Nelson Rockefeller
39. James (Jimmy) Earl Carter, Jr. (1924—)	Plains, Georgia	Democrat	1977—1981	Walter Mondale
40. Ronald Wilson Reagan (1911— 2004)	Tampico, Illinois	Republican	1981—1989	George H. W. Bush
41. George H. W. Bush (1924—)	Milton, Massachusetts	Republican	1989—1993	James Danforth (Dan) Quayle
42. William (Bill) Jefferson Clinton (1946—)	Hope, Arkansas	Democrat	1993—2001	Al Gore
43. George W. Bush (1946—)	New Haven, Connecticut	Republican	2001—2009	Richard Cheney
44. Barack Obama (1961—)	Honolulu, Hawaii	Democrat	2009—2017	Joseph Biden
45. Donald Trump (1946—)	Queens, New York	Republican	2017—2021	Mike Pence
46. Joseph Biden (1942—)	Scranton, Pennsylvania	Democrat	2021—	Kamala Harris

Appendix 3　U.S. History Timeline

Year	Events
1492	Christopher Columbus, financed by Spain, makes the first of four voyages to the New World. He lands in the Bahamas (Oct. 12).
1513	Spanish explorer Juan Ponce de León lands on the coast of Florida.
1565	Saint Augustine, Florida, settled by the Spanish, becomes the first permanent European colony in North America.
1607	Jamestown, the first permanent English settlement in America, is established by the London Company in southeast Virginia (May 14 o.s.).
1619	The House of Burgesses, the first representative assembly in America, meets for the first time in Virginia (July 30 o.s.). The first African slaves are brought to Jamestown (summer).
1620	The Plymouth Colony in Massachusetts is established by Pilgrims from England (Dec. 11 o.s.). Before disembarking from their ship, the *Mayflower*, 41 male passengers sign *The Mayflower Compact*, an agreement that forms the basis of the colony's government.
1650	Colonial population is estimated at 50,400.
1664	English seize New Amsterdam (city and colony) from the Dutch and rename it New York (Sept.).
1752	Britain and the British colonies switch from the Julian to the Gregorian calendar (Sept. 2).
1754—1763	French and Indian War
1770	Boston Massacre
1773	Boston Tea Party: A group of colonial patriots disguised as Mohawk Indians board three ships in Boston harbor and dump more than 300 crates of tea overboard as a protest against the British tea tax (Dec. 16).
1774	First Continental Congress meets in Philadelphia, with 56 delegates representing every colony except Georgia. Delegates include Patrick Henry, George Washington, and Samuel Adams (Sept. 5—Oct. 26).
1775—1783	American Revolution
1776	Continental Congress adopts *the Declaration of Independence* in Philadelphia (July 4).
1777	Continental Congress approves the first official flag of the United States (June 14). Continental Congress adopts the Articles of Confederation, the first U.S. constitution (Nov. 15).

Appendixes

(Continued)

Year	Events
1786	Shays's Rebellion erupts (Aug.); farmers from New Hampshire to South Carolina take up arms to protest high state taxes and stiff penalties for failure to pay.
1787	Constitutional Convention, made up of delegates from 12 of the original 13 colonies, meets in Philadelphia to draft the U.S. Constitution (May – Sept.).
1789	George Washington is unanimously elected president of the United States in a vote by state electors (Feb. 4). U.S. Constitution goes into effect, having been ratified by nine states (March 4). U.S. Congress meets for the first time at Federal Hall in New York City (March 4). Washington is inaugurated as president at Federal Hall in New York City (April 30).
1790	U.S. Supreme Court meets for the first time at the Merchants Exchange Building in New York City (Feb. 2). The court, made up of one chief justice and five associate justices, hears its first case in 1792. The nation's first census shows that the population has climbed to nearly 4 million.
1791	First ten amendments to the Constitution, known as the Bill of Rights, are ratified (Dec. 15).
1793	Washington's second inauguration is held in Philadelphia (March 4). Eli Whitney's invention of the cotton gin greatly increases the demand for slave labor.
1797	John Adams is inaugurated as the second president in Philadelphia (March 4).
1800	The U.S. capital is moved from Philadelphia to Washington, D.C. (June 15). U.S. Congress meets in Washington, D.C., for the first time (Nov. 17).
1801	Thomas Jefferson is inaugurated as the third president in Washington, D.C. (March 4).
1803	Louisiana Purchase: United States agrees to pay France $15 million for the Louisiana Territory, which extends west from the Mississippi River to the Rocky Mountains and comprises about 830,000 sq mi (treaty signed May 2). As a result, the U.S. nearly doubles in size.
1804	Lewis and Clark set out from St. Louis, Mo., on expedition to explore the West and find a route to the Pacific Ocean. (May 14).
1805	Jefferson's second inauguration (March 4). Lewis and Clark reach the Pacific Ocean (Nov. 15).
1809	James Madison is inaugurated as the fourth president (March 4).
1812—1814	War of 1812
1817	James Monroe is inaugurated as the fifth president (March 4).

(Continued)

Year	Events
1819	Spain agrees to cede Florida to the United States (Feb. 22).
1820	Missouri Compromise
1821	Monroe's second inauguration (March 5).
1822	Denmark Vesey, an enslaved African American carpenter who had purchased his freedom, plans a slave revolt with the intent to lay siege on Charleston, South Carolina. The plot is discovered, and Vesey and 34 coconspirators are hanged.
1823	Monroe Doctrine
1825	John Quincy Adams is inaugurated as the sixth president (March 4). Erie Canal, linking the Hudson River to Lake Erie, is opened for traffic (Oct. 26).
1828	Construction is begun on the Baltimore and Ohio Railroad, the first public railroad in the U.S. (July 4).
1829	Andrew Jackson is inaugurated as seventh president (March 4).
1830	President Jackson signs the Indian Removal Act, which authorizes the forced removal of Native Americans living in the eastern part of the country to lands west of the Mississippi River (May 28). By the late 1830s the Jackson administration has relocated nearly 50,000 Native Americans.
1831	Nat Turner, an enslaved African American preacher, leads the most significant slave uprising in American history. He and his band of about 80 followers launch a bloody, day-long rebellion in Southampton County, Virginia. The militia quells the rebellion, and Turner is eventually hanged. As a consequence, Virginia institutes much stricter slave laws.
1833	Jackson's second inauguration (March 4).
1836	Texas declares its independence from Mexico (March 1). Texan defenders of the Alamo are all killed during siege by the Mexican Army (Feb. 24—March 6). Texans defeat Mexicans at San Jacinto (April 21).
1837	Martin Van Buren is inaugurated as the eighth president (March 4).
1838	More than 15,000 Cherokee Indians are forced to march from Georgia to Indian Territory in present-day Oklahoma. Approximately 4,000 die from starvation and disease along the "Trail of Tears."
1841	William Henry Harrison is inaugurated as the ninth president (March 4). He dies one month later (April 4) and is succeeded in office by his vice president, John Tyler.
1845	U.S. annexes Texas by joint resolution of Congress (March 1). James Polk is inaugurated as the 11th president (March 4). The term "manifest destiny" appears for the first time in a magazine article by John L. O'Sullivan (July-August). It expresses the belief held by many white Americans that the United States is destined to expand across the continent.

(Continued)

Year	Events
1846	Oregon Treaty fixes U.S.-Canadian border at 49th parallel; U.S. acquires Oregon territory (June 15).
1846—1848	Mexican War
1848	Gold is discovered at Sutter's Mill in California (Jan. 24); gold rush reaches its height the following year. Women's rights convention is held at Seneca Falls, N.Y. (July 19—20).
1849	Zachary Taylor is inaugurated as the 12th president (March 5). Harriet Tubman escapes from slavery and becomes one of the most effective and celebrated members of the Underground Railroad.
1850	President Taylor dies (July 9) and is succeeded by his vice president, Millard Fillmore.
1852	Harriet Beecher Stowe's novel, Uncle Tom's Cabin is published. It becomes one of the most influential works to stir anti-slavery sentiments.
1853	Franklin Pierce is inaugurated as the 14th president (March 4). Gadsden Purchase treaty is signed; U.S. acquires border territory from Mexico for $10 million (Dec. 30).
1854	Congress passes the Kansas-Nebraska Act, establishing the territories of Kansas and Nebraska (May 30). The legislation repeals the Missouri Compromise of 1820 and renews tensions between anti-and proslavery factions.
1857	James Buchanan is inaugurated as the 15th president (March 4). Dred Scott v. Sanford: Landmark Supreme Court decision holds that Congress does not have the right to ban slavery in states and, furthermore, that slaves are not citizens.
1858	Abraham Lincoln comes to national attention in a series of seven debates with Sen. Stephen A. Douglas during Illinois state election campaign (Aug.—Oct.).
1859	Abolitionist John Brown and 21 followers capture federal arsenal at Harpers Ferry, Va. (now W. Va.), in an attempt to spark a slave revolt (Oct. 16).
1860	Abraham Lincoln is elected president (Nov. 6). South Carolina secedes from the Union (Dec. 20).
1861	Mississippi, Florida, Alabama, Georgia, and Louisiana secede (Jan.). Confederate States of America is established (Feb. 8). Jefferson Davis is elected president of the Confederacy (Feb. 9). Texas secedes (March 2). Abraham Lincoln is inaugurated as the 16th president (March 4).
1861—1865	Civil War
1863	Homestead Act becomes law, allowing settlers to claim land (160 acres) after they have lived on it for five years (Jan. 1).
1865	Lincoln is assassinated (April 14) by John Wilkes Booth in Washington, D.C., and is succeeded by his vice president, Andrew Johnson. Thirteenth Amendment to the Constitution is ratified, prohibiting slavery (Dec. 6).

(Continued)

Year	Events
1867	U.S. acquires Alaska from Russia for the sum of $7.2 million (treaty concluded March 30).
1868	President Johnson is impeached by the House of Representatives (Feb. 24), but he is acquitted at his trial in the Senate (May 26). Fourteenth Amendment to the Constitution is ratified, defining citizenship (July 9).
1869	Ulysses S. Grant is inaugurated as the 18th president (March 4). Central Pacific and Union Pacific railroads are joined at Promontory, Utah, creating first transcontinental railroad (May 10).
1870	Fifteenth Amendment to the Constitution is ratified, giving blacks the right to vote (Feb. 3).
1873	Grant's second inauguration (March 4).
1877	Rutherford B. Hayes is inaugurated as the 19th president (March 5). The first telephone line is built from Boston to Somerville, Mass.; the following year, President Hayes has the first telephone installed in the White House.
1881	James A. Garfield is inaugurated as the 20th president (March 4). He is shot (July 2) by Charles Guiteau in Washington, DC, and later dies from complications of his wounds in Elberon, N.J. (Sept. 19). Garfield's vice president, Chester Alan Arthur, succeeds him in office.
1885	Grover Cleveland is inaugurated as the 22nd president (March 4).
1886	Statue of Liberty is dedicated (Oct. 28). American Federation of Labor is organized (Dec.).
1889	Benjamin Harrison is inaugurated as the 23rd president (March 4). Oklahoma is opened to settlers (April 22).
1890	National American Woman Suffrage Association (NAWSA) is founded, with Elizabeth Cady Stanton as president. Sherman Antitrust Act is signed into law, prohibiting commercial monopolies (July 2). Last major battle of the Indian Wars occurs at Wounded Knee in South Dakota (Dec. 29). In reporting the results of the 1890 census, the Census Bureau announces that the West has been settled and the frontier is closed.
1893	Grover Cleveland is inaugurated a second time, as the 24th president (March 4). He is the only president to serve two nonconsecutive terms.
1897	William McKinley is inaugurated as the 25th president (March 4).
1898	Spanish-American War
1898	U.S. annexes Hawaii by an act of Congress (July 7).
1899	U.S. acquires American Samoa by treaty with Great Britain and Germany (Dec. 2).
1900	Galveston hurricane leaves an estimated 6,000 to 8,000 dead (Sept. 8). According to the census, the nation's population numbers nearly 76 million.

(Continued)

Year	Events
1901	McKinley's second inauguration (March 4). He is shot (Sept. 6) by anarchist Leon Czolgosz in Buffalo, N.Y., and later dies from his wounds (Sept. 14). He is succeeded by his vice president, Theodore Roosevelt.
1903	U.S. acquires Panama Canal Zone (treaty signed Nov. 17). Wright brothers make the first controlled, sustained flight in heavier-than-air aircraft at Kitty Hawk, N.C. (Dec. 17).
1905	Theodore Roosevelt's second inauguration (March 4).
1908	Bureau of Investigation, forerunner of the FBI, is established (July 26).
1909	William Howard Taft is inaugurated as the 27th president (March 4). Mrs. Taft has 80 Japanese cherry trees planted along the banks of the Potomac River.
1913	Woodrow Wilson is inaugurated as the 28th president (March 4). Seventeenth Amendment to the Constitution is ratified, providing for the direct election of U.S. senators by popular vote rather than by the state legislatures (April 8).
1914—1918	World War I
1914	Panama Canal opens to traffic (Aug. 15).
1915	First long distance telephone service, between New York and San Francisco, is demonstrated (Jan. 25).
1916	U.S. agrees to purchase Danish West Indies (Virgin Islands) for $25 million (treaty signed Aug. 14). Jeannette Rankin of Montana is the first woman elected to the U.S. House of Representatives (Nov. 7).
1917	Wilson's second inauguration (March 5). First regular airmail service begins, with one round trip a day between Washington, D.C., and New York (May 15).
1918	Worldwide influenza epidemic strikes; by 1920, nearly 20 million are dead. In U.S., 500,000 perish.
1919	League of Nations meets for the first time; U.S. is not represented (Jan. 13). Eighteenth Amendment to the Constitution is ratified, prohibiting the manufacture, sale, and transportation of liquor (Jan. 16). It is later repealed by the Twenty-First Amendment in 1933. Nineteenth Amendment to the Constitution is ratified, granting women the right to vote (Aug. 18). President Wilson suffers a stroke (Sept. 26). Treaty of Versailles, outlining terms for peace at the end of World War I, is rejected by the Senate (Nov. 19).
1921	Warren G. Harding is inaugurated as the 29th president (March 4). He signs resolution declaring peace with Austria and Germany (July 2).
1923	President Harding dies suddenly (Aug. 2). He is succeeded by his vice president, Calvin Coolidge. Teapot Dome scandal breaks, as Senate launches an investigation into improper leasing of naval oil reserves during Harding administration (Oct.)
1925	Coolidge's second inauguration (March 4). Tennessee passes a law against the teaching of evolution in public schools (March 23), setting the stage for the Scopes Monkey Trial (July 10—25).

(Continued)

Year	Events
1927	Charles Lindbergh makes the first solo nonstop transatlantic flight in his plane The Spirit of St. Louis (May 20—21).
1929	Herbert Hoover is inaugurated as the 31st president (March 4). Stock market crash precipitates the Great Depression (Oct. 29).
1931	The Star-Spangled Banner is adopted as the national anthem (March 3).
1932	Hattie Wyatt Caraway of Arkansas is the first woman elected to the U.S. Senate, to fill a vacancy caused by the death of her husband (Jan. 12). She is reelected in 1932 and 1938. Amelia Earhart completes first solo nonstop transatlantic flight by a woman (May 21).
1933	Twentieth Amendment to the Constitution, sometimes called the "Lame Duck Amendment," is ratified, moving the president's inauguration date from March 4 to Jan. 20 (Jan. 23). Franklin Roosevelt is inaugurated as the 32nd president (March 4). New Deal recovery measures are enacted by Congress (March 9—June 16). Twenty-First Amendment to the Constitution is ratified, repealing Prohibition (Dec. 5).
1935	Works Progress Administration is established (April 8). Social Security Act is passed (Aug. 14). Bureau of Investigation (established 1908) becomes the Federal Bureau of Investigation under J. Edgar Hoover
1937	F. Roosevelt's second inauguration (Jan. 20).
1938	Fair Labor Standards Act is passed, setting the first minimum wage in the U.S. at 25 cents per hour (June 25).
1939—1945	World War II
1945	United Nations is established (Oct. 24).
1946	The Philippines, which had been ceded to the U.S. by Spain at the end of the Spanish-American War, becomes an independent republic (July 4).
1947	Presidential Succession Act is signed into law by President Truman (July 18). Central Intelligence Agency is established.
1948	Congress passes foreign aid bill including the Marshall Plan, which provides for European postwar recovery (April 2). Soviets begin blockade of Berlin in the first major crisis of the cold war (June 24). In response, U.S. and Great Britain begin airlift of food and fuel to West Berlin (June 26).
1949	Truman's second inauguration (Jan. 20). North Atlantic Treaty Organization (NATO) is established (April 4). Soviets end blockade of Berlin (May 12), but airlift continues until Sept. 30.
1950—1953	Korean War
1950—1975	Vietnam War

(Continued)

Year	Events
1951	Twenty-Second Amendment to the Constitution is ratified, limiting the president to two terms (Feb. 27). President Truman speaks in first coast-to-coast live television broadcast (Sept. 4).
1952	Puerto Rico becomes a U.S. commonwealth (July 25). First hydrogen bomb is detonated by the U.S. on Eniwetok, an atoll in the Marshall Islands (Nov. 1).
1953	Dwight Eisenhower is inaugurated as the 34th president (Jan. 20). Julius and Ethel Rosenberg are executed for passing secret information about U.S. atomic weaponry to the Soviets (June 19).
1954	Sen. Joseph R. McCarthy accuses army officials, members of the media, and other public figures of being Communists during highly publicized hearings (April 22—June 17). Brown v. Board of Education of Topeka, Kans.: Landmark Supreme Court decision declares that racial segregation in schools is unconstitutional (May 17).
1957	Eisenhower's second inauguration (Jan. 21). President sends federal troops to Central High School in Little Rock, Ark., to enforce integration of black students (Sept. 24).
1958	Explorer I, first American satellite, is launched (Jan. 31).
1959	Alaska becomes the 49th state (Jan. 3) and Hawaii becomes the 50th (Aug. 21).
1961	U.S. severs diplomatic relations with Cuba (Jan. 3). John F. Kennedy is inaugurated as the 35th president (Jan. 20). Bay of Pigs invasion of Cuba fails (April 17—20). A mixed-race group of volunteers sponsored by the Committee on Racial Equality—the so-called Freedom Riders—travel on buses through the South in order to protest racially segregated interstate bus facilities (May).
1962	Lt. Col. John Glenn becomes first U.S. astronaut to orbit Earth (Feb. 20). Cuban Missile Crisis: President Kennedy denounces Soviet Union for secretly installing missile bases on Cuba and initiates a naval blockade of the island (Oct. 22—Nov. 20).
1963	Rev. Martin Luther King, Jr., delivers his "I Have a Dream" speech before a crowd of 200,000 during the civil rights march on Washington, D.C. (Aug. 28). President Kennedy is assassinated in Dallas, Tex. (Nov. 22). He is succeeded in office by his vice president, Lyndon B. Johnson.
1964	President Johnson signs the Civil Rights Act (July 2).
1965	In his annual state of the Union address, President Johnson proposes his Great Society program (Jan. 4). L. Johnson's second inauguration (Jan. 20). State troopers attack peaceful demonstrators led by Rev. Martin Luther King, Jr., as they try to cross bridge in Selma, Ala. (March 7). President Johnson signs the Voting Rights Act, which prohibits discriminatory voting practices (Aug. 6). In six days of rioting in Watts, a black section of Los Angeles, 35 people are killed and 883 injured (Aug. 11—16).
1966	Miranda v. Arizona: Landmark Supreme Court decision further defines due process clause of Fourteenth Amendment and establishes Miranda rights (June 13).

(Continued)

Year	Events
1967	Twenty-Fifth Amendment to the Constitution is ratified, outlining the procedures for filling vacancies in the presidency and vice presidency (Feb. 10).
1968	Rev. Martin Luther King, Jr., is assassinated in Memphis, Tenn. (April 4). Sen. Robert F. Kennedy is assassinated in Los Angeles, Calif. (June 5—6).
1969	Richard Nixon is inaugurated as the 37th president (Jan. 20). Astronauts Neil Armstrong and Edwin Aldrin, Jr., become the first men to land on the Moon (July 20).
1971	The Twenty-Sixth Amendment to the Constitution is ratified, lowering the voting age from 21 to 18 (July 1).
1972	Nixon makes historic visit to China (Feb. 21—27). U.S. and Soviet Union sign strategic arms control agreement known as SALT I (May 26). Five men, all employees of Nixon's reelection campaign, are caught breaking into rival Democratic headquarters at the Watergate complex in Washington, D.C. (June 17).
1973	Nixon's second inauguration (Jan. 20). Roe v. Wade: Landmark Supreme Court decision legalizes abortion in first trimester of pregnancy (Jan. 22). Senate Select Committee begins televised hearings to investigate Watergate cover-up (May 17—Aug. 7). Vice President Spiro T. Agnew resigns over charges of corruption and income tax evasion (Oct. 10). President Nixon nominates Gerald R. Ford as vice president (Oct. 12). Ford is confirmed by Congress and sworn in (Dec. 6). He is the first vice president to succeed to the office under the terms laid out by the Twenty-Fifth Amendment.
1974	House Judiciary Committee recommends to full House that Nixon be impeached on grounds of obstruction of justice, abuse of power, and contempt of Congress (July 27—30). Nixon resigns; he is succeeded in office by his vice president, Gerald Ford (Aug. 9). Nixon is granted an unconditional pardon by President Ford (Sept. 8). Five former Nixon aides go on trial for their involvement in the Watergate cover-up (Oct. 15); H. R. Haldeman, John D. Ehrlichman, and John Mitchell eventually serve time in prison. Nelson Rockefeller is confirmed and sworn in as vice president (Dec. 19).
1977	Jimmy Carter is inaugurated as the 39th president (Jan. 20). President Carter signs treaty (Sept. 7) agreeing to turn control of Panama Canal over to Panama on Dec. 31, 1999.
1978	President Carter meets with Egyptian president Anwar Sadat and Israeli prime minister Menachem Begin at Camp David (Sept. 6); Sadat and Begin sign Camp David Accord, ending 30-year conflict between Egypt and Israel (Sept. 17).
1979	U.S. establishes diplomatic ties with the People's Republic of China (Jan. 1). Malfunction at Three Mile Island nuclear reactor in Pennsylvania causes near meltdown (March 28). Panama takes control of the Canal Zone, formerly administered by U.S. (Oct. 1). Iranian students storm U.S. embassy in Teheran and hold 66 people hostage (Nov. 4); 13 of the hostages are released (Nov. 19—20).

(Continued)

Year	Events
1980	President Carter announces that U.S. athletes will not attend Summer Olympics in Moscow unless Soviet Union withdraws from Afghanistan (Jan. 20). FBI's undercover bribery investigation, code named Abscam, implicates a U.S. senator, seven members of the House, and 31 other public officials (Feb. 2). U.S. mission to rescue hostages in Iran is aborted after a helicopter and cargo plane collide at the staging site in a remote part of Iran and 8 servicemen are killed (April 25).
1981	Ronald Reagan is inaugurated as the 40th president (Jan. 20). U.S. hostages held in Iran are released after 444 days in captivity (Jan. 20). President Reagan is shot in the chest by John Hinckley, Jr. (March 30). Sandra Day O'Connor is sworn in as the first woman Supreme Court justice (Sept. 25).
1982	Deadline for ratification of the Equal Rights Amendment to the Constitution passes without the necessary votes (June 30).
1983	U.S. invades Caribbean island of Grenada after a coup by Marxist faction in the government (Oct. 25).
1985	Reagan's second inauguration (Jan. 21).
1986	Space shuttle Challenger explodes 73 seconds after liftoff, killing all seven crew members (Jan. 28). It is the worst accident in the history of the U.S. space program. U.S. bombs military bases in Libya in effort to deter terrorist strikes on American targets (April 14). Iran-Contra scandal breaks when White House is forced to reveal secret arms-for-hostages deals (Nov.).
1987	Congress holds public hearings in Iran-Contra investigation (May 5—Aug. 3). In a speech in Berlin, President Reagan challenges Soviet leader Mikhail Gorbachev to "tear down this wall" and open Eastern Europe to political and economic reform (June 12). Reagan and Gorbachev sign INF treaty, the first arms-control agreement to reduce the superpowers' nuclear weapons (Dec. 8).
1989	George H. W. Bush is inaugurated as the 41st president (Jan. 20). Oil tanker Exxon Valdez runs aground in Prince William Sound, spilling more than 10 million gallons of oil (March 24). It is the largest oil spill in U.S. history. President Bush signs legislation to provide for federal bailout of nearly 800 insolvent savings and loan institutions (Aug. 9). U.S. forces invade Panama in an attempt to capture Gen. Manuel Noriega, who previously had been indicted in the U.S. on drug trafficking charges (Dec. 20).
1990	Iraqi troops invade Kuwait, leading to the Persian Gulf War (Aug. 2).
1991	Persian Gulf War
1991	U.S. and Soviet Union sign START I treaty, agreeing to further reduce strategic nuclear arms (July 31). Senate Judiciary Committee conducts televised hearings to investigate allegations of past sexual harassment brought against Supreme Court nominee Clarence Thomas by Anita Hill, a law professor at the University of Oklahoma (Oct. 11—13).

(Continued)

Year	Events
1992	Following the breakup of the Soviet Union in Dec. 1991, President Bush and Russian president Boris Yeltsin meet at Camp David and formally declare an end to the cold war (Feb. 1). The acquittal of four white police officers charged in the 1991 beating of black motorist Rodney King in Los Angeles sets off several days of rioting, leading to more than 50 deaths, thousands of injuries and arrests, and $1 billion in property damage (April 29). President Bush authorizes sending U.S. troops to Somalia as part of UN relief effort (Dec. 4). President Bush grants pardons to six officials convicted or indicted in the Iran-Contra scandal, leading some to suspect a cover-up (Dec. 24).
1993	Bill Clinton is inaugurated as the 42nd president (Jan. 20). Bomb explodes in basement garage of World Trade Center, killing 6, injuring 1,000, and causing more than $500 million in damage (Feb. 26). After 51-day standoff with federal agents, Branch Davidian compound in Waco, Tex., burns to the ground, killing 80 cult members (April 19). President Clinton orders missile attack against Iraq in retaliation for alleged plot to assassinate former President Bush (June 26). Eighteen U.S. soldiers are killed in ambush by Somali militiamen in Mogadishu (Oct. 3—4). President Clinton signs North American Free Trade Agreement into law (Dec. 8).
1994	Paula Jones, a former Arkansas state employee, files a federal lawsuit against President Clinton for sexual harassment (May 6).
1995	Bombing of federal office building in Oklahoma City kills 168 people (April 19). U.S. establishes full diplomatic relations with Vietnam (July 11). President Clinton sends first 8,000 of 20,000 U.S. troops to Bosnia for 12-month peacekeeping mission (Dec.). Budget standoff between President Clinton and Congress results in partial shutdown of U.S. government (Dec. 16—Jan. 6).
1997	Clinton's second inauguration (Jan. 20).
1998	President Clinton denies having had a sexual relationship with a White House intern named Monica Lewinsky (Jan. 17). President Clinton releases 1999 federal budget plan; it is the first balanced budget since 1969 (Feb. 2). In televised address, President Clinton admits having had a sexual relationship with Monica Lewinsky (Aug. 17). U.S. launches missile attacks on targets in Sudan and Afghanistan following terrorist attacks on U.S. embassies in Kenya and Tanzania (Aug. 20). U.S. and Britain launch air strikes against weapons sites in Iraq (Dec. 16). House of Representatives votes to impeach President Clinton on charges of perjury and obstruction of justice (Dec. 19).
1999	Senate acquits Clinton of impeachment charges (Feb. 12). NATO wages air campaign against Yugoslavia over killing and deportation of ethnic Albanians in Kosovo (March 24—June 10). School shooting at Columbine High School in Littleton, Colo., leaves 14 students (including the 2 shooters) and 1 teacher dead and 23 others wounded (April 20). U.S. and China sign historic trade agreement (Nov. 15).

(Continued)

Year	Events
2000	According to the census, the nation's population numbers are more than 280 million (April 1). No clear winner is declared in the close presidential election contest between Vice President Al Gore and Texas governor George W. Bush (Nov. 7). More than a month after the presidential election, the U.S. Supreme Court rules against a manual recount of ballots in certain Florida counties, which it contends would violate the Constitution's equal protection and due process guarantees. The decision provokes enormous controversy, with critics maintaining that the court has in effect determined the outcome of the election (Dec. 12). Bush formally accepts the presidency, having won a slim majority in the electoral college but not a majority of the popular vote (Dec. 13).
2001	George W. Bush is inaugurated as the 43rd president (Jan. 20). Two hijacked jetliners ram twin towers of World Trade Center in worst terrorist attack against U.S.; a third hijacked plane flies into the Pentagon, and a fourth crashes in rural Pennsylvania. More than 3,000 people die in the attacks (Sept. 11). U.S. and Britain launch air attacks against targets in Afghanistan after Taliban government fails to hand over Saudi terrorist Osama bin Laden, the suspected mastermind behind the Sept. 11 attacks (Oct. 7). Following air campaign and ground assault by Afghani opposition troops, the Taliban regime topples (Dec. 9); however, the hunt for bin Laden and other members of al-Qaeda terrorist organization continues.
2002	In his first State of the Union address, President Bush labels Iran, Iraq, and North Korea an "axis of evil" and declares that U.S. will wage war against states that develop weapons of mass destruction (Jan. 29). President Bush signs legislation creating a new cabinet department of Homeland Security. (Nov. 25).
2003	Space shuttle Columbia explodes upon reentry into Earth's atmosphere, killing all seven astronauts on board (Feb. 1). War waged by the U.S. and Britain against Iraq begins (March 19). President Bush signs $350 billion tax-cut bill (May 28).
2004	The U.S. returns sovereignty to an interim government in Iraq, but maintains roughly 135,000 troops in the country to fight a growing insurgency (June 28). Four hurricanes devastate Florida and other parts of the southern United States (Aug. and Sept.).
2005	The U.S. engagement in Iraq continues amid that country's escalating violence and fragile political stability. Hurricane Katrina wreaks catastrophic damage on Mississippi and Louisiana; 80% of New Orleans is flooded (Aug. 29—30). All levels of government are criticized for the delayed and inadequate response to the disaster.
2006	The U.S. Census Bureau estimates that the population of the United States has reached 300 million (Oct. 17).

(Continued)

Year	Events
2007	California Democrat Nancy Pelosi becomes the first woman Speaker of the House of Representatives (Jan. 4). Attorney General Alberto Gonzales admits that the Justice Department made mistakes and exercised poor judgment in firing nine federal prosecutors in late 2006 (March 13). Male student kills two in a Virginia Tech dorm. Two hours later, he kills 30 more in a classroom building before committing suicide. The shooting rampage is the most deadly in U.S. history. Fifteen others are wounded (April 16). The minimum wage in the U.S. increases to $5.85, up from $5.15. It's the first increase in 10 years. The wage will increase 70 cents each year through 2009, when it reaches $7.25 an hour (July 24). An eight-lane interstate bridge in Minneapolis, Minnesota, that is packed with cars breaks into sections and falls into the river, killing 13 people (Aug. 1). The White House announces that Alberto Gonzales, the beleaguered attorney general, has submitted his resignation to President Bush (Aug. 27). In highly anticipated testimony, Gen. David Petraeus tells members of the House Foreign Affairs and Armed Services committees that the U.S. military needs more time to meet its goals in Iraq. Petraeus rejects suggestions that the U.S. shift from a counterinsurgency operation to training Iraqi forces and fighting terrorists. Instead, he says the U.S. must continue all three missions (Sep. 10).
2008	After months of campaigning and primary races, Barack Obama and John McCain are finally chosen as the presidential nominees for the Democratic and Republican parties, respectively (June 3). After months of unraveling, the economy finally comes crashing down in 2008, with the Dow Jones Industrial Average tumbling 4.4% in one day, Lehman Brothers filing for bankruptcy, and Bush putting mortgage giants Fannie Mae and Freddie Mac under government conservatorship (Sept.). Democrats perform well across the board in the November elections. Barack Obama becomes the first African-American to be elected President, with 52.8% of the vote. In Congress, Democrats retain majorities in both the House and the Senate, with 57 Senators and 178 Representatives (Nov. 4).
2009	President Obama signs executive orders closing all secret prisons and detention camps run by the CIA, including the infamous Guantanamo Bay prison in Cuba, and banning coercive interrogation methods (Jan. 22). The Senate votes in favor of a $168 billion package that gives rebates of $300—$600 for individuals earning up to $75,000 and to couples with incomes up to $150,000. Families will be eligible for up to $300 in rebates for each child (Feb. 7). President Obama signs the $787 billion stimulus package into law. The president's hope is that the package will create 3.5 million jobs for Americans in the next two years (Feb. 17). Insurance giant American International Group reports a $61.7 billion loss for the fourth quarter of 2008. A.I.G. lost $99.3 billion in 2008. The federal government, which has already provided the company with a $60 billion loan, will be giving A.I.G. an additional $30 billion. Nearly 80% of A.I.G. is now owned by the federal government (March 2). After confirming 20 cases of swine flu in the United States, including eight in New York City, the U.S. declares the outbreak a public health emergency (April 26). Michael Jackson, lifelong musician, pop singer, and superstar, dies at age 50 (June 25). The Senate approves, 68 to 31, the nomination of Sonia Sotomayor to the U.S. Supreme Court. She's the first Hispanic Supreme Court justice and the third woman to serve on the Court. (Aug. 25) Senator Edward "Ted" Kennedy, a fixture in the

(Continued)

Year	Events
	Senate for 46 years, dies of brain cancer at the age of 77 (Aug. 6). A shooting at the Fort Hood army post in Texas kills 13 and injures 29. Ten of those killed are military personnel. Maj. Nidal Malik Hasan, an army psychiatrist, is charged with 13 counts of premeditated murder (Nov. 5). A Nigerian man on a flight from Amsterdam to Detroit allegedly attempted to ignite an explosive device hidden in his underwear. The alleged bomber, Umar Farouk Abdulmutallab, told officials later that he was directed by the terrorist group Al Qaeda (Dec. 25).
2010	An explosion and fire on the Deepwater Horizon oil rig in the Gulf of Mexico sends millions of gallons of oil into the sea. The spill kills 11 and is the largest offshore spill in U.S. history as well as one of the largest spills in world history(Jan. 22). The United States Senate votes 63 to 37 to confirm President Obama's most recent nominee to the U.S. Supreme Court, Elena Kagan, as the newest Justice. Kagan is only the fourth woman to ever hold this position, and she'll be the third female member of the current bench, joining Ruth Bader Ginsburg and Sonia Sotomayor. Kagan is the former dean of Harvard Law School; she'll be the only member of the current Supreme Court to have no previous experience as a judge (Aug. 5). The Senate votes 65 to 31 in favor of repealing Don't Ask, Don't Tell, the Clinton-era military policy that forbids openly gay men and women from serving in the military. Eight Republicans side with the Democrats to strike down the ban. The repeal is sent to President Obama for his final signature. The ban will not be lifted officially until Obama, Defense Secretary Robert Gates, and Admiral Mike Mullen, the chairman of the Joint Chiefs of Staff, agree that the military is ready to enact the change and that it won't affect military readiness (Dec. 18).
2011	Arizona Representative Gabrielle Giffords is among 17 shot by a gunman who opened fire on the congresswoman's constituent meeting outside a local grocery store. The gunman, who police identify as Jared Lee Loughner, is apprehended (Jan. 8). President Obama announces his intention to reduce the federal deficit by $400 billion over 10 years. His plan for enacting this dramatic reduction includes budget cuts and freezes, including a spending freeze on many domestic programs (Jan. 24). The Obama Administration determines that the Defense of Marriage Act is unconstitutional. The Justice Department will stop defending the law in court (Feb. 23). With less than two hours to spare, an agreement on the federal budget is made, avoiding a government shutdown. Republicans demand a provision to restrict financing to Planned Parenthood and other groups that provide abortions. Obama and the Democrats refuse to budge on the abortion provision, but they do agree to tens of billions in spending cuts (April 1). Legendary Boston crime boss, James "Whitey" Bulger is found and arrested by federal authorities in Santa Monica, Calif. Bulger is on the FBI's 10 Most Wanted list and has been indicted in 19 murders (June 22). Congress makes an 11th-hour deal to prevent a national default. The deal raises the debt ceiling in two steps to $2.4 trillion and cuts an initial $1 trillion in spending over ten years (Aug. 1). For the first time in history, the U.S. has its credit rating lowered. Credit agency Standard & Poor's lowered the nation's credit rating from the top grade of AAA to AA+, removing the U.S. from its list of risk-free borrowers (Aug. 5). The Congressional Supercommittee in charge of finding $1.2 trillion in deficit reductions fails to agree on what programs to cut. Therefore, automatic cuts to military and domestic programs will go into effect in 2013 (Nov. 21).

(Continued)

Year	Events
2012	The Pentagon announces that women will now be permanently assigned to battalions. Many women already serve in those battalions due to demand in Iraq and Afghanistan. The new ruling only makes these job assignments official and upholds the ban on women serving in combat (Feb. 9). Hurricane Sandy causes at least 132 deaths and an estimated 82 billion in damages, making it the second costliest hurricane in the U. S., behind Katrina. New Jersey, New York, and Connecticut are hardest hit (Oct. 29). President Obama is re-elected, narrowly defeating Republican nominee Mitt Romney. Democrats keep their majority in the Senate. Key victories for the Democrats include a win for Tammy Baldwin in Wisconsin. Her victory makes her the first openly gay candidate to capture a seat in the Senate. The Republicans keep the majority in the House of Representatives with 232 seats to 191 for the Democrats(Nov. 6). Adam Lanza, age 20, forces his way into Sandy Hook Elementary School, in Newtown, Connecticut, and kills 26 people, including 20 children between the ages of six and seven. Then Lanza takes his own life while still inside the school (Dec. 14).
2013	Multiple bombs explode near the finish line of the Boston Marathon. Three people are killed and more than 170 people are injured (April 15). The Guardian receives information that reveals that the National Security Agency (NSA) is using PRISM to spy on the web activities, including email, of U.S. citizens. Through PRISM, a clandestine national security surveillance program, the NSA has direct access to Facebook, YouTube, Skype, Google, Apple, Yahoo and other websites (June 6). *The Guardian* publishes a report on another NSA tool called Boundless Informant, used by the U. S. government to watch activity in every country in the world. President Obama confirms the existence of PRISM and its use to spy on the online activity of U. S. citizens(June 8). Edward Snowden, a former CIA employee, comes forward and admits that he is the source of the recent NSA leaks (June 9). Congress fails to agree on a budget and pass a spending bill, causing the government to shut down. The government shutdown forces about 800,000 federal workers off the job (Oct. 1). The night before the debt ceiling deadline, both the House and Senate approve a bill to fund the government until January 15, 2014, and raise the debt limit through February 7, 2014. The bill ends the 16-day government shutdown. It also ends the Republican standoff with President Obama over the *Affordable Care Act* (Oct. 16). The Senate deploys the "nuclear option," voting 52—48 to end the right of the minority to filibuster executive and judicial branch nominees. The vote is called a monumental, once in a generation change to Senate procedure (Nov. 21). The first ruling against the NSA surveillance program is handed down by Judge Richard Leon of Federal District Court for the District of Columbia. He says the program is "significantly likely" to violate the Fourth Amendment which addresses protection against unreasonable searches (Dec. 16). Just days after Judge Leon's ruling, an advisory panel commissioned by President Obama releases a 300-page report that recommends 46 changes to the NSA surveillance program (Dec 18).

重点参考书目和网站

[1] Axelrod, Alan. (2006) *The Complete Idiot's Guide to American History*. Washington D.C.：Alpha.
[2] Bennett, Michael J. (1996) *When Dreams Came True：The GI Bill and the Making of Modern America*. London：Brassey's.
[3] Beschloss, Michael R. (2007) *Presidential Courage：Brave Leaders and How They Changed America 1789—1989*. New York：Simon & Schuster.
[4] Boyer, Paul S. (2001) *The Oxford Companion to United States History*. New York：Oxford University Press, USA.
[5] Collier, Christopher. (1987) *Decision in Philadelphia：The Constitutional Convention of 1787*. New York：Random House.
[6] Cook, Timothy E., ed. (2005) *Freeing the Presses：The First Amendment in Action*. Baton Rouge, LA：Louisiana State University Press.
[7] Current, Richard N., Alan Brinkley & Harry Williams. (2001) *American History：A Survey*. New York：McGraw-Hill Companies.
[8] Eggleston, Edward. (2001) *A First Book in American History*. Atlanta：Lost Classics Book Co.
[9] Faragher, John Mack, et al.. (2005) *Out of Many：A History of the American People, Combined Edition*. Illinois：Prentice Hall.
[10] Foner, Eric. (1997) *The New American History：Critical Perspectives On the Past*. Philadelphia：Philadelphia Temple University Press.
[11] Heidler, David Stephen, et al.. (2000) *Encyclopedia of the American Civil War. Vols. 1—5：A Political, Social, and Military History*. Santa Barbara, Calif.：ABC-CLIO.
[12] Hofstadter, Richard. (2000) *Great Issues in American History, Vol. III：From Reconstruction to the Present Day, 1864—1981*. California：Vintage Publishing House.
[13] Johnson, Paul M. (1999) *A History of the American People*. New York：Harper Perennial.
[14] Labunski, Richard. (2006) *James Madison and the Struggle for the Bill of Rights*. New York：Oxford University Press.
[15] Purvis, Thomas L. (1997) *A Dictionary of American History*. Cambridge, Mass.：Blackwell Publishers.
[16] Zinn, Howard. (2005) *A People's History of the United States：1492 to Present*. New York：Harper Perennial Modern Classics.
[17] 范悦. (2006) 美国历史概况[M]. 北京:对外经济贸易大学出版社.
[18] 范悦. (2006) 美国历史文化阅读教材[M]. 北京:对外经济贸易大学出版社.
[19] 房龙. (2006) 美国史纲[M]. 尹继武译. 西安:陕西师范大学出版社.
[20] 美国新闻署. (2004) 美国历史概况[M]. 杨俊峰等译. 沈阳:辽宁教育出版社.
[21] 王波. (2004) 20世纪美国重要历史文献导读[M]. 北京:北京大学出版社.
[22] 王波. (2004) 美国历史与文化选读[M]. 北京:北京大学出版社.
[23] 王加丰,周旭东. (2007) 美国历史文化[M]. 杭州:浙江大学出版社.
[24] American Historical Association (AHA)：http://www.historians.org/index.cfm
[25] Biography of America：http://www.learner.org/biographyofamerica/
[26] Digital History：http://www.digitalhistory.uh.edu/
[27] Documents for the Study of American History：http://www.ku.edu/carrie/docs/amdocs_index.html
[28] Gilder Lehrman Institute of American History：http://www.gilderlehrman.org/
[29] History Matters：http://historymatters.gmu.edu/
[30] Organization of American Historians (OAH)：http://www.oah.org/
[31] The Historical Society：http://www.bu.edu/historic/
[32] The Library of Congress American Memory：Historical Collections for the National Digital Library http://memory.loc.gov/ammem/
[33] Virtual Library：History：United States http://vlib.iue.it/history/USA/
[34] We the People：http://www.wethepeople.gov

美国国情：美国历史文化（第3版）

尊敬的老师：

　　您好！

　　为了方便您更好地使用本教材，获得最佳教学效果，我们特向使用该书作为教材的教师赠送本教材配套课件资料。如有需要，请完整填写"教师联系表"并加盖所在单位系（院）公章，免费向出版社索取。

北京大学出版社

教 师 联 系 表

教材名称	美国国情：美国历史文化（第3版）					
姓名：		性别：		职务：		职称：
E-mail：			联系电话：		邮政编码：	
供职学校：			所在院系：			（章）
学校地址：						
教学科目与年级：				班级人数：		
通信地址：						

　　填写完毕后，请将此表邮寄给我们，我们将为您免费寄送本教材配套资料，谢谢！

北京市海淀区成府路 205 号
北京大学出版社外语编辑部　李　颖　　　　邮 购 部 电 话：010-62534449
邮政编码：100871　　　　　　　　　　　　市场营销部电话：010-62750672
电子邮箱：evalee1770@sina.com　　　　　　外语编辑部电话：010-62754382